WHEN THE
GUILLOTINE
FELL

The
Bloody Beginning
and Horrifying End
to France's River of Blood,
1791–1977

—

JEREMY MERCER

—

WHEN THE
GUILLOTINE

FELL

St. Martin's Press
New York

www.stmartins.com

Book design and map assembly by Jonathan Bennett

Library of Congress Cataloging-in-Publication Data
Mercer, Jeremy.
  When the guillotine fell : the bloody beginning and horrifying end to France's river of blood, 1791–1977 / Jeremy Mercer.—1st ed.
      p. cm.
  Includes bibliographical references.
  ISBN-13: 978-0-312-35791-7
  ISBN-10: 0-312-35791-5
  1. Guillotine—France—History. 2. Capital punishment—France—History.
3. Djandoubi, Hamida, d. 1977. I. Title.
  HV8555.M47 2008
  364.660944—dc22

                                                    2008012873

First Edition: July 2008

10   9   8   7   6   5   4   3   2   1

For my parents

WHEN THE
GUILLOTINE
FELL

THE OFFICIAL WITNESSES began to arrive at the prison shortly before four in the morning.

As decreed by French law, there was the sentencing judge, the prosecutor, the defense lawyers, and an official representative of the sitting government. Counting the guards, the clerks, the doctor, and the other prison functionaries, the audience would number more than twenty. This figure did not, of course, include the executioner and his two assistants. These men had to be considered more actors than spectators in the production.

The guillotine itself had been erected an hour earlier, before the crowd had begun to gather. The base had been laid down with the help of a spirit level and thin wooden wedges to assure its proper balance. The two wooden uprights, almost fifteen feet in height, were lifted into place and a trio of support arms attached on each side. The curiously named *mouton* (sheep), a sixty-five-pound weight that would propel the blade downward, was slipped into the copper runners along the inside of each upright. The crossbar was secured at the top of the two uprights, and the blade itself was bolted onto the *mouton*. Then the entire cutting apparatus was hoisted upward using a rope and pulley system. It clicked perfectly into a clasp known as the *grenouille* (frog), where it would stay until the executioner pulled the lever that sent the blade on its lethal descent.

Next, the long wooden plank on which the man would lie, the *bascule,* was bolted into place. Then came the *lunette,* a wooden clamp with the carved-out hollow for the condemned man's neck. A small metal bucket was placed in front of the machine and a large wicker basket was set beside the plank at the back. In keeping with the rather blithe system of nomenclature, the former was called the *baignoire* (bathtub) because it caught the blood, and the latter was called the *corbeille* (wastebasket) because the headless body was rolled into it once the blade had done its work. One final gruesome detail, a screen, called the *paravent,* was placed in front of the guillotine to protect spectators from the spurting blood. Then all the bolts were tightened and the mechanism was tested to ensure that the blade fell quick and true.

The chief executioner, a man by the name of Chevalier, was especially meticulous in his work on this morning. He was still new to the job. Although he had assisted in the executions of more than twenty men, this would be only the second time he was in command of the entire process—and responsible for any mishaps.

There was, needless to say, a rich history of botched guillotinings in France. Perhaps the most famous occurred in the town of Pamiers, near the Spanish border. On that occasion, the guillotine had been assembled, the condemned man strapped onto the *bascule,* and his neck clamped into the *lunette.* But when the lever was pulled, the blade jammed before it could complete its downward journey, and it merely bit into the back of the man's neck. Five times the blade was raised and five times it fell, but the head was never severed. The chief executioner and his assistants hurried to diagnose the mechanical problem. Amid the confusion, the condemned man managed to free himself from the guillotine and staggered away, spraying onlookers with his blood. This sorry tale ended only when one of the executioner's assistants, noted for his quick thinking, pulled out a butcher's knife, leaped on the condemned man's shoulders, and hacked off the head by hand.

"It happened. It was seen to happen. Deny it if you dare," wrote Victor Hugo, one of the many appalled by this clumsy execution.

That had been a dark day for the guillotine indeed, and the incident fueled the movement to abolish the death penalty in France for decades afterward. Now, with the guillotine once again under siege by abolitionists, Chevalier knew that another bungled execution wouldn't be tolerated. So, long after his assistants had gone to drink their coffees and smoke their cigarettes, he stayed with the machine, methodically examining each bolt and joint, testing the sharpness of the thick metal blade.

When the guillotine was finally pronounced ready and the official witnesses had all arrived, the prisoner was fetched from his cell. As a precaution, the corridor had been covered with old blankets so that the footsteps wouldn't echo out. If either the condemned man or his fellow inmates awoke to the sound of this approaching horde of officials, it would ignite a violent panic. For there was but one reason for the officials to be visiting death row before dawn, and that reason was death itself.

The cell door was unlocked and swung open. Seen through the grille that covered the thin slit of a window, the sky was still dark with night. The man was asleep on his concrete bunk. He was shaken awake, and those fateful words were pronounced: "Your appeal has been rejected and your request for clemency refused."

The man blinked several times but didn't say a word. He splashed cold water onto his face. Then he followed the cortège back along the blanket-covered corridor.

They arrived at a small room where the executioner Chevalier was waiting with his two assistants. There was a table covered in wax paper. On top was the traditional bottle of cognac, a glass of water, a package of cigarettes, and a pen and paper in case the man wanted to write any last words.

The man pushed away the paper but accepted the cognac. The first glass was emptied in a single swallow. A second was poured. This too went in one gulp.

The man smoked a cigarette. Then he asked for a second and smoked that until the ember burned his fingers. When he asked for a third, the executioner became impatient. As per French custom, the man was to be guillotined precisely at dawn and outside the prison walls; a thin line of gray could already be seen to the east. The sun was coming.

"*Ah non,*" Chevalier said. "That's enough. We've already lost enough time."

There would be no third cigarette.

The prisoner's *toilette* was still to be performed. One of the assistants took a pair of scissors and cropped off the man's hair. Then the collar and back of the man's shirt were cut away. There was to be no buffer of cloth or hair when the blade met the skin of the neck.

The man's hands were bound behind his back with a thin rope. The assistants each took an arm and lifted him from the chair. A door was opened. And there, in a small courtyard, stood the guillotine.

Everything happened quickly then. The man was strapped onto the *bascule.* The *lunette* was clamped around his neck. The blade fell.

It was September 10, 1977. The guillotine had just claimed its final head.

I

THE FIRST THING PEOPLE noticed about Hamida Djandoubi was his looks. He was dead handsome: dark eyes, thick hair, and a smile that danced between playfulness and seduction. Women would actually turn and stare after him when he passed on the street. One writer even compared him to Harry Belafonte.

Hamida was Tunisian by birth, the eldest of seven children. The family was raised in Carthage, the city so famously razed by the Romans, which by the mid-twentieth century had become just another poor suburb of Tunis. His father, Hédi, worked odd construction jobs and ran a black market veterinary clinic. He didn't have a license, but he did have a knack for healing cattle.

As a teenager, Hamida dreamed of Europe. The adventure, the money, and, yes, the women with such liberal reputations. When he finished high school, he took a job selling advertisements for a local business magazine. It took him almost a year, but he saved enough to make the voyage.

France was the obvious destination. Like Algeria and Morocco, Tunisia was a former French colony. Although it had gained its official independence in 1956, the two countries maintained close diplomatic ties, including a guest worker program. Hamida qualified for a visa and received his passport shortly before his nineteenth birthday. In September 1968 he booked his passage from Tunis to Marseille, the major port on the Mediterranean Sea and main entry point to France for North Africans.

*
* *

MARSEILLE IS THE anti-Paris. Lodged among the rocky cliffs on France's southern coast, it is a brash and sun-scoured city. Instead of

7

the refined culture and polished façades of the capital, this sweaty port exudes a raw humanity difficult to find in the north. There is little of the wealth of Paris and none of the rush; in Marseille, it is still custom to take a siesta in the afternoon and to spend the early evening sipping *apéros* under the cooling sky.

For centuries, Marseille was the most important port on the Mediterranean and, at one point in the nineteenth century, the fourth-largest port in the world after London, Liverpool, and New York. At the height of the French Empire it was also one of the most prosperous cities in Europe as colonial riches poured in from Indochina, the Caribbean, and Africa. In *The Count of Monte Cristo*, Alexandre Dumas describes the city's main street, La Canebière, as so luxurious that even Parisians were jealous.* And when Mark Twain visited Marseille in 1867, he too was awed and recounted the event in his travel diaries: "On every hand were bright colors, flashing constellations of gas burners, gaily dressed men and women thronging the sidewalks— hurry, life, activity, cheerfulness, conversation, and laughter everywhere!"

But by the second half of twentieth century, most of this glory had faded. France had renounced or lost most of her colonies, and instead of ships laden with spices and fabric, it was boatloads of colonial refugees that were docking in Marseille. When the main port was moved to an autonomous tax-free zone outside the city, the local economy faltered. Unemployment crept higher and the crime families became entrenched. With the release of the Gene Hackman movie *The French Connection* in 1971, Marseille became synonymous with heroin and corruption.

But if Marseille had lost its European luster, it remained the destination of choice for North Africans. For a young man growing up in Oran

---

* As the Marseille-born composer Vincent Scotto so famously sang, "Our Cane, Cane, Canebière / Is popular everywhere."

or Rabat or Tunis, the easiest route to Europe was a ferry ride across the Mediterranean to Marseille. In the decade after the Second World War, with so much labor needed to rebuild the country, the influx of immigrants from the Maghreb was so great the city became a peculiar hybrid of French café and Arab souk. In the rest of France, Marseille started to be called, often with a hint of derision, "the most northern city in Africa."

*
*   *

THIS WAS THE MARSEILLE that greeted Hamida Djandoubi when he descended from the ferry on September 10, 1968. Thanks to an Italian contractor he met in Tunis, he had the address of a Marseille couple who had once lived in Tunisia. Vincent and Katherine Comandé owned a grocery store in the city's sixth arrondissement, an affluent residential neighborhood just a few miles south of the Old Port. As four of their five children had already left home to study or start their own families, the Comandés took in guests for the companionship and for help with their business. There was a bedroom in the back of the grocery store, and Hamida was invited to live there and eat with the family in return for stocking the shelves and minding the till a few hours every day.

The grocery store was on rue Christophe Colomb. Christopher Columbus street. A new world for Hamida to explore.

So his life in France began. He studied law for a term at the local university. He courted women in the discos. He played soccer on weekends. He took holidays across Western Europe.

By that fated fall of 1971, Hamida had left the grocery store and was living in a men's residence close to the Pointe-Rouge beach. He was twenty-two years old and worked full-time for a landscaper named Désiré Boyer. But this was only a temporary position. His plan was to move to Paris, get his license for heavy trucks, and then drive rigs around Europe. He'd already given his notice, and his last day on the job was scheduled for October 15, 1971. He'd bought a ticket on the train that left for Paris the very next day.

As it happened, it was a good time for a young Tunisian man to be leaving the south of France. Two weeks earlier, one of the most atrocious crimes of the decade had been committed outside Nice by a group of four Tunisian laborers. The men broke into a farmhouse in search of money and ended up slitting the throat of a seven-year-old girl and stabbing a pregnant woman in the womb. The depravity of the crime left the region stunned. Suddenly young Arab men, already accustomed to a certain discrimination, were treated with a little more scorn, greeted with a little more fear.

The day in question, October 9, 1971, was a Saturday. The weather was typical of the south of France in early fall, that is, nearly ideal. It was sunny and warm enough for the beach, the air scented with sea and pine. But, this being Marseille, there was the wind.

The mistral is a violent wind that swoops southward from the center of France and along the Rhône valley. It torments the Mediterranean coast, particularly the stretch between Toulon and Marseille. It shakes windows, it steals laundry from clotheslines, it tears clay tiles from roofs. The people of Marseille like to say the mistral even causes temporary insanity.

That morning, Hamida was driving a tractor with an industrial tiller hooked to the back. The company was installing an irrigation canal and landscaping the adjoining banks. An iron plate had been left on the construction road, and the wind quickly covered it with a thin layer of dust and dirt. Hamida never saw it. The tractor's wheels skidded and slipped when they hit the metal. In an instant, the tractor overturned and Hamida was pinned underneath. His leg was sucked into the tiller's churning blades. He blacked out.

When he came to, everything was numb. Blood dripped into a pool beneath the tiller. He could see a piece of his foot. It made him think of hamburger meat. He blacked out again.

Firefighters spent more than two hours trying to extract the shreds of his leg from the rototiller.* It couldn't be done. They were going to have to cut.

Hamida woke up at the Hôpital de la Conception that evening. His right leg had been amputated at the knee.

---

* I was told the accident report was lost during a fire in the department's archives. Subsequent discussions with hospital and firefighting personnel left me with the impression that if the victim had been "French," more might have been done to save his leg.

2

TO BEST UNDERSTAND how primitive human beings conducted their daily affairs, one must spend a great deal of time sifting through pottery shards or spelunking through caves.

Some of the most important clues have come from the African nation of Tanzania. Here, at the Laetoli site, there are footprints preserved in volcanic ash that are 3.7 million years old—the first evidence of bipedalism, that fateful moment when our hominid ancestors first thrust their heads into the air and rose up onto their hind legs. A few dozen miles north is the Olduvai Gorge, where a two-million-year-old hand axe was found, a discovery so remarkable that Arthur C. Clarke chose to drop his black monolith at this very spot in *2001: A Space Odyssey*.

In terms of social conventions, the indicators date from more recent times. Near Nice on the Côte d'Azur, for example, a prehistoric village known as Terra Amata was home to a group of *homo erectus* roughly 380,000 years ago. It was used as a base camp to hunt the elephants and meadow rhinoceroses that once thrived in the south of France, and the arrangement of foundation stones suggests there were communal fire pits and other shared amenities.

As for the less tangible aspects of Stone Age culture, these require yet another leap forward. The first cave paintings date from roughly thirty-five thousand years ago. Drawn with charcoal or red ocher, these paintings show animals, hunting rituals, or, often, someone's fascination with their own handprint. Among the more celebrated samples of this work are the Lascaux caves in southwestern France, a World Heritage Site since 1979, and the Altamira caves in Spain, grandly known as the Sistine Chapel of cave painting. An especially spectacular cave was discovered beneath the Calanques, the cliffs that jut into the Mediterranean Sea just outside Marseille. In 1985, the deep-sea diver Henri Cosquer swam through a labyrinthine underwater tunnel and surfaced inside a cave. The walls were decorated with paintings of penguins and seals. The work dated back thirty thousand years, before the glaciers of the last Ice Age melted and the Mediterranean waters rose to cover the cave mouth.

But perhaps the most curious of all cave paintings are to be found at Cingle de la Mola Remigia, on the eastern coast of Spain. It was the German researcher Hugo Obermaier who brought the extraordinary news to the world in the 1930s. Four paintings here, dating from 6500 B.C., depict what appear to be organized killings. In the most vivid, a single man is shown lying in the foreground, his arms and legs bound with rope. His body is riddled with arrows. Behind him, a group of seventeen other men raise their bows in exultation.

Whether the dead man was a captured enemy or a member of the tribe who had run afoul of communal rules is impossible to know. What is abundantly clear is that it wasn't an ordinary killing. It was a prehistoric execution.*

---

* These cave paintings were an elusive quarry: from a throwaway line in William A. Schabas's *Abolition of the Death Penalty in International Law* to *La Peine de mort: Esquisse historique et juridique* by Paul Savey-Casard, to the Hugo Obermaier Society in Regensburg, Germany, and, finally, to Dr. Christian Züchner of the University of Erlangen-Nürnberg, who solved the mystery and identified the caves for me.

3

ELISABETH BOUSQUET's friends and family thought of her as naïve or inexperienced or perhaps a little slow. Others were less generous. They called her a *simplette,* a simpleton.

One of the reasons for these characterizations was her appearance. As a little girl, she wore thick glasses that magnified her already large eyes, and her heavy lips caused her to speak with a slight lisp. But a better reason had to do with her upbringing. It was, to put it mildly, sheltered.

Elisabeth was the youngest daughter of Alphonsine and Pierre Bousquet, a small-town couple from the southern interior of France. They married in 1944, when Pierre was twenty-one years old and Alphonsine was twenty-five. It was a typically fruitful Catholic union at a time when birth control was still illegal. There were seven children, although three died as infants. That left Jean-Pierre, Marie-Josée, Roland, and Elisabeth.

Until 1950 the couple lived in Estaing, a storybook village of about six hundred people tucked into a river valley a hundred miles north of Montpellier. It was unquestionably scenic and was even voted one of the most beautiful villages in France. It was also unquestionably eerie. A stone castle loomed over Estaing, dominating the tiny village houses like an ogre among schoolchildren. It belonged to the wealthy Giscard d'Estaing family, who, after a slight tweaking of their family tree, traced their ancestry back to one of the senior aides to Richard the Lionheart.

Pierre's parents managed a local hotel and restaurant, and after the wedding he worked as a waiter in the family business. Once the children began to arrive, Pierre and Alphonsine looked to improve their lot. In 1950 they moved to Marseille, the largest city in Provence and the second largest in France. Big cities have long lured youth in search of a better life, and, in the popular imagination, what Émile Zola wrote in *Les Mystères de Marseille* in 1867 remained true in 1950: "In Marseille, faced with several great fortunes earned in just a few years, there isn't a young man who doesn't dream of a parallel windfall."

Sadly for the Bousquets, they arrived in the city just as things were beginning to economically disintegrate.

*

*   *

MARSEILLE'S ECONOMY began to decline in earnest after the Second World War. There was a rash of strikes on the docks as the Communist-dominated unions clashed with more conservative police and political forces. Traditional sectors such as olive oil and soap making—the famous *savon de Marseille*—faced increased competition from Italy, Spain, and other Mediterranean countries. Then there was the hardship of absorbing the tens of thousands of men and women who were returning to France via Marseille as the troubles began to flare in the French colonies in North Africa.

Like the rest of Europe, Marseille also had to deal with the consequences of the war. At first, after the fall of Paris and the dawn of Vichy France in 1940, Marseille remained an essentially free city. The port was open, the city attracted a number of prominent exiles, including André Breton and the surrealists, and its narrow streets became home to a large Resistance network. There was even a lively business in providing passage to Jews escaping the expanding reach of the Nazis. The author Anna Seghers, who spent weeks in a dismal downtown hotel, described Marseille as the sewer that channeled the flood of lost European souls to the sea.

Once the Allies landed in North Africa in November 1942, the Nazis could no longer allow such a strategic port to remain free. With help from collaborationists in the local government, police department, and even organized crime, Marseille quickly fell under Nazi control. The Nazi elite regarded this motley city with open disdain.

Karl Oberg, the SS officer in charge of police, announced: "This city is the cancer of Europe. And Europe cannot live as long as Marseille hasn't been purified."

And purify they did. After members of the Resistance launched a series of attacks against the occupying forces, including a bomb planted in a tramcar full of Nazi soldiers, the Germans attempted to tame the city. In January 1943, in what is known as the Battle of Marseille, close to six thousand people were arrested, and two thousand were shipped to internment camps. Then Oberg announced he would clean the city with "mines and fire." There was no more obvious target than Le Panier, the oldest neighborhood in Marseille, a locale where opium dens and legalized prostitution once flourished and where the Resistance made its headquarters during the war. In all, more than fifteen hundred buildings were dynamited in Le Panier, and thirty thousand people found themselves homeless.

Insult was added to injury when American bombers swarmed over Marseille in May 1944 and dropped 288 tons of bombs on the city. The newspaper *Le Petit Marseillais* called it part of the "*aggressions de l'aviation anglo-américaine*" (the Anglo-American air attacks), and the sorry result was more than two thousand dead and a dozen neighborhoods left in ruin.

This was the Marseille that greeted the young Bousquet family when they arrived in 1950, a grim city still recovering from its wartime wounds. But fate would make it even grimmer for the family, as they carried an extra burden: their very name.

In an unhappy coincidence, the head of police services for Vichy France and the man who came to Marseille to enthusiastically oversee the dynamiting of Le Panier was named René Bousquet. He was an ardent supporter of Nazi policies, surpassing their deportation quotas and lobbying to lower the age at which Jewish children could be sent to the camps. Such devotion led Heinrich Himmler to say he was "impressed" by Bousquet and declare him a "precious collaborator." But in Marseille, in the years following the war, the very mention of Bousquet brought a snarl to the lips and sent a spray of spittle to the sidewalk. Even though the two families were not related, the Bousquets couldn't have carried a more damning name as they embarked upon their new lives.

*

*   *

ONCE IN MARSEILLE, Pierre found another restaurant job, but the money was less than the family had hoped for. The couple rented a small apartment in the neighborhood known as La Plaine and struggled along with their first two children, Jean-Pierre and Marie-Josée. But life was so cramped that when their third child, Roland, arrived, he was sent to live with Alphonsine's parents in the town of Langogne, four hours northwest of Marseille by car. And when Elisabeth was born, on April 29, 1953, she too was sent away.

It was in the quiet, rural town of Langogne that her simple ways began. Her elderly grandparents were out of touch with the needs of a young girl and dressed her in whatever mishmash of clothes they could find. She was doted on by her uncle, Father Rigaud, the town priest, but she never really had any friends her own age. The grandparents kept four or five sheep, and Elisabeth spent much of her time with the animals. She was often seen leading them through the cobbled streets so they could graze outside of town.

Maryse Hugon ran a grocery store near the grandparents' home in Langogne. Almost every day for seven years, Elisabeth would stop in to buy her favorite toffee candies, Carambars. "She was a little bit behind all the other children. She was closed in on herself," Hugon recalled.

At school, she gradually fell behind the others. When she was twelve years old, she was in a class with nine-year-olds. Eventually, she was transferred to the Centre Ste-Marie, a special technical class where girls were taught cooking and sewing. It was for those who weren't "intellectually gifted," as one of the teachers, Sister Odette Lafout, so delicately put it.

Elisabeth saw her parents on holidays and vacations, but for the most part her family was foreign to her. She became even more isolated when her brother Roland was called back to Marseille to rejoin the family.

At last, when Elisabeth was fifteen years old, her parents were in a position to bring her to live with them as well. She packed up her suitcase in Langogne and prepared for Marseille. Those who knew her were leery of the move.

"When I found out she would be joining her family in Marseille, I was very worried," said Hugon. "She was naïve. She wasn't ready for a big city."

And there was certainly reason to worry. This girl of fifteen went from a rural town of little more than four thousand people to a tumultuous metropolis of close to eight hundred thousand. Even for one with a deft mind and street smarts, it would have been difficult to adapt. And young Elisabeth hadn't been blessed with either.

Having always struggled in school, even under the guidance of the nuns, she dropped out altogether shortly after arriving in Marseille. This only made the transition more difficult, and she ended up spending most of her time in the apartment watching television or going on walks with her sister, Marie-Josée.

"She certainly wasn't prepared for her new life," her sister-in-law would write some three decades later. "No experience, too naïve, she sank into a hyperemotional state that she couldn't overcome."*

Her father found Elisabeth a job as a full-time babysitter for a physiotherapist by the name of François Ceccaldi. The work was neither challenging nor well paid, but Elisabeth turned out to be a loving

---

*Elisabeth Bousquet's brothers, Jean-Pierre and Roland, both declined to be interviewed for this book. Their reluctance might be due to their deceased mother's request that a curtain of silence be drawn across this tragic episode. In a letter dated March 16, 2007, Roland's wife asked: "Do you know how much suffering this family has endured and how long it has taken to overcome it? . . . Do you not think that this has gone far enough now and that it is time to let us live our last years in peace?"

nanny, and the Ceccaldi children, a boy and a girl, were delighted by her. She took them to the park, she played board games with them, she listened to their stories.

"She was a very, very sweet girl," remembered Dr. Ceccaldi. "She wasn't too smart—but sweet. A bit of a *simplette*."

Dr. Ceccaldi's wife, Paulette, remembers Elisabeth complaining about her lack of friends. Paulette tried to help. "I encouraged her to go to parties or meetings for young people. She always would say yes, then no, then yes, and finally never go," Paulette said. "She was very, very shy."

But Elisabeth desperately wanted friends, particularly a boyfriend.

"I knew how it was going to be," Paulette remembered. "The first man to speak nicely to her and voilà."

*

*   *

THE HONDA 750 was Pierre Bousquet's passion. He loved the motorcycle and he loved to ride it fast—even though, like his daughter Elisabeth, he was cursed with poor vision. There was a string of minor accidents, and, according to his former son-in-law, Noël Patel, after less than five thousand miles he was forced to change the rear tire because it had been worn away by excessive braking.

"He shouldn't have been on that motorcycle," said Noël. "I'm not sure he ever had real control of it."

But this didn't deter Pierre, certainly not on that fateful morning of October 9, 1971. It was a Saturday, and, along with the mistral, the talk of the city was of two subjects dear to the hearts of the Marseillais: liquor and soccer. The day before, a fire at a distillery had sent two and a half million gallons of alcohol up in flames; that night, the national soccer team was to play a crucial European Cup match against Hungary. And as Marseille was also an unabashedly religious city with a statuette of the Virgin Mary carved above most every street corner, the newspapers and radio stations assiduously noted that October 9 was the feast day of St. Denis, the Paris bishop whose head was lopped off atop Montmartre in A.D. 250.

Pierre had invited his daughter Marie-Josée along with him for a ride that morning. The cause of the accident was never known. On a harmless curve, Pierre lost control and the motorcycle caromed into the concrete sidewall of the motorway. Pierre's legs were broken and Marie-Josée suffered major head trauma. Both were rushed to Hôpital de la Conception by ambulance.

The Bousquet family was duly notified. That evening, Elisabeth arrived at the hospital to visit her father. Upon entering his room, she couldn't help noticing the handsome young man who lay in the next bed.

It was Hamida Djandoubi.

4

ACCORDING TO THE COMMONLY accepted chronology, Hammurabi ascended to the throne of Babylon upon the death of his father, Sin-muballit, in 1792 B.C. At the time, Babylon was the political and economic capital of Mesopotamia. And since Mesopotamia was the most advanced civilization the planet had ever known, Hammurabi found himself in a very powerful position indeed.

In Hammurabi's day, Mesopotamia stretched from the Gulf of Arabia to the Mediterranean Sea, and Babylon itself stood on the banks of the Euphrates River, about sixty miles south of modern-day Baghdad. The region is known as the cradle of civilization for good reason: eighteen centuries before the birth of Christ, Mesopotamia had an intricate written language, Akkadian; astronomers had cataloged the stars into the twelve signs of the zodiac; and there was an advanced system of mathematics using the base 60, the reason why, to this day, minutes are divided into sixty seconds and hours into sixty minutes.

Another Mesopotamian feat was a legal system that allowed people to live with a relative degree of order and security. While most of the world still operated under crude tribal custom, including practices such as marriage by capture and blood vendettas, in Mesopotamia there had been written laws since the reign of Urukagina in the twenty-fourth century B.C. and a civil code was introduced by Ur-Nammu in the twenty-first century B.C. And it was here, in the realm of justice, that Hammurabi would surpass his predecessors and forever lodge himself in the history books by introducing the first-ever complete criminal code.

About 1760 B.C. he declared himself "a shepherd who brings peace" and had a set of 282 laws etched into a seven-foot-tall black rock he nicknamed "the King of Justice." He then erected this mammoth tablet at the Temple of Shamash, the God of the Sun. Though the vast majority of Babylonians couldn't actually read, this public display was revolutionary: the people's rights had literally been carved in stone.

"That the strong may not oppress the weak, so to give justice to the orphan [and] the widow, I have inscribed my precious words on my monument," Hammurabi proclaimed.*

Under Hammurabi's Code, minor offenses were punished with fines, exile, or physical mutilation. Law 195, for example, states, "If a son strikes his father, they shall cut off his fore-hand." More important, Hammurabi was the first person to codify the concept of death as a legal punishment. In all, there were twenty-eight capital offenses in the code, from murder to more mundane trespasses such as cheating clients of their beer in a tavern, stealing from a temple, or having sex with your son's wife. Another five crimes involved a quasi death penalty: at a time when few people could swim, the offender was thrown in the river.

By doing this, Hammurabi forever entrenched the belief that certain crimes so threaten a community that the only reasonable remedy is to promise death to the malefactors. As Sir Henry Maine wrote in his landmark 1893 work, *Ancient Law,* "The punishment of death is a necessity of society in certain stages of the civilizing process. . . . Without it, the community neither feels that it is sufficiently revenged, nor thinks that the example of his punishment is adequate to deter others from imitating him."

Hammurabi also brought us the *lex talionis,* the law of retaliation that is so imbued in the concept of justice. It legislates one of the most primal instincts, the animal reality behind the majesty of criminal law: if we are hurt, we want to hurt back. Five centuries before a similar passage appeared in the Old Testament, Hammurabi wrote:

*I relied on the translation of Hammurabi's Code found in *The Babylonian Laws,* edited by G. R. Driver and John C. Miles (Oxford: Clarendon Press, 1955).

LAW 196: *If a man has put out the eye of a free man, they shall put out his eye.*

LAW 200: *If a man knocks out the tooth of a man equal to him, they shall knock out his tooth.*

Hammurabi died in 1750 B.C., but his code was reproduced, distributed, and used as the basis of law in the region for more than one thousand years. One of the original copies was discovered by a team of French archaeologists in 1901 and is now on display at the Louvre in Paris. In America, Hammurabi's image is enshrined at both the House of Representatives and the Supreme Court.

5

PIERRE BOUSQUET WAS astonished by the torrent of people who came to see his fellow invalid. And, even more remarkably, most of Hamida Djandoubi's visitors were attractive young women.

This wouldn't have been such a surprise if Pierre had known Hamida before their time together in that twin-bed hospital room. Hamida had always captivated women. He was good-looking, he was tall, he was endowed with an athlete's physique. And then there was his voice: soft and deep, a perfect tool for seduction.

The first heart he won was that of his own mother, Cherifa. His first name is evidence enough of her devotion. Hamida is a derivative of Muhammad, the Muslim prophet. But in Tunisia and most other Muslim countries, men are called Hamid and women Hamida, similar to the Western tradition of Chris and Chrissie. A doting Muslim mother might occasionally coo "my little Hamida" to her baby boy, just like a Chris might occasionally become Chrissie while looking so adorable in the crib. But this practice would normally be abandoned once the infant was out of diapers. In Hamida's case, Cherifa was so smitten, the feminine version of the boy's name was used through adolescence and into manhood.

Hamida would always make the most of the attraction women felt to him. One episode from his childhood would be especially portentous. When he was ten years old, there was a party at the family home, and he began playing with a neighbor's daughter. Things became a little too intimate, and his mother dragged him away from the girl. That night, after the last guest had left, Cherifa beat her young son's back raw with a belt. Then she went and got a tube of harissa, the searing hot chili pepper paste. She squirted out a spoonful and thrust it up into the boy's rectum to make sure he got the message.

While the incident would evoke great interest when Hamida re-counted it for psychologists years later, the punishment did little to dampen his youthful ardor. He later boasted he'd lost his virginity at the age of fifteen, and he was seldom without at least one girlfriend in Tunis. When he arrived in France, his success with women continued. A regular at the bars and discos around the Old Port, he would intro-duce himself as Joe, a peculiar transformation of Djandoubi that he came up with. With his looks and his charm, he had dates most every night of the week. At one point, he found a job with a local florist and showered his women with bouquets of slightly wilted flowers.

Bruno Comandé, the oldest of the five Comandé children, remem-bers the phenomenon well. Even after Hamida left the grocery store on rue Christophe Colomb, he would return to eat dinner with the family several times a month. He was often accompanied by a date, and he always brought flowers for Madame Comandé.

"The pretty girls would run after him," Bruno said. "I never saw anything like it."

Another close friend of Hamida's, Louis Bugia, tells a similar story. On the occasion of Louis's *fiançailles*, his engagement celebration, Hamida brought an attractive curly-haired brunette as a date. In the photographs, they make a most handsome couple, arm in arm with broad smiles.

"To be honest, I could never keep his girlfriends straight," said Bu-gia. "That's just the way he was. Women loved him. When he walked down the street, they would turn to look."

Perhaps it was inevitable, then, that when young Elisabeth Bous-quet walked into that hospital room, she noticed Hamida lying in the next bed over.

*

*   *

MARSEILLE IS A CITY of raconteurs. Men and women sit around in cafés or bars and tell tales that always feel one size too large. There is even a tasteful word for this art of exaggeration: *broderie*. It's not telling lies; it's just embroidering the truth.

Nowhere is this more evident than in the city's foundation myth. The truth of the matter is that Marseille is the oldest city in France, and one of the more prominent authors to record the city's origins was Aristotle. He visited "Massalia" in 350 B.C. to study the political infrastructure. His major work from that period, *The Republic of the Massalians,* is lost, the last copy believed to have burned with the library in Alexandria. But his account of the city's birth was widely cited by his contemporaries and is considered the most reliable.

According to Aristotle, Marseille was founded by sailors from the Greek colony of Phocaea, a city-state on what is today the western coast of Turkey. These Phocaean Greeks were the most dogged of explorers, setting out in their longboats and founding settlements throughout the Mediterranean basin.

The Phocaeans arrived in what would become Marseille in 594 B.C. Led by a captain named Euxene, they espied the natural port created by the mouth of the river Lacydon and stopped to gather wood and water. At the time, the surrounding hills were the home of a tribe of Ligurians known as the Saylens. In such a savage era, the Saylens had creative means of discouraging invaders: they sliced off the heads of their fallen enemies, stuck them on poles, and set them up in concentric rings around their villages. Such was the Saylens' fervor for decollation that when the archaeologist Achille Peigné-Delacourt discovered a stone blade in the south of France in 1866, he actually claimed it to be a Ligurian guillotine.

Although they were a rather hostile group, Euxene softened the Saylens with a bounty of traditional Hellenic gifts—wheat, grape vines, and olive trees—and their chief, Nann, eventually granted the Phocaeans the right to set up a trading post on their shores. Euxene returned to Phocaea, where he consulted with the governors, and then went on to Delphi, where he consulted the Oracle. Both gave encouraging responses, and the colony of Massalia was founded more than 2,600 years ago.

As riveting as this official history is, it never quite satisfied the Marseillais taste for romantic intrigue. Over the centuries, the story was embroidered into one that better reflected the city's image of itself. Like all ports, Marseille is a vast medley of people, and as Casanova noted in his memoirs after visiting the city in the 1740s, it is a "mixture of nationalities, the grave Turk and the glittering Andalusian, the French dandy, the gross Negro, the crafty Greek, the dull Hollander." Racial stereotypes aside, it is an apt description, and city officials often stumble over themselves to vaunt Marseille's unique *brassage culturel*— its intermingling of different cultures.

In this vein, the popular myth is that Marseille was founded when a ship captained by a handsome young Greek named Protis dropped anchor one sunny afternoon in 600 B.C. By chance, Protis arrived the day of a grand celebration: the local Ligurian king had declared it time for his ravishing daughter, Gyptis, to marry. Eligible young men had traveled from far and wide to win her heart and, out of *politesse,* the king invited Protis to the feast.

The Ligurian custom was for the bride-to-be to hide behind a curtain during the feast and observe the wit and grace of her suitors. At the end of the meal, she would emerge and present a chalice of water to her chosen husband. To the amazement of all on hand, Gyptis offered her water to Protis. There was no refusing, and as a dowry, Protis received the land that is now Marseille.

It is an idyllic tale, a mixed marriage at the root of a mixed city. Of course, the malady of racism being what it was, especially in those turbulent years when Hamida and Elisabeth met, the reality for a mixed couple in Marseille could be ruthlessly different.

*

* *

ELISABETH WAS ONE of those young women who began appearing regularly at Hamida's bedside. She was eighteen years old, with curly brown hair and a plump but voluptuous figure. She was lonely, he was eager for distraction, and there was that dance of pheromones that draws men and women together. But there was also a little something more. Elisabeth was desperate to escape her family's apartment.

There can be no doubt that the material situation of the Bousquets had vastly improved since their arrival in Marseille. Pierre was now a well-established waiter at an Alsatian restaurant on cours Estienne d'Orves near the Old Port. The large public square, once a docking basin for tall ships and home to the Marseille arsenal, had been filled in, paved over, and named after Honoré Étienne d'Orves, a hero of the French Resistance. By the 1970s, it had become an almost-thriving tourist district, and Pierre's restaurant had a reputation for charcuterie that guaranteed a steady clientele. This meant the money was good, and as it happened, Pierre was good with the money.

Over the years he saved enough for a down payment on an apartment on rue Consolat. It was in the heart of Marseille, just up the way from the famous Canebière, and it was large enough for the entire Bousquet family to be united at last. A few years later this same scrimping enabled Pierre to buy that sporty and speedy Honda 750.

Although Pierre's frugality had its benefits, it didn't make life easy for his wife, Alphonsine Bousquet. Noël Patel, who married Marie-Josée Bousquet, said the family grated under the stern budgetary measures.

"Pierre was strict and very controlling with the finances," Noël said. "It was hard on them, but it wasn't an entirely bad thing. It wasn't as if he was gambling or drinking. He used the money to buy an apartment for the family. It was a good deed."

But there was more than the parsimony. Pierre also had a reputation as being *caractériel* (moody), and it made for a difficult household. Fissures began to appear in the Bousquet marriage, and the couple spent time apart. "It was always Alphonsine who had to be flexible. She always had to adapt to her husband's behavior, always bending to his will," recalled Noël.

It must be said that Noël can't be considered a completely objective source when it comes to the relationship between Pierre and Alphonsine. By 1971 the family situation had become extremely complicated. The marriage between Noël, an electrician, and Marie-Josée, a clerk in a downtown cheese shop, had already crumbled. The marriage between Pierre and Alphonsine was in the midst of crumbling. And, most troublesome of all, there were suspicions that Alphonsine and Noël were seeking consolation in each other's arms.

This was the rather ignominious atmosphere that Elisabeth lived in, and she was eager to escape it. Paulette Ceccaldi says that when Elisabeth came to work, she would often complain about her mother and the situation at home. "I think they were very difficult times for her," Ceccaldi says. "She was emotionally all alone there."

So Elizabeth began spending long hours at Hamida's bedside. She often overstayed visiting hours, but nobody at the hospital seemed to mind such details. At the time, nurses across the country were preoccupied with more serious matters. A few weeks before the twin accidents of October 9, a nurse was killed during a hostage taking at Clairvaux prison in the north of France. The crime had not only outraged the country, it had also cast a harsh light on the working conditions of certain public employees. With all the talk of work stoppages and union solidarity, one visitor who stayed a few extra hours at the hospital was barely noticed.

Elisabeth would bring little gifts for Hamida or make him cakes and crumbles. She would make a point of removing her glasses before entering his room in hopes of appearing more fetching. It was an innocent flirtation. After his amputation, Hamida was certainly in no shape for anything more serious. At least not yet.

6

NOTHING SPARKS A GOOD debate about crime and punishment like a law that makes stealing cabbage a capital offense.

In 621 B.C., shortly before the founding of Marseille and amid the general blossoming of Greek civilization, a fellow named Draco was asked to compile a new criminal code for the polis of Athens. In his disciplinary zeal, he decided that practically every offense, from laziness to murder to vegetable theft, should result in the death penalty. "Small ones deserve that, and I have no higher for greater crimes," Draco is cited as saying.

To no great surprise, this severity caused some sensation. One commentator, Demades, insisted Draco's laws were actually written in blood. Another, Suidas, wrote that Athenians were so pleased with the legal code that when Draco entered a theater, they showered him with their cloaks as a tribute. Ultimately, these laws were used for only thirty years before being replaced by the more lenient Solonian Constitution, but the controversy they spurred marked the beginning of the great philosophical inquiry into the purpose of punishment.

Even after the Solonian reforms, Greek justice remained rather, well, Draconian. The death penalty was used to punish robbery, embezzlement, adultery, treason, and murder, while execution methods included stoning, poisoning, hurling from a high rock, and impaling the condemned individual on sharp spikes. Although there were early voices of opposition, capital punishment wasn't truly questioned until early in the fourth century B.C. and the trial of Socrates.

Athens was in dire shape at the time. There had been the plague of 430 B.C. that led the citizens to build pyres of corpses in the streets and then the exhausting Peloponnesian War with Sparta that ended in embarrassing defeat in 404 B.C. The city needed a scapegoat, and it so happened that Socrates was stirring up intellectual trouble at the time. He challenged people to live virtuously, he urged them to forsake material goods, he questioned leading politicians, he generally acted the gadfly.

The official charges were that Socrates was corrupting the youth and promoting atheism. At a trial before five hundred of his peers, Socrates not only refused to apologize but actually continued to agitate. According to Plato, Socrates asked why Athenians "care so much about laying up the greatest amount of money and honor and reputation, and so little about wisdom and truth and the greatest improvement of the soul?" Not the way to woo one's judges, and, sure enough, in 399 B.C., Socrates was sentenced to death by hemlock.

For Plato, the execution of his mentor was a breaking point. Already discouraged by the corruption in Athens, he now devoted himself to his vision of a truly just society. His most widely read discourse, *The Republic*, actually begins with the question "What is justice?" and proposes a civilization ruled by philosopher kings and a population that values virtue above all. It is here, in discussing law and order, that Plato becomes the first to introduce the concept of rehabilitation, saying "only the unreasonable fury of a beast" punishes merely as an act of retribution.

"The proper office of punishment is twofold," Plato elaborated in *Gorgias*. "He who is rightly punished ought either to become better and profit by it, or he ought to be made an example to his fellows, that they may see what he suffers, and fear and become better."

Plato wasn't an abolitionist by any means; he accepted that there were "incurable" criminals who needed to be excised from society. He concluded in *Laws* that if, "after receiving such an excellent education and training from youth upward, he has not abstained from the greatest of crimes, his punishment shall be death."

About the same time, another Athenian author accounts for the first reasoned argument against the death penalty. In *History of the*

Peloponnesian War, the retired general Thucydides writes of the dilemma facing Athens when the colony of Mytilene attempted to join forces with the Spartans. A general named Cleon, "remarkable among Athenians for the violence of his character," proposed that every adult male be put to death to deter other potential rebellions. Another general, Diodotus, disagreed.

"Now, in human societies the death penalty has been laid down for many offenses less serious than this one. Yet people still take risks," Diodotus told the assembly. "We must not, therefore, come to the wrong conclusions through having too much confidence in the effectiveness of capital punishment."

Already, one of the principal arguments for capital punishment—deterrence—was being questioned. In this particular case, the assembly agreed with Diodotus and voted to spare the Mytilenes.

7

A CATACLYSMIC DEPRESSION overpowered Hamida Djandoubi after the amputation. He couldn't bring himself to look at his bandaged stump. He would jolt awake in the night, wet with sweat, grasping for his missing foot. He had no appetite.

"The first thing I thought," he told the police, "was that I should commit suicide."

Hamida had been a *sportif*, as they say in Marseille. He played soccer regularly, sometimes telling people he was a member of the reserve squad for Olympique de Marseille. This was quite the claim. "OM" was and is the most popular professional sports franchise in France, the equivalent of the New York Yankees or Manchester United. For decades, it has drawn bigger home crowds, sold more replica jerseys, and had larger national television audiences than any other team in the country. In Marseille itself, the team is nigh religion, and even the reserve squads consist only of elite athletes. In any case, Olympique de Marseille has no actual records of a player named "Djandoubi," "Djendoubi," or "Jendoubi." But he still liked to tell the story, and it seldom failed to impress.

Now it appeared there would be no more soccer at any level. Nor would there be a job working construction or landscaping. Nor would there be late nights dancing. "I knew I was never going to be normal," he said.

Hamida wasn't the only one to lapse into despondency after having a leg amputated at the Hôpital de la Conception. More famously, it was here in this same surgery ward that Arthur Rimbaud had his right leg cut off in May 1891.

Rimbaud is known for his symbolist poetry and his torrid affair with fellow poet Paul Verlaine. But by 1891 the author of *A Season in Hell* had forsaken writing for more lucrative pursuits, such as gunrunning in Africa. It was on one of these adventures that he was diagnosed with carcinoma of the leg and was forced to return to France. His illness was so grave that he didn't get any farther than Marseille.

"*La vie m'est devenu impossible,*" Rimbaud wrote to his mother after the surgery. "*Que je suis donc malheureux! Que je suis donc malheureux!*"

How unhappy he was indeed. Six months after the amputation, Rimbaud was dead.

Hamida wasn't going to die, but that was small consolation. More than a month after the accident, the claws of depression hadn't yet released him, and friends began to worry. Louis Bugia had known him since the summer of 1969. They'd met at the Pointe-Rouge beach and had an immediate rapport. Louis had been born in Tunisia, his father having moved there from Sicily in search of work. Altogether, Bugia spent eight years in Tunis, knew many of the same neighborhoods as Hamida, and could still speak a little Arabic.

"We had a lot to talk about," Bugia remembered. "It quickly went from a random encounter at the beach to friendship."

Hamida began visiting the Bugia family to eat dinner and talk Tunisia with Bugia's father, Salvatore. Everyone was happy. It gave Salvatore a chance to reminisce and speak Arabic, while Hamida was the perfect guest: always polite and sociable, always arriving with a bouquet of flowers for the mother.

The first time Louis Bugia visited Hamida in the hospital, he was taken aback by the changes in his friend. "He was depressed, but I thought that was normal considering what happened. What struck me was his anger. He refused to consider that there might be a future."

Vincent and Katherine Comandé were equally distressed by Hamida's mental state. He had been practically part of their family for the year he lived in their grocery store, sharing meals, watching the Sunday-night movies on television, spending days at the beach together. Hamida even went so far as to tell Vincent Comandé he was the father he never had. Of course, he neglected to mention that his real father, Hédi, was alive and well in Tunis.

What always struck the Comandés was how lighthearted Hamida could be. One time, at a beach near the Camargue, the mistral started blowing and picked up one of the children's beach balls. Hamida ran for nearly a mile before finally catching up with it. He came back panting, the ball held aloft in pride.

"We couldn't stop laughing," Bruno Comandé remembered. "He had this enthusiasm that made everything seem funny."

Now the Comandés barely recognized him. Not only was he in immense physical pain, he was inconsolable. He kept repeating, "*Ma vie est gâchée. Ma vie est gâchée.*"

My life is ruined.*

*

*   *

TO UNDERSTAND THE Marseille that Hamida Djandoubi and Elisabeth Bousquet found themselves in during those first years of the 1970s, one needs to understand the impact of the Algerian situation on the city.

In one of its most haunting colonial chapters, France first invaded Algeria in 1830 on the twin grounds of a slight to one of its diplomats and allegations that the country was willfully harboring the pirates who pillaged the Mediterranean shipping lanes. In a forewarning of all that was to come, what was supposed to be a swift victory by French forces became a tortured occupation that wasn't fully realized until the end of the nineteenth century.

The country eventually became a French *département* (administrative district), and at the peak of the colonial period, there were more

---

* In one of those coincidences that feel charged with greater meaning, near the end of my work on this book I fell off my bicycle and ruptured the tendon in my right ankle. Though it was nothing compared to Hamida's injury, for three months I was reduced to hobbling, was dependent on others for help, and was surprisingly lethargic and depressed. It was a brief glimpse into what my subject may have felt.

than one million French nationals among Algeria's total population of nine million people. Yet, to no great surprise, the French were never truly accepted. Always present, the Algerian independence movement truly took flight after World War II. Algerian soldiers fought alongside the Allies, yet returned to find they were still second-class citizens in their own country. The wealth, the power, and even the beaches were reserved for the French. Algerians began to lobby for more individual rights, and this coincided with the movement by fundamentalist Muslim groups to turn Algeria into an Islamic state. With widespread social unrest and a motivated revolutionary cadre, the hostilities began in November 1954, when the nationalist group Front de Libération Nationale (FLN) attacked key French sites in Algeria and broadcast radio calls from its base in Cairo for all Muslims to take up arms. In France, the response from the minister of the interior, François Mitterrand, was blunt: "The only possible negotiation is war."

War it was, eight years of butchery on both sides. Typical were the Philippeville massacres of 1955, when the FLN executed 123 French residents in hopes of prompting an exodus of French settlers. In response, French troops went on a rampage. The official tally states 1,273 Algerians were killed in retaliation, although Algerian sources put the number closer to 12,000. As Albert Camus, born in a small Algerian town near present-day Annaba, wrote, "To justify himself, each relies on the other's crime."

Despite assurances from Charles de Gaulle that France would never cede the colony, in June 1962 the French military left Algeria, and there was a rush of refugees back across the Mediterranean. More than 1.4 million people arrived in France, in two main groups: the *pieds-noirs* (black feet), French nationals who'd been born in Algeria; and the *harkis,* Algerians who had fought alongside the French in the war and were now the target of vicious reprisals. The saying among both groups was *"La valise ou le cercueil."* The suitcase or the coffin.

Most of those émigrés from Algeria ended up coming through

Marseille, and many stayed. The numbers spoke for themselves: in 1954 metropolitan Marseille had a population of 661,462; by 1968 that number had jumped to 894,000. These masses were a logistical and economic nightmare for the government and an unwelcome intrusion for many French people. While there were networks of volunteers to help the refugees, there was also the predictable backlash to such an explosion in population. The new arrivals, particularly the Arabs, were blamed for everything from the lack of jobs to the rise in crime. Predictably, there was also a surge in support for far-right parties that promised to curb immigration and get tough on delinquency.

*

* *

HAMIDA DJANDOUBI could never have guessed this new political trend would intimately concern him. All he wanted was a fair disability pension.

In one way, Hamida was incredibly lucky. At a time when tens of thousands of North Africans were working illegally in France, he at least had an official contract. This made him eligible for an injury settlement and a pension, although he would have to struggle through the miasma of French bureaucracy to secure it. On the advice of the landscaper's insurance company, Hamida was referred to a Marseille lawyer named Jean Goudareau to aid him in this daunting legal task. It was to become the most unusual of relationships.

In the fall of 1971, Jean Goudareau was fifty-eight years old, married, and the father of two girls. He was old-school France and proudly traced his ancestors back to the Welsh archers—the "Good Arrows" who came into Normandy during the Hundred Years' War. Marseille became the family's home when Goudareau's father was appointed director of one of the major shipping companies that was based in the city. Goudareau himself was supposed to follow the same path and was scheduled to head a shipping office in Buenos Aires until World War II intervened.

During the war, Goudareau first fought with the French troops in Norway, then joined the Resistance network in Marseille. Afterward, he forgot about the shipping business and began practicing law in earnest. His work consisted mostly of contracts, real estate, and insurance settlements, with the occasional criminal case flung into the mix. His very first case was typical of his workload, although on that occasion it happened to involve a major French celebrity. The singer Charles Trenet had missed a concert in Nice, claiming he'd caught a cold while taking a bath. Goudareau represented the concert producer. It was a simple affair: a signed contract hadn't been respected. Goudareau got the producer his money back.

But, in reality, by the 1970s law was only a part-time occupation for Goudareau. His true passion was politics. It had begun when he was a law student in Paris and he edited a far-right newspaper, *Le National*. World War II only entrenched his beliefs. He was appalled by how quickly France fell to the Germans, and took it as proof the country needed a stronger national ethic. He was fiercely opposed to the wave of immigration from North Africa and the French withdrawal from Algeria. His convictions led him to enter local politics, and he was eventually elected to the Marseille city council.

Goudareau was one of the politicians whose boat rose on this ugly tide of anger and fear following the Algerian War. When Hamida Djandoubi's file crossed his desk, the irony was that his new client was one of the immigrants he so often railed against.

"For me, who didn't have any particular sympathy for the Maghrebians, I had to admit to myself that he was a very likable," Goudareau said decades later. "Actually, he was a very handsome boy, very elegant, very angelic, not at all your typical Arab."*

---

* Jean Goudareau, ninety-three years old, kindly invited me into his home in Marseille to conduct a series of recorded interviews between 2005 and 2007. It is perhaps a sign of aging that I was able to thoroughly enjoy my afternoons with this accomplished gentleman despite the incompatibility of many of our political opinions.

As for Hamida, he either wasn't aware of or wasn't concerned with his new lawyer's attitudes. He needed the money.

*

*   *

IN DECEMBER 1971, after two months at the Hôpital de la Conception, Djandoubi was transferred to the Notre Dame de Bon Voyage rehabilitation center in La Ciotat.

It should have been an ideal setting for his recovery. La Ciotat was a coastal town east of Marseille with postcard views of the Mediterranean, while the rehab center itself was one block from the beach and the strip of restaurants and bars that catered to the beach-going crowd. The center itself looked out over the blue waters of the Golfe d'Amour, and most of the patients had rooms with a view of the sea. The doctors were hopeful that Hamida would be able to build a normal life for himself. Although he had never done particularly well at school—he had failed the major high school exam that would have allowed him to go to a university—he was bright enough. Reports show his faculties of analysis were "of a very high level" while IQ tests placed him "at the limit of the superior category."

In theory, he should have been able to adapt well. But things weren't working out that way. While waiting for the amputation wound to heal so he could be fitted for a prosthesis, Hamida faced a daily exercise regime to keep his leg muscles in shape. Not only did this prove painful, but he often needed help standing and walking, and he detested appearing helpless in front of others, especially the female nurses.

This may have been partly due to Hamida's paranoid obsession with the idea that women would no longer find him attractive because of his missing leg. "I felt like I wasn't a man like the others anymore," he would tell psychologists. "I didn't want anybody to laugh at me."

This fixation was either the root or the exacerbation of another of Hamida's problems. He was losing his sexual appetite. He told doctors he used to be able to make love two or three times in a single afternoon; now he had trouble getting an erection.

Hamida couldn't accept what had happened to him. He was constantly tormented by stress and battled bouts of trembling. His cigarette consumption doubled to two packs a day. The doctors prescribed Binoctal and Nozinan so he could sleep at night. Tranquilizers and antidepressants became part of his daily diet.

It was at this point that the signs of violence began to emerge. First he slapped a cleaning lady who worked at the center, because he thought she had smirked when looking at his leg. Then he got in a fight with another patient whom he accused of mocking his injury. He passed it off as a bad case of the nerves.

"I keep having breakdowns," he told the doctors. "I used to be so calm."

8

FOR ROUGHLY TEN CENTURIES, the Romans honed their legal pro-cedures, introduced courts of law across their territories, and created the very profession of lawyer. The whole business culminated in A.D. 529, when Emperor Justinian compiled the majestic *Corpus Iuris Civilis,* the fruit of all Roman legal wisdom and the foundation of all modern law. Quite the legacy. But, alas, not their most notorious con-tribution to the world of criminal justice.

Although it was Plato who formulated the idea that public punish-ment might act as a deterrent, it was the Romans who so enthusiastically embraced the concept. For a society that loved a spectacle, executions became one of the most popular public entertainments. There were gladiatorial combats between convicts; condemned men were fed to li-ons; and the punishment for killing your father was to be stuffed into a goatskin sack with a dog, a rooster, a viper, and a monkey, and then thrown into the water while the crowds cheered on the riverbanks.

"The more public the punishments are, the greater the effect they will produce upon the reformation of others," the orator Seneca the El-der famously proclaimed. (Seneca did have some qualms about the public administration of justice. For instance, he didn't think it wise to decapitate criminals in the presence of men wearing sandals.)

From Rome's earliest days, punishment was meted out as publicly as possible, all in the name of dissuasion. Under the Twelve Tables, a com-bination bill of rights and criminal code dating from 451 B.C., public executions were prescribed for a range of offenses, including:

Publishing libels and insulting songs

Furtively cutting or causing to be grazed crops raised by plowing, by an adult

> *Knowingly and maliciously burning a house or a pile of grain near a house*
>
> *Willful murder of a freeman*
>
> *Making disturbances in the City at night*

And the execution methods were truly spectacular. Arsonists, for example, were chained to walls, their legs were broken, and then the public was invited to come forward and beat the criminal to death with rocks and clubs. There were, however, unforeseen problems. Friends of the condemned man would often run up and quickly crack him on the head so he would mercifully lose consciousness. This was enormously frustrating for the audience, so it became standard practice that if the criminal was knocked out too early, the person responsible would be beaten as a side event. (Acts of mercy have always been a problem with participatory executions. In tenth-century England, misbehaving slaves were stoned to death by their fellow slaves. If a slave failed to hit his condemned colleague three times in a row, he was whipped.)

The most familiar manifestation of execution as a combination of entertainment and example was the gladiatorial combat. Unlike prisoners of war or slaves who could win their liberty, condemned criminals were under special contracts stating that they had to be killed within a year of becoming a gladiator.

But there were even more creative means of administering the death penalty. In A.D. 62, Nero had his friend Marcus Caius executed before a rapt crowd at Circus Maximus. Caius was whipped until his skin hung in shreds, then placed in the hollow belly of a sculpted bronze bull. A fire was then kindled so Caius was slowly roasted to death. To the delight of the spectators, the bull's horns had been designed to amplify the dying man's screams.

Nero's uncle, Caligula, transformed executions into a sporting competition. Soldiers were challenged to behead prisoners using increasingly difficult techniques. In the early rounds, the criminals had their necks on a chopping block; later, the prisoners knelt so there was no brace to ease the task. The goal was to take the head off in one clean swipe, and score was kept like in golf: the soldier with the fewest strokes at the end of the event won. Prizes included a night with one of Caligula's most talented prostitutes, extra vacation time, or a raise in pay for the champion's entire unit.

Amazingly, these sorts of customs were endorsed by the greatest legal mind of the time. Cicero argued that gladiatorial combats instructed the crowds in "courage and, above all, self-control." Born in 106 B.C., Cicero is more famous for being the prosecutor who delivered the most damning request for the death penalty in ancient history. When Lucius Catilina hatched a plan to overthow the Roman Republic, it was Cicero who prosecuted him before the Senate and demanded the death for all involved in the Catiline conspiracy. Despite Julius Caesar's argument that such executions would set a dangerous precedent and Lucius Catalina's own offer to exile himself to Massilia, as Marseille was then known, Cicero won out and the conspirators were killed.

Critics of the death penalty often argue that it fuels society's endless cycle of violence. And it is true that, throughout the centuries, the greatest enthusiasts of blood justice often succumb to it themselves. In Cicero's case, after prosecuting the Catiline conspirators and applauding the assassination of Julius Caesar, he himself fell victim to the deadly whims of justice. In 43 B.C., guilty of having publicly mocked Mark Antony, Cicero suffered true "capital" punishment—he had his *caput* (Latin for head) cut off by Antony's henchmen, making the punishment *capitalis* (the corresponding Latin adjective). Afterward the head was displayed at the Forum, where Antony's wife, Fulvia, jabbed Cicero's lifeless tongue with her hairpin in return for the insults he'd heaped upon her husband.

In the end, Cicero could be said to have been a victim of the predominant Roman philosophy: individuals could be sacrificed for the greater good. Nobody argued this more fervently than Cassius Longinus, one of the conspirators against Caesar and a prominent member of the Senate. When a law was proposed that would condemn all the slaves in a household to death if one among them killed his or her master, Cassius was its most vociferous supporter.

"The individual injustice involved," Cassius explained, "is redeemed by the public utility."

9

ELISABETH GEORGETTE BOUSQUET was in love. After months of hospital visits and cute little get-well cards, she and Hamida Djandoubi were dating. She told her brother Jean-Pierre she had her new boyfriend *"dans ma peau"* (in my skin).

By all accounts, she couldn't stop talking about Hamida. Her employer, François Ceccaldi, remembers endless stories about the handsome young Arab man she met in the hospital. He also remembers warning her that nothing good would come of it.

"It didn't sound like this fellow would be right for her," Ceccaldi said. "But you know how it is with young girls: if they are in love, you have to chain them up to keep them away."

The affair took its time developing. In the hospital, Hamida appreciated the distraction of Elisabeth's visits, but nothing even vaguely romantic occurred. His move to the rehabilitation center in La Ciotat put an end to those bedside conversations, but Elisabeth still wrote him notes and sent him little gifts in the mail. During the dark and violent gloom of his recuperation, this attention from a young woman made Hamida think that maybe, just maybe, he might still have a little of his old charm left.

Hamida was initially discharged from Notre Dame de Bon Voyage on Valentine's Day 1972, but was readmitted a short while later due to complications with his leg. He couldn't get used to his prosthesis, the flesh of his stump became raw and irritated, and he continued to suffer from phantom limb sensations.

After a second round of rehab and a fitting for a new prosthesis, he was released for good in July 1972. He could walk upward of a mile at a time, and his limp was barely noticeable. Most people who saw him assumed he had a mild ankle sprain or a problem with his calf.

Once back in Marseille, Hamida moved into the Sonacotra men's residence at Pointe-Rouge, the beach community in the south end of the city. Sonacotras were apartment complexes built by a government agency, the Société Nationale de Construction pour les Travailleurs, as a cheap housing solution for the legions of men arriving in France after the Algerian war. There were a half dozen Sonacotras in Marseille by 1972, each building divided into shared apartments with their own kitchen and bathroom. At a time when landlords weren't eager to rent to North Africans, the Sonacotras filled a vital housing role. But that didn't make them an especially charming place to live, and on the street they were known as "foyers of solitude."

Hamida had been staying at that Sonacotra on and off since leaving the Comandés' grocery store in 1969. It was considered the Rolls-Royce of Marseille Sonacotras, as it was in a wealthy neighborhood, close to shops and cafés, and, most tantalizing of all, about three hundred feet from the sea. After his amputation, they welcomed him back and gave him a ground-floor room. There was no elevator.

The rent was 150 francs a month. His lawyer, Jean Goudareau, had negotiated a temporary pension of 330 francs a months, which allowed Hamida to pay his rent and buy a few groceries, but little else.

That August, Hamida briefly returned to Tunisia to renew his visa. He didn't contact his parents. He didn't want anybody to know about his accident.

When he returned to Marseille, he decided to call Elisabeth, and the two went on their first date in September 1972. They had a surprising amount in common. Like Elisabeth, Hamida had been separated from his family at an early age because of family financial difficulties. There were two sons and five daughters in the Djandoubi family, and his parents couldn't manage all the children. Just before his twelfth birthday, Hamida and his brother, Ali, were sent off to live with an uncle while the five daughters stayed at home with Hédi and Cherifa.

Whether it was this mutual sense of abandonment or the less complicated magic of sexual attraction, Hamida and Elisabeth made plans to see each other again. It was something of a courageous decision because of the backlash from the bigots who feared that Arab men were taking the "French" women. If a white woman was seen on the streets with an Arab man, it wasn't unusual for her to be called *pute* or *pétasse*—slut or whore. Sadly, this sort of racism isn't rare in such culturally diverse cities; it is the inevitable *revers de la médaille,* the backside of the medal, as the French say. Marseille has long exhibited a certain hatred for its newest arrivals, whether they were the Italians in the nineteenth century or the Armenians early in the twentieth. In Claude McKay's novel *Banjo,* an undulating homage to African American men in Marseille in the 1920s, a black prostitute named Latnah embodies these racial divisions when she finds her boyfriend flirting with a white woman.

"I go with white man, but only for money. White race no love my race. My race no love white," she says.

But Hamida and Elisabeth forged ahead. On their next date, in early October, Hamida snuck her into his room at the Sonacotra. On that day, they made love for the first time.

In many ways, for a man who was suddenly so wretchedly insecure, Elisabeth was a safe choice as a girlfriend. Her combination of desperate loneliness and helpless naïveté meant she was neither a challenge to his ego nor a threat to leaving him. And she had seen him at his very worst in the hospital and accepted his amputation . . . though it might be argued that, for a man who couldn't accept his physical diminution himself, this type of devotion might not have been a healthy thing.

She was also his first lover since the accident. Whatever worries he might have had about women finding him attractive should have been soothed. As should any apprehensions about his sexual performance. In terms of the mechanics of intercourse, everything was back in working order.

Within weeks of their first intimacy, Elisabeth started spending nights with Hamida. This broke all the rules: residents of the Sonaco-tra weren't allowed female visitors, let alone a girlfriend who spent the night, and Elisabeth's parents expressly forbade their daughter to sleep outside the family apartment.

But Elisabeth was in love. I'm an adult, she kept telling her family. I can take care of myself. Marie-Josée Bousquet just shook her head. Her baby sister had always been headstrong.

Her father, Pierre, was still recovering from his motorcycle accident and was struggling with the problems in his own marriage. He was slightly out of touch with his daughter. But, in principle, he wasn't op-posed to the relationship. In the hospital, Hamida had come across as a nice, normal sort of fellow. He just didn't want his daughter getting a bad reputation.

This would turn out to be the least of his concerns.

*
*   *

ONE OF THE GREAT PARADOXES of France in the 1970s was that this country renowned for its liberties still clung to many of its conserva-tive traditions.

The very month that Hamida and Elisabeth's relationship was con-summated, the two men who carried out the hostage taking at the Clairvaux prison, Claude Buffet and Roger Bontems, were guillotined at a prison in Paris. Thus, not only was France the last democracy in Europe to use the death penalty, it continued to decapitate its con-demned men with a device born of the French Revolution.

Then there was the plight of women. Even though Elisabeth Bous-quet was nineteen years old in the fall of 1972, she was still considered a minor under French law. Until 1974, the age of majority was twenty-one in France, which meant that Elisabeth didn't have the right to vote or even to leave her parents' home without their permission.

Part of this was the specter of Charles de Gaulle. As leader of the Free French Forces during World War II, de Gaulle had become the country's greatest hero, mostly because glorifying him, and the small numbers who joined the French Resistance, was one way for France to salvage her pride. Images of de Gaulle leading the French army along the Champs-Élysées helped blur more painful memories of France's quick surrender and the Vichy government's collaboration with the Nazis.

After the war, de Gaulle led the provisional French government but chose to resign in 1946 because of a constitutional squabble. It was in 1958 that he returned to power. The Algerian question had so destabilized the country that French paratroopers in Corsica were preparing a military coup. De Gaulle, the only one with the influence to resolve the crisis, was elected president and ushered in a new constitution that founded the Fifth Republic.

It led to a Dickensian period for France. It was the best of economic times, a period of unprecedented economic growth known as *les Trente Glorieuses,* the thirty glorious years after World War II. France became the fifth-largest economy in the world, it built an arsenal of nuclear weapons, and de Gaulle oversaw a series of projects, from the expansion of the Marseille port to the foundation of the French aviation industry. But, politically, it was among the worst of times. The war in Algeria spurred a string of terrorist attacks in mainland France, and when de Gaulle eventually agreed to the independence of Algeria, a large part of the country was opposed. In Marseille, Jean Goudareau launched a campaign against the withdrawal, warning that France would descend into civil war.

But what ultimately undid de Gaulle was his inability to respond to society's changing mores. He was seventy-seven years old when the student uprising took over Paris in May 1968. He embodied a France of another epoch, and a generation of men and, more important, women was clamoring for more rights, more freedoms, more equality. One widely distributed May '68 poster was symbolic of the frustration: a silhouette of de Gaulle demanding: *Sois Jeune et Tais-Toi.* Be young and shut up.

De Gaulle resigned in 1969, but the new president, Georges Pompidou, was one of his protégés, the former director of the Anne de Gaulle Foundation for Down syndrome, no less. Though Pompidou was twenty years younger than de Gaulle, the new government continued in much the same direction.

So, by 1972, not only was France the last democracy in Europe to use capital punishment, but abortion was still illegal, contraception was available only by a doctor's prescription, only 2 percent of the representatives to parliament were women. And if a nineteen-year-old girl spent the night with her boyfriend, she was considered a runaway.

*

* *

THE FIRST TIME Elisabeth "ran away," her brother Jean-Pierre went to the Sonacotra to fetch her. Elisabeth hid in the closet. At first, Hamida played along, denying that Elisabeth was with him. Finally, he relented and her brother took her home.

It was enough to make the family anxious. And it only got worse a few weeks later, when Elisabeth started behaving strangely. She admitted she'd smoked hashish with Hamida and had taken some yellow pills he'd given her. She said she hadn't wanted to, but he'd insisted and she hadn't known how to say no.

This sort of doleful aquiescence was nothing new for Elisabeth. Sister Odette Lafout, her teacher in Langogne, remembers how easily influenced she was by the other children at school. She was the type of girl who, if asked for her chocolate pudding at lunchtime, would give it up no matter how badly she wanted the dessert for herself.

"She had a very difficult time saying no," Sister Lafout remembers. "There was very little self-esteem in that girl."

The news of the drugs was a breaking point for her older brother Jean-Pierre. Deciding she was too impulsive, he marched her to the local police precinct. An officer lectured her on the dangers of drugs and the rules governing minors in France. Jean-Pierre hoped it would scare her enough to keep her away from Hamida Djandoubi. It didn't.

She kept dating Hamida, letting her life unravel. She quit her job taking care of the Ceccaldi children. She started to fight relentlessly with her mother. And then she ran away again.

It was straight to Hamida. This time, her mother and sister went to the Sonacotra to get her. After she was dragged home once again, she asked her father, Pierre, for legal permission to live full-time with Hamida.

"I refused," Pierre said. "Ever since she knew this Hamida she didn't want to work anymore."

But if the family was worried about Elisabeth's sudden rebellious streak, they were terrified by what happened just before Christmas in 1972. For the first time, Hamida became violent with Elisabeth.

It was Alphonsine who noticed it. Elisabeth had blisters on her left hand. She asked her daughter what had happened. After some hedging, she admitted Hamida had burned her with his cigarette, both on her hand and across her back. He'd also beaten her with his belt. She told her mother Hamida had suspected her of cheating on him.

Momentarily, at least, the crisis with Elisabeth and Hamida overshadowed the Bousquet family's personal problems. Alphonsine and Pierre got together and ordered Elisabeth to stop seeing Hamida. This time, she promised to stay away from the man she loved.

10

THE BIBLE IS A FUNNY BOOK. On one hand, it is a remarkably rigorous set of laws. In the Old Testament, there are more than two dozen offenses punishable by death, including homosexuality, witchcraft, and blasphemy. Strictly speaking, you could be executed if your ox gores a person to death (Exodus 22:29), if you work with your ox on the Sabbath (Exodus 35:2), if you worship your ox (Deuteronomy 17:5), or if you have sex with your ox (Leviticus 20:15).

Yet God delivered the first draft of these stringent laws to none other than a murderer. When touring a slave camp as a young man, Moses saw an Egyptian guard abusing a Jewish worker and was so outraged, he "looked this way and that way, and when he saw there was no man, slew the Egyptian, and hid him in the sand" (Exodus 2:12).

Such ironies would only be subject to theological debate if the Bible had remained a purely spiritual text. Instead, just as the Romans defined the mechanics of Western justice, it was the Bible that defined the morality underlying the judicial apparatus. To this day, our system of crime and punishment reflects the edicts of the Bible, while several crucial Old Testament passages continue to influence the debate on capital punishment. Some evoke compassion. When Cain killed his brother Abel in a fit of jealousy, for example, God chose exile over execution, taking extra pains to protect Cain's life. "And the Lord set a mark upon Cain, lest any finding him should kill him" (Genesis 4:15).

Later, after the Great Flood, God was more uncompromising. About the time of Noah's six-hundredth birthday, God gave the following order: "Whoso sheddeth man's blood, by man shall his blood be shed: for in the image of God made he man."

If taken as prescriptive, this passage, from Genesis 9:6, is a divine order for the death penalty in cases of murder or manslaughter. Unless it is considered descriptive, in which case it merely describes the dismal cycle of retribution that stems from human violence.

God's intentions were further clarified when the Ten Commandments were passed down to that famous murderer Moses. Exodus 21:23 mimics the *lex talionis* of Hammurabi's Code, announcing: "Thou shalt give life for life, eye for eye, tooth for tooth, hand for hand, foot for foot."

Clear enough. Unless one is talking about slaves, who weren't held in the same regard. Exodus 21:27 tells us, "And if he smite out his manservant's tooth, or his maidservant's tooth; he shall let him go free for his tooth's sake."

There are other loopholes. In Deuteronomy 4:42, Moses, perhaps thinking of his own criminal past, created cities of refuge. The towns of Bezer, Ramoth, and Golan became sanctuaries for a murderer: upon "fleeing unto one of these cities, he might live."

With such a moral tangle, it is no wonder early religious courts were cautious in their interpretation of Mosaic Law. In Jewish tradition, crimes were tried by the Sanhedrin, a court of twenty-three judges, and a record of verdicts was kept in the Mishnah (the first written recording of the oral Torah) to ensure continuity. It appears Jewish leaders decided it was technically impossible to sentence anyone to death, because the requirements were too strenuous to meet. According to Deuteronomy 19:15, for example, the death penalty could be meted out only if there were two eyewitnesses to a crime, and those witnesses couldn't be women, slaves, relatives of the victims, or people of bad reputation.

So the Jews came up with a when-pigs-can-fly type of compromise. Yes, God's law provided for the death penalty; but in practice, the circumstances in which it was legal were so rare that the penalty was essentially unusable. The Mishnah declared that a Jewish court that sentenced a person to death even once during seven years would be "ruinous." Rabbi Eliezar ben Azariah upped this to "even seventy years," and then Rabbis Akiba and Tarfon topped it all, declaring, "Had we been in the Sanhedrin, none would ever have been put to death."

For Christians, of course, Jesus put a fresh spin on things.

Among the very first pages of the New Testament, Jesus begs people to reconsider the concept of vengeance. According to Matthew, during his Sermon on the Mount, Jesus announced: "Ye have heard that it hath been said, An eye for an eye, and a tooth for a tooth: But I say unto you, That ye resist not evil; but whosoever shall smite thee on thy right cheek, turn to him the other also."

Jesus expands on his philosophy of nonviolence at the temple on the Mount of Olives. A group of scribes and Pharisees brought forward a woman caught in the act of adultery and declared: "Now Moses in the law commanded us that such should be stoned: but what sayest thou?" Jesus, unable to openly contradict the law, subverted the death penalty by proclaiming: "He that is without sin among you, let him cast the first stone" (John 8:5–7).

All of this preaching eventually led to the most famous execution in human history. In approximately A.D. 29, in the fifteenth year of the rule of the Roman emperor Tiberius, Jesus was accused of "perverting the nation" and was duly crucified. According to Luke 24:34, among his last words were "Father, forgive them, for they know not what they do."

Throughout Western history, no text has had as much impact on judicial values as the Bible. When it comes to that most complicated of subjects, the death penalty, both its opponents and proponents quote it to support their positions. That's the difficulty with such a diverse text: it is like a jumbo box of LEGOs, and any sophist worth his salt can pick out individual bricks and build whatever argument he chooses.

Still, at the end of the day, one thing from the Bible seems rather clear: Thou Shalt Not Kill.

II

HAMIDA DJANDOUBI WAS in a dark place. He drank, he drugged, he rarely left his apartment. Even his own brother didn't want anything to do with him.

Ali was two years younger than Hamida and of roughly the same height and build. Alas, he wasn't blessed with the same eye-widening good looks, and the women who remember Ali describe him as tough-looking and even a bit frightening.

Like his older brother, Ali was drawn to Europe for a chance at a better, less oppressive life. In Tunis, he worked as a gas station attendant after high school and saved enough money to visit Hamida in Marseille. He liked what he saw, so he returned to Tunisia, filled out the proper forms, and received a French work visa in the spring of 1972.

The brothers should have been close. They had been sent away together to live with their uncle Ahmed and had grown up sharing a bedroom. This could have been a bonding experience, endowing them with an us-against-the-world mentality. Instead, it was only a source of bad memories. Ali would later tell police that his older brother was sickly as a child, always needing injections and special treatment, always enjoying the attention his maladies earned him. Worse, he was a bully. Of all those who knew Hamida, Ali is the only one who reported any signs of violence or manipulative behavior before his accident and amputation.

"From the time he was very young, he always did whatever pleased him. He always liked to order people around and never admitted when he was wrong," Ali would tell police.

And apparently it wasn't just at home that Hamida's haughty attitude was ill appreciated. As a teenager in Carthage, he mouthed off to the wrong person at a party and got cracked on the head with a two-pound barbell. He was knocked unconscious and spent the night in the hospital. The scar remained visible, just beneath his hairline.

If it was hard to be Hamida's younger brother back in Tunisia, it was worse in Marseille after the accident had so soured his demeanor. For months, the two young men lived in the same four-bedroom apartment at the Pointe-Rouge Sonacotra. Ali found his brother taciturn and moody. He would stay locked in his room for weeks without seeing anybody. And worst of all, he still bossed Ali around.

"I didn't like to be around him too much," he said. "He had a bad character and was always on edge."

Not that Ali was reputed to have the best of characters himself. According to Bruno Comandé, Ali, like his older brother, was given a free room in the back of the grocery store when he first arrived in Marseille. And, like Hamida, he soon tired of this life and moved to the Sonacotra. Unlike his older brother, Ali reportedly emptied the till the night before he left.

*

*   *

ONE OF THE PECULIAR aspects of the Hamida Djandoubi case is the onomastics. The name *Djandoubi* derives from the Tunisian city of Jendouba. Sixty miles east of the Algerian border, the city was for centuries a crossroads for travelers and camel caravans. Today, it is mostly known as the jumping-off point for tourists who want to visit Bulla Regia, the underground city built by the Romans about A.D. 100.

According to some elderly residents of Jendouba, the city's name stems from an old desert legend. A warrior who'd had his head cut off walked into the village and begged for help. Local healers covered his neck in pomades and potions, then replaced the head. Miraculously, the warrior recovered. A short while later, the village was raided by desert pirates, and the warrior successfully drove them off. That warrior's name was Jendouba.*

But if Jendouba was the name of the warrior and Jendouba was the name of the city, not all of Jendouba's children carry this exact name. Over the centuries, it has been transmogrified into a handful of variants: Jendoubi, Djendoubi, Djandoubi. . . . In the case of Hamida and Ali, they were born to the "Djendoubi" family in Tunis, but both men saw their names altered when they arrived in France. Ali became "Jendoubi" when the immigration officials forgot the *D* on his visa. Hamida's case was a little more unusual. When he arrived in France, he still used "Djendoubi." This was the name he himself wrote on his bank passbook, and this was the name that police have on file from their earliest dealings with him. But when things got serious, a court clerk mistook the *e* for an *a*, and it was as "Djandoubi" that his name became infamous.

*

*   *

HAMIDA HAD NOW DISTANCED himself from all of his old friends. Before his accident, he used to visit Louis Bugia and his wife, Colette, as often as once a week. "I was just learning to cook, but he really loved to eat with us," Colette remembered. "He told me my meals were wonderful. He always was a real flatterer."

Now months would pass with no sign of him. And when he finally did appear, he seemed depressed and vacant. "I noticed he'd started drinking after the accident," Louis said. "Before, he never touched it, never. Not even at our *fiançailles*. I don't think he had one glass. But after . . ."

The Bugias tried to reach out to Hamida, but he didn't respond.

---

*The story of the headless warrior Jendouba came to me through the Franco-Tunisian artist Anicée Driss, with whom I shared an atelier in 2005. During one of her trips to Tunisia, the gentleman next to her on the airplane happened to be from Jendouba. He told her of the legend, which she helpfully shared with me.

"Maybe if he was in his own country, with his whole family around him, he would have been able to handle the shock of what happened better," Louis said. "Maybe things would have turned out differently."

The Comandés had also lost contact with Hamida. "There were two Djandoubis, one before and one after the accident," explained Bruno Comandé. "Since the accident he was hardened. By the end, we just stopped seeing him."

Adding to Hamida's frustrations was his lack of a job. He had been an enterprising worker since arriving in France. There'd been the grocery store, the flower shop, the landscaping company. The entire time, he took side jobs working in construction or painting to earn money to travel. Even when he went on vacation, he found ways to earn money. When he was in Paris for three months to visit a friend in 1970, he found two part-time jobs: he drove a minibus for the company Les Calèches de France, chauffeuring airline pilots and stewardesses to and from the airport; and three days a week he got up at four in the morning to sell vegetables at one of the outdoor markets in the eighteenth arrondissement. Before his amputation, his employers applauded his work ethic and determination.

"He learned everything quickly, he was very intelligent, he worked hard," said Désiré Boyer, the owner of the landscaping company. "I never had a single complaint."

After the accident, it would be a different story. An industrious young man can always find work as a laborer. An industrious young man with one leg has fewer options.

On the advice of Jean Goudareau, Hamida registered with ANPE, the national employment agency, in order to learn another trade. It was best to prepare for the future. Hamida wouldn't qualify for a full pension, as he wasn't fully disabled. He was still mobile and was learning to drive a car again. He qualified for an array of desk jobs and retail positions.

Starting in the fall of 1972, Hamida made repeated visits to the employment office to see Alberte Joubert. She was the reinsertion counselor who worked with handicapped applicants, matching their disabilities to jobs. It wasn't an enviable task. In Marseille in the 1970s, there was 20 percent unemployment, and jobs of all types were scarce. Still, Hamida did his best to stand out.

"He particularly wanted to get a job," Joubert said. "He was always very well dressed, elegant even. He made an excellent impression."

But that didn't mean a job. Months passed and there was no work for him. Early in 1973, Hamida decided that maybe a trip would change his luck. Growing up in Tunisia, he'd dreamed of exploring all of Europe, and before his accident, he'd been to Holland, Belgium, Germany, and Sweden. During the last trip, he'd acquired a twenty-volume collection of Swedish pornography that was one of his most cherished possessions.

Now he took advantage of his free time and went on a bus trip through Italy and Yugoslavia. And, sure enough, when he got back to Marseille his luck changed.

In March 1973, seventeen months after his accident, Madame Joubert found him a temporary position in a bakery on avenue de Toulon. France still had compulsory military service in the 1970s, and the regular pastry chef had been called up to fulfill his twelve-month obligation to the army. Hamida had to be at the bakery at 6 A.M. every morning, but it was decent work and there were fringe benefits: all the pastries and pizza he could eat.

With the new job and the interim pension payments, Hamida had enough for a down payment on a used car. He picked out a white four-door Simca 1000, known as a Simca Mille. This was a boxy car, one step up from economy, and very popular with bachelors. In fact, it had such a playboy reputation, the group Les Chevaliers du Fiel paid musical tribute to the car with "*Dans la Simca 1000*." Part of the chorus went:

> *I am going to have you naked in the Simca 1000*
> *I am going to be naked in the Simca 1000*
> *We are going to be naked in the Simca 1000*

Even after their violent parting, Hamida didn't forget about Elisabeth Bousquet. One of his frequent stops in those days was Jean Goudareau's law office. The insurance company had scheduled a series of medical exams to determine the extent of his incapacitation, and he was eager to have the results.

He also went to the office because he enjoyed talking with Goudareau's secretary, Lucie Le Manchec. She'd wanted to go to university and become a French teacher, but her father lost his job and her sister had a serious accident, so she quit school to work in the law office. The two got on well. Hamida would bring her flowers or chocolates or treats from the bakery, and they would spend the afternoon chatting between phone calls. Le Manchec says he often spoke of Elisabeth. How they met in the hospital, how they had dated, how she had wanted them to get an apartment together.

"He said they got on very, very well," remembered Le Manchec. "But I think that with his problem with his leg, he had a complex. He was ill at ease with people and he got angry at the girl and broke it off. But he kept talking about her."

Hamida never told Le Manchec he'd accused Elisabeth of cheating on him, burned her with cigarettes, and whipped her with his belt.

*
* *

IN THE END, IT WAS Elisabeth who came to Hamida.

It wasn't an easy time for the teenager. Alphonsine had finally announced she wanted a divorce and left the family apartment. To her family's great dismay and suspicion, she moved in with her former son-in-law, Noël Patel, who was living with his uncle in the suburbs of

Marseille. It had all the appearances of a scandalous situation, and Pierre Bousquet himself told the police that his wife and former son-in-law were lovers. But Noël Patel denies it to this day.

"I was happy to help this woman. I was proud of her. It took great courage for her to leave like that," he said. "That was it, though, nothing more intimate than that. If a woman comes to live at your house, people just start talking."*

Whatever the exact truth of the Bousquet family's situation, it clearly wasn't a stable one. Between the lingering pain from his motorcycle injuries and the raw emotional wounds left by his impending divorce, Pierre couldn't cope. He chose to move away for a year. "I lost sight of my family," he admitted.

That left Elisabeth adrift. Sometimes she stayed with friends. Other times, she checked herself into women's shelters. Occasionally, she went to see her old employers, the Ceccaldis, for a meal.

"She was very alone," recalled Paulette Ceccaldi. "I don't think her family was there for her."

Perhaps this is why, in April 1973, she decided to go find Hamida Djandoubi at the Sonacotra Pointe-Rouge. That first time, he was nice to her and fixed her a meal in his room. The next time, they became lovers again. Elisabeth even asked if she could move into the foyer with Hamida. He reminded her there were rules against women spending even one night at the Sonacotra.

Still, Elisabeth continued with her visits. One afternoon, she was surprised alone in Hamida's room by Michel Dos, the manager of the Sonacotra. When he explained the rules, she announced she was Hamida's fiancée and refused to leave. Dos asked to see her papers. When he realized she was a minor, he escorted Elisabeth to the door and told her to wait for her "fiancé" outside.

---

* Although Noël Patel denied having an affair with Alphonsine Bousquet, during an interview in the summer of 2007 he took out a black-and-white photo of her that he'd kept with him for more than three decades. As he gazed at the long-ago image of the woman, his eyes moistened with tears.

"She wasn't behaving like a normal person," Dos later reported to the police.

Predictably, it didn't take long for the relationship to turn violent once more. Hamida hit Elisabeth again toward the end of April 1973. He said it was to straighten her out. She'd been telling him about her parents' impending divorce and how her mother had taken up with her sister's ex-husband. According to Hamida, Elisabeth also had confessed to having had sex with Noël Patel. Although this accusation appeared completely groundless, Hamida punished her with his belt. It was ugly violence. But Elisabeth stayed.

It is hard to blame her. She was lost and alone and had nobody else to turn to. She thought things would work out, that it was just a fit of temper, that soon Hamida would get over his amputation and become the boyfriend she'd always dreamed of, the man who would protect her from the vagaries of the world and make her life happy.

Instead, a week later, she was having sex with Hamida's friends for twenty francs a go.

12

AS BEAUTIFUL AS THE IDEALS of Jesus were, early Christians had to be practical. They were, after all, already the victims of ruthless persecution—and execution—at the hands of the Romans. Were they supposed to go and aggravate their ordeal by denouncing Roman law because it didn't adhere to the principles of nonviolence and forgiveness?

In an early case of Realpolitik, the first Christian philosophers carved out a nifty plot of moral high ground based on the teachings of Paul. The key passage is found in Romans I when Paul orders Christians to respect the Roman government: "The powers that be are ordained by God. Whosoever therefore resisteth the power, resisteth the ordinance of God."

With this logic, Christians could accept Roman law and its brutalities because the Romans only ruled by the grace of God and thus their violence must be ordained by the heavenly powers. But early Christians themselves were still compelled to avoid bloodshed. As Minucius Felix, one of the more vocal supporters of the early Christian movement, wrote in the second century while defending Christians from the accusation that they drank the blood of infants, "We, however, are not allowed to witness or to hear of human slaughter."

This inherent pacifism led to the belief, as voiced by Tertullian in the third century A.D., that Christians couldn't act as judges if it meant delivering a death sentence. Tertullian, a leader of the Christian church in Carthage, even questioned whether a true Christian could serve as a soldier. "Gospel is one and the same for the Christian at all times whatever his occupation in life," Tertullian wrote.

But it didn't take long for the compromises to come. Origen, the Alexandrian scholar who died around A.D. 250, decided that an execution simply quickened a criminal's journey to heaven: "Sin is absolved through the death penalty," he would write.

This intellectual dynamic of Christians-as-outsiders changed forever in the year 312, when Emperor Constantine had his vision of a cross with the message "Under this sign you will conquer." The next year, he issued the Edict of Milan, legalizing Christianity throughout the Roman Empire. Constantine himself converted on his deathbed, and, shortly after, Christianity became the official religion of Rome.

With Christianity now the ruling power, everything had to be reconsidered. The tenet of mercy and forgiveness was no longer a moral ideal; it now had to be reconciled with the practical administration of justice and government. There were conflicts from the beginning. Emperor Julian banned Christians from public office because he feared they would refuse to carry out executions. He had good reason. When a Christian judge asked Ambrose, the bishop of Milan, how to handle the death penalty, Ambrose cited Romans 13:4, and said: "You will be excused if you do it; but you will be admired if you refrain when you might have done it."

Ambrose considered the question again in his treatise *On Cain and Abel,* concluding, "God, in His providence, gives this sort of verdict so that magistrates might learn the virtues of magnanimity and patience."

But it was Ambrose's protégé, Augustine, who would shape the Christian philosophy of punishment by arriving at a dramatically different conclusion.

Augustine was born in present-day Algeria in 354, and, by all accounts, he was a randy young man. He fathered a child with one of his mistresses while studying in Carthage and once famously prayed, "Grant me chastity . . . but not yet."

After converting to Christianity in 386, Augustine served in Hippo Regius, today the city of Annaba in Algeria, and began his writings. Although personally opposed to the death penalty—he sought to have it banned in North Africa—Augustine wrote works that became the essential Christian justification for both war and capital punishment. In 391, five years after converting, he wrote in *Commentary on the Sermon on the Mount*: "Noble and saintly men inflicted death as a punishment . . . so that the living would be struck with a salutary fear."

"The same divine law which forbids the killing of human beings allows certain exceptions, as when God authorizes killing by general law," Augustine continued. "It is in no way contrary to the commandment 'Thou shalt not kill' to wage war at God's bidding, or for representatives of the State's authority to put criminals to death."

It was on these grounds that communities across the Roman territory were governed and would be governed for centuries to come. In France, the conversion of Clovis, the first king of all the Franks, in 496 brought the country in step with Roman law and Christian thought; three centuries later, Charlemagne, known as the Father of France, embedded these principles of sanctified judicial killing in his nascent country after being named the ruler of the new Holy Roman Empire.

Any last doubts about the New Testament's view on war and execution were banished by Thomas Aquinas. Born in Italy in 1225, he so alarmed his family with his religious leanings that they locked him in his castle bedroom with a prostitute to tempt him. It didn't work.

Aquinas ended up studying and teaching in Paris, and in *Summa theologiae,* he defined the ultimate goals of Christian punishment: to better the individual who had sinned; to deter others from sinning; and to balance the moral order. In *Summa theologiae,* he concluded that the death penalty was necessary to meet these goals.

"If anyone is dangerous or corrupting to the community on the account of some sin, it is praiseworthy and salubrious that he be killed, in order to preserve the common good," he wrote.

Ultimately, Aquinas declares the notion that "Thou shalt not kill" forbids state executions as "frivolous." In *Summa contra gentiles*, he notes that the Commandment is followed by the passage "Wrongdoers thou shalt not suffer to live" (Exodus 22:18). Sinners, according to Aquinas's interpretation, had forfeited their right to life.

"Although it is evil in itself to kill a man who preserves his human dignity, nevertheless to kill a man who is a sinner can be good, just as it can be good to kill a beast; for an evil man is worse than a beast."

Aquinas's work cemented Christian philosophy as Europe entered the Middle Ages. This is despite the fact that, shortly before his death, he dismissed his entire body of work after having an unexplained mystical experience.

"All that I have written seems to me like so much straw compared to what I have seen," he said.

At the time of this revelation, several monks insisted they found Aquinas levitating.

13

PROSTITUTION IS THE GHOST that haunts the case. The accusations are many. The facts are few. Out of such a morass came only the inevitable provocative headlines and tenuous suppositions.

What are known, more or less, are the events of May 1973. It was on May 24 of that year that Elisabeth arrived at the Prevention and Protection office at the Marseille police station. Accompanying her was a counselor from Foyer Ariane, a women's shelter in downtown Marseille that catered to young women trying to escape prostitution or domestic violence. Elisabeth was there to lodge a complaint against Hamida Djandoubi. This is what she told Inspector Jean Sardou:

Hamida had started complaining that she didn't have enough money. He wanted Elisabeth to buy things for him. Like cigarettes. With her savings left over from the babysitting job, she did her best, but it was never enough.

The first weekend of May 1973, just days after her twentieth birthday, Elisabeth said she arrived at the Sonacotra for a normal visit with her boyfriend. Instead, Hamida told her he knew how they could earn some extra money. He would ask around and see if any of the men at the residence would pay to have sex with Elisabeth.

He charged men twenty francs to sleep with her. He pocketed the money and then stood outside the door and waited while the transaction was completed.

"He took me to the rooms of his friends at the foyer and I had to make love," she told Inspector Sardou.

Elisabeth couldn't remember how many men. She guessed eight. She did specify that none were violent and that none of them took her by force. "I was consenting," she confirmed.

According to Elisabeth, Hamida wanted to keep the operation

going. He also wanted to raise the price. Twenty francs didn't amount to much in 1973. At the supermarket, a can of sliced Dole pineapples cost three francs. With twenty, you could barely buy lunch for two in a café.

But Elisabeth refused to sleep with any more men, no matter the price. Still, she stayed with Hamida that night, and for the rest of the weekend. They even had sex several times. She said she left him on Sunday, May 6. He'd beaten her again. She'd had enough.

All told, she waited three weeks to complain to the police. She told Inspector Sardou she was too frightened to come forward earlier.

"He told me that if something happened to him, he was going to kill me," Elisabeth said.

*

*　　*

THE FOYER ARIANE, on rue d'Aubagne, was founded by Catholic nuns in 1968. It was a sanctuary amid the urban chaos, with clean rooms and a quiet garden with a stout plane tree out back.* The mission was to help young women escape domestic violence or prostitution, though the nuns rarely refused anyone who appeared at their door.

The counselors who were there in the early 1970s remember Elisabeth Bousquet as a young woman in desperate need of love, affection, and attention. They were the ones who convinced her to go to the police. It was an agonizing decision: they knew it would be an ordeal for the troubled young woman, but they felt Hamida posed an enormous danger to women and wanted the police to deal with him.

"I still think about it, the way we pushed her to go to make the com-

---

* Fate behaves in a curious fashion. In the summer of 2005, I took a spot in an artists' atelier on rue d'Aubagne to work on this very manuscript. At the time, I wasn't aware of the Foyer Ariane or its connection to the case. It was an eerie moment when I realized the window of the atelier looked out over the foyer's garden and the plane tree that surely must once have shaded Elisabeth Bousquet.

plaint," says Marie-Solange Guiard, who worked at the foyer at the time. "How can you not feel guilty about something like that? How can you not think about it?"*

The counselors also remember Hamida. They say that during the time Elisabeth stayed at the residence, he would appear at all hours, buzzing relentlessly at the door, demanding to speak with her. When they wouldn't let him up, he would lurk outside on rue d'Aubagne. The counselors agreed that Elisabeth should go out only with an escort.

"He would be there waiting for us and then he would limp after us, block after block," said Marie-Solange. "He was trying to intimidate us and Elisabeth."

Curiously, the street where Foyer Ariane was located, rue d'Aubagne, had no kind history toward young women. It was at a hotel just two blocks down from the shelter that the Marquis de Sade and his valet, Latour, organized their sexual debaucheries while in Marseille. The most famous incident occurred in July 1772, when the men lured three adolescent girls up to their room. Sade fed them aniseed candies laced with Spanish fly and then descended upon them. Afterward, the girls complained to the police, and Sade and Latour were charged with sodomy and poisoning. Sade escaped to Italy before he could be arrested, so the high court in Aix-en-Provence was forced to try him in absentia. He was sentenced to death and his straw effigy was beheaded with an axe.

The Marseille hotel that was the scene of these crimes has since been torn down and replaced with a newer building.

*

*   *

FRANCE, LIKE SO MANY countries, has long been obsessed with crime, and one offshoot of this fascination is a genre of journalism that takes

---

* Marie-Solange Guiard was typical of the women I encountered who worked in shelters in Marseille: brave, dedicated, and incredibly compassionate. During her time at Foyer Ariane, one woman even attempted to abduct Guiard's infant child. Amazingly, this didn't dissuade her from her commitment to the shelter.

two steps into territory prohibited by the standards of more respectable news-gathering organizations. One foot goes into the gory details and photographs that are censored in the mainstream press; the other goes into the shadowy world of half fact and unconfirmed rumor. In France, this market has been ably filled by *Détective* magazine and its successor, *Le Nouveau Détective*.

In the 1970s, *Détective* featured such running investigations as "Inside the Harems of the Oil Kings" and had front-page headlines such as "HE SHARED HIS WIFE WITH HIS FATHER." They inevitably wrote about Hamida Djandoubi and these allegations of prostitution under the bold headline "HER TENDER FIANCÉ WAS A DANGEROUS PIMP."

Citing a friend of Elisabeth's known only as Ginette, *Détective* reported that Elisabeth was in constant fear after the incident at the Sonacotra. Ginette told the magazine that Elisabeth broke into tears when the two women happened to meet at a bus stop:

> *I took her into a nearby café. There, she let out a terrible secret!
> "You can do absolutely nothing for me. If only you knew! I live
> in fear, in terror even! I am under the control of Hamida. He
> put me against the wall and told me, 'You live with me and you
> have to obey me. I want you to earn money as a prostitute. You
> have no choice, because if you run away, I will make you pay for
> your betrayal.'*
>
> *"I didn't know what else to do," she continued. "I was so
> happy to meet the tender fiancé I'd always dreamed of. Now he
> keeps me with these threats. . . ."*

This was *Détective*'s take on the prostitution question. It should be taken with an ample dose of skepticism.

*

*   *

THE CASE PROBABLY wasn't a priority for the police. It wasn't until two weeks after Elisabeth's complaint, on June 7, that Inspector Sardou sought out Hamida Djandoubi for questioning. Amazingly, his story was almost identical to Elisabeth's. Save for one important detail. He told the police it was all her idea.

In Hamida's version, Elisabeth arrived at the foyer and complained she had no place else to go. She stayed with him for three nights, then announced she had an idea for how to make them some money.

According to Hamida, Elisabeth confessed she was regularly prostituting herself. She apparently told him she had a Corsican pimp and worked the strip on avenue du Prado, a boulevard in Marseille's rich south end where hookers turned tricks out of parked vans and converted pizza trucks. He also alleged that Elisabeth admitted to sleeping with the owner of a store in downtown Marseille in exchange for new clothes. It must be noted that there was never an iota of evidence to support these claims.

As for the Friday night in question, Hamida told the police that Elisabeth asked him to get her clients. He said he brought her to five rooms. Elisabeth took the first twenty francs, then afterward he collected the money.

"She wanted to continue, but I wouldn't allow it," Hamida told Inspector Sardou.

Once everything was done, Hamida told police he and Elisabeth went grocery shopping. While they were making dinner, her mother, Alphonsine, arrived at the Sonacotra. Elisabeth hid in the closet. Hamida told Alphonsine he hadn't seen her daughter in a week.

That night, Elisabeth decided she never wanted to live with her mother again. She asked Hamida for help. He gave her twenty francs from what was left of the prostitution money, and she went to a women's shelter.

Hamida admitted to seeing Elisabeth only two more times. Once, they had sex at the Sonacotra. The second time, he went by the women's shelter to pick up a sweater she had borrowed. Then he broke up with her.

"I know I was wrong to take her to those rooms that night, and to have taken most of the money," Djandoubi told Inspector Sardou. "You can see I sincerely regretted what I did, because it didn't happen again."

So the investigation began. Inspector Sardou went to the Sonacotra. He spoke to the director, Michel Dos, who said he had heard no rumors about the night of prostitution. The police canvassed the Sonacotra. They couldn't find any resident willing to admit to having paid for sex with Elisabeth.

With the conflicting stories, the next step was a "confrontation." This was a French investigative technique in which the two parties were brought together and asked to repeat their stories. Police would observe and ask questions in hopes of discerning who was lying.

When Inspector Sardou sought out Elisabeth for the confrontation toward the end of June 1973, he found out that she'd been hospitalized.

She'd had a nervous breakdown. She was being treated by a neurologist by the name of Dr. Boudouresques at Hôpital de la Timone. The doctor told police Elisabeth was too emotionally fragile to cope with the anguish of a confrontation.

During that same visit to the hospital, Inspector Sardou asked around after Elisabeth. He found out she "wandered into the men's wing of the hospital a little too often." He noted this in his report and evidently decided it was a sign of poor character in a woman. And so Inspector Sardou let the matter drop.

Hamida Djandoubi wouldn't.

14

THE COMBINATION OF ROMAN LAW and Christian philosophy that shaped Europe in the Middle Ages is like that clichéd glass of water. It was definitely filled with good things, laying the legal and spiritual foundation for the grand civilizations to come. But, at least when it came to criminal justice, the mix of the Church-approved executions and the Roman penchant for public punishment turned out to be a glass-half-empty judicial phenomenon.

In principle, by the end of the thirteenth century there were two legal systems in Europe: courts set up by individual kings or rulers and based on the Roman *Corpus Iuris Civilis*; and the Church's ecclesiastical courts, governed by the body of canon law compiled by Gratian of Bologna in 1140, the sublimely titled *Concordance of Discordant Canons*. But in practice, the two systems were irrevocably intertwined, as the Church was so powerful that few rulers contradicted its wishes.

An obvious example was the inquisitions. It was Thomas Aquinas who so eloquently justified the first of the medieval inquisitions with his argument that heretics "deserve not only to be separated from the Church by excommunication, but also to be severed from the world by death." And once the Lateran councils declared that any king who didn't help root out heresy could be deposed with the support of the Church, there was little opposition to the movement to eradicate non-believers.

Among the earliest victims were the Cathars, a gnostic group that vowed never to lie or have sex and ate only vegetables and fish. When their creed started gaining popularity in the south of France, the Church decided to present them with an ultimatum: accept the Roman Catholic doctrine or face the penalty for heresy.

The Cathars (or the "Good Men and Good Women," as they preferred to call themselves) chose their faith. The most famous massacre occurred outside Béziers, where as many as twenty thousand people were said to have been killed in a single day. At one point, hundreds of Cathars and Catholics rushed into the cathedral for safety. When the cathedral was set ablaze, the papal legate, the abbot of Cîteaux, was asked whether they should douse the flames to protect the Catholics. "Let them all die," the abbot is said to have answered. "God will recognize his own."

One can't be too critical of this attitude, as death wasn't seen as a penalty but a blessing, a way to liberate people from their earthly errors and expedite their passage to heaven. With this sort of moral assurance, death could be meted out freely to anybody who didn't quite fit the norms of the new order.

The first French witch was legally burned in Toulouse in 1245. In Lorraine, nine hundred witches were executed between 1581 and 1591, while a single judge in Saint-Claude sentenced six hundred witches to be burned alive. In the Basque territories, a royal commission was appointed to purge the countryside of witches. Some sources indicate as many as thirty thousand people were burned at the stake over the years, and the head of the commission, a man named Pierre de Lancre, wrote in his final report that when the last witch died a swarm of toads burst from her head.

This zealous cleansing extended even to French animals. In 1266, at Fontenay-aux-Roses outside of Paris, a pig was burned to death for having eaten a child. A century later, in 1386, another pig was charged with mutilating a young boy in Normandy. After the court found the pig guilty, the animal was dressed in a vest and pants, and a human mask was placed over its snout. Then the pig was led to the gallows and hanged before a crowd of hundreds. Another case involving pigs had a slightly more merciful ending. In 1457 at Lavegny, a sow and her six babies were charged with murdering a child. At trial, the mother pig was found guilty and sentenced to death, but the piglets were acquitted because of their age.*

With Cathars, witches, and pigs meeting such gruesome ends, one can only imagine the fate reserved for a genuine criminal. Take François Ravaillac.

On May 14, 1610, Ravaillac stabbed King Henri IV to death in Paris. This was a wildly bad decision. Henri, the first Bourbon king, was extremely popular, having promised—and delivered—the famous chicken in every pot for the people of France. A Protestant by birth, he had converted to Catholicism to end the Wars of Religion and was one of the first European rulers to embrace freedom of religion, announcing: "Those who follow their consciences are of my religion."

Ravaillac, a Catholic, had come under the notion that Henri was going to revert to Protestantism, and in order to prevent this apostasy, he leapt into the royal carriage with a knife. Two swift thrusts ended the king's life.

To nobody's surprise, Ravaillac was sentenced to death, and his execution at the place de Grève in Paris was one of the most grisly in French history. Eyewitness accounts, such as *The Terrible and Deserved Death of Francis Ravilliack,* which was published in Edinburgh, were instant bestsellers.

According to this breathless account, Ravaillac was tied to a wood and iron cross, then the arm he used to stab King Henri was placed in a furnace until it caught fire and the melting flesh dripped from the bone. Ravaillac "yelled out with such horrible cries as if he had bin a Devil."

Next, the executioner used large iron pincers to peel strips of flesh

---

* Pigs have always had a rough time before the courts. A peculiar case unfolded in New Haven, Connecticut, in 1642 when a sow gave birth to a deformed piglet with a single milky eye. That one eye bore an eerie resemblance to the eyes of a farmhand by the name of Spencer, and, sure enough, this Spencer admitted to having sex with the animal. He was found guilty of bestiality and was hanged on April 8, 1642. The pig was killed with a sword, and the two were buried in a joint grave.

from Ravaillac's chest, arm, thighs, and calves. Each strip was held up before the audience and then thrown into the furnace. After that, a mixture of boiling oil, tar, and sulfur was poured into the open wounds. The executioner then took a doughnut-shaped device and placed it on Ravaillac's stomach so that his navel was in the center. Molten lead was poured into the aperture.

Finally, four horses were yoked to Ravaillac's arms and legs and sent off in four directions. But "so strongly was his flesh and joynts knit together that of long time, these four horses could not dismember him, nor any way teare one joynt from the other, so that one of the horses fainted."

The afflicted horse was replaced, but even then Ravaillac would not come apart. Finally, the executioner used a razor to cut the bothersome cartilage, and he was torn into five pieces. The crowds chased after the horses so they could cut the arms and legs into even smaller pieces and, of course, collect souvenirs.

When only the bones of Ravaillac remained, they were thrown into the furnace and the ashes scattered in the wind.

The author ends this account with the old hope that such an execution will act as a deterrent since the same punishment will be used against others who "attempt to lift their hands against God's anointed."

15

THE SAME JUNE WEEK Hamida Djandoubi was interrogated by police for prostituting Elisabeth, he met his next girlfriend.

Annie V. was sixteen years old. She was a short girl with dark hair, dark eyes, and a shy smile. If not conventionally beautiful, she was schoolgirl cute. And, by all accounts, susceptible.

Most people considered Annie somewhat slow. In the early grades, she couldn't follow along at school, so the principal put her in remedial classes. When that didn't work, she was transferred to a technical institute to learn industrial sewing.

Her mother blamed these academic shortcomings on the fact that Annie was left-handed. She told the police that such a handicap was an "obvious disadvantage."

Annie and Hamida met at the LunaParc, a beachside amusement arcade near Pointe-Rouge. Annie thought Hamida was handsome. Within a week, they were lovers.

That summer Hamida was twenty-three, seven years older than his new girlfriend. Almost every day he drove his white Simca across Marseille to pick up Annie. It proved difficult for her to sneak out of the apartment without her parents knowing. There were seven children in Annie's family, and five of them still lived at home. Once, two of her younger brothers spied her getting into Hamida's car. Annie bribed them not to tell.

Eventually, Annie's mother discovered her daughter was dating. She wanted to be introduced to the new boyfriend, so Annie invited Hamida to have dinner with her family. He refused.

Annie's parents were postal workers and took a monthlong vacation in August 1973. They brought their children to visit family in Lodève, a town in the hills north of Montpellier. Since Hamida's bakery closed for several weeks in August, he decided to follow Annie. They had secret dates. He told Annie he loved her. He said they should get married.

Annie said she thought she loved Hamida too.

*

*   *

ON THAT SAME AUGUST trip to Lodève, Hamida met his second girl-friend.

Amaria M. was walking in the park outside her low-income housing project with three other teenage girls when Hamida spotted her. He had a few hours before his rendezvous with Annie, so he began to flirt. Amaria agreed to meet him again.

For the next four days, he would see Amaria every afternoon. They kissed a little, but nothing more. He asked to see her in the evenings as well. She had to say no. Her parents wouldn't let her go out after dark.

Amaria was sixteen years old too, an emerging beauty who was tall and thin with rich long hair. She was an only child and lived with her parents in a one-bedroom apartment. Amaria slept on a pullout couch in the living room.

The family came from Tlemcen, Algeria, where her father was a *harki*, having fought alongside the French troops during the war. In 1962 the family had had little choice but to leave. Amaria was six years old when she arrived in France. They spent a year in a temporary housing camp before her father found a job working for the forestry department in Lodève. His wife was hired at a local carpet factory.

That summer of 1973, Amaria was caught between two cultures. At home, it was the Maghreb. Her mother didn't speak French, and her father was trying to arrange a marriage for her with the son of a friend back in Algeria. With her friends at high school, it was another world. Different clothes, different music, different values. Still, her parents did their best.

"They made big sacrifices to raise her," said Sadia, a school friend of

Amaria's. "She was always dressed in style, she fit in, her parents gave her whatever she wanted."

When Annie's family vacation ended, Hamida also left Lodève. Once back in Marseille, he wrote Amaria a flurry of love letters. He addressed them to a friend since Amaria wasn't allowed to receive mail at home.

The last week of September 1973, to celebrate his twenty-fourth birthday, Hamida drove up to Lodève to see Amaria. He only stayed six hours, arriving at eleven in the morning and leaving at five in the afternoon. But there was enough time to get a hotel room. The couple went to bed together for the first time. Afterward, Amaria admitted she'd been a virgin.

Before leaving Lodève, Hamida asked her to come live with him in Marseille.

Amaria told her friend Hamama about the invitation. Hamama had also met Hamida during the August vacation. He had also asked Hamama to go out on a date with him. "Don't do it," she advised Amaria. "Think of your parents."

So Amaria told Djandoubi no. Or rather, not yet.*

*

*   *

THAT SEPTEMBER, Hamida left the Sonacotra and rented an apartment of his own on rue Villa Paradis near the center of Marseille. It was on the second story of a small house that had been divided into four apartments. His windows overlooked the street.

He'd told the landlord, Victor Barrielle, that he was getting married and needed an apartment quickly. Barrielle wasn't inclined to rent to

---

*One of the dilemmas I faced while researching this book was whether or not to contact Annie and Amaria. I knew that having their past surge up might wrench apart their new lives; I also knew that if they ever discovered the existence of this book, they might resent not having had the chance to share their side of the story. In the end, after numerous discussions with the counselors and lawyers who worked with Annie and Amaria, I decided it was best to leave the women in peace and not risk shattering the new lives they had painstakingly built for themselves.

Hamida, but given his handicap and the upcoming marriage, he relented.

The house was in the shadows of Notre-Dame de la Garde. Victor Hugo once mocked Marseille as a city without monuments, and it is true that there is a dearth of veritable postcard attractions. But there is one soaring icon: the Good Mother, the church Notre-Dame de la Garde that watches over Marseille like the Cristo Redentor in Rio de Janeiro.

The Christian tradition is deep in Marseille. Local legend claims that the resurrected Lazarus came to the city after Jesus was crucified. At the St. Victor Abbey, there are Christian coffins from the third century A.D. And it was from here that another Lazarus, the bishop of Marseille, launched the campaign to convert Provence in the fifth century A.D. The site of Notre-Dame de la Garde itself was a Christian refuge starting in the thirteenth century, although the current church wasn't completed until 1864.

Some visit the church only for the view. From its wide terraces, one can see the twisting urbanity of Marseille, the distant ships crossing the Mediterranean, the bleached mountains that border the city. Others come for more inspired reasons. It is at Notre-Dame de la Garde that the families of sailors pray when there are storms at sea. If the sailors return safely, it is the custom to render tribute, so the church's inner walls are crowded with a century and a half of paintings showing the Virgin Mary protecting ships in raging seas.

Hamida was able to get this apartment in the shadows of the church because his accident money had finally come through. After a final examination by the labor tribunal doctor, it was determined that he was eligible for 70 percent of a full disability pension. This meant a total of 7,100 francs a year. The settlement was retroactive to the time of the accident, so even after the advances were accounted for, he received a bulk payment of more than 5,000 francs.

The money was vital. Though the rent for his new apartment was just 268 francs a month, Barrielle insisted Hamida pay an entire year's rent in advance. This wasn't such an unusual practice in Marseille; it was a way to discourage unwanted tenants.

Most assuredly, Hamida wasn't going to be missed by the management at Sonacotra. There were the troubles with Elisabeth staying in his room, then the hassles of the police investigation following the prostitution complaint. Henri Ardourel, a temporary director at the foyer, denounced him as arrogant. "I can tell you this," Ardourel said. "He had an anti-French attitude."

Nor was Hamida winning any friends at the bakery on avenue de Toulon. It wasn't his work ethic. He was on time every day, no small feat, as his shift ran from 6 A.M. to 1 P.M. And by all accounts, he did his job well, making an especially delicious *tarte aux pommes*. The problem was his personality. "He had a persecution complex," said Roger Columban, the bakery owner. "He was always complaining that people weren't treating him fairly."

*

*   *

IN JANUARY 1974, Hamida finally convinced Amaria to leave Lodève and come live with him at the rue Villa Paradis apartment. His argument was compelling: he told her he would break up with her if she didn't.

"I was scared I was going to lose him, so I accepted," Amaria would later tell the police.

The police came to a less romantic conclusion. "It seems Amaria M. couldn't reconcile the attraction of the French lifestyle with the tribal moral restraints imposed by her parents," stated a Lodève police report. "Her desire for liberty pushed her to follow the first individual who showed her a flicker of easy pleasure."

It was true that Amaria's life was overwhelmingly dull in Lodève. She'd already quit high school. Like Annie, Amaria wasn't an academic achiever. Her report card for the school year that ended in June 1970 read: "Very disruptive, thinks only of amusing herself in class, because the level is too elevated for her."

The next year, June 1971, her report card read: "Student with very little talent, bad spirit, debauched, rude, and very turbulent."

And finally, in June 1972, she was so rarely in class there was no report card.

As the assistant principal of the high school noted, "This young woman was not at all in the academic spirit, she showed absolutely no interest in her studies, and her only visible goal was to quit school."

That meant that Amaria spent most of the fall of 1973 at home, waiting to get a job at the same carpet factory where her mother worked. Worse, her parents were putting more pressure on her about the arranged marriage.

"They took me to Algeria to get to know him, but for my part, I refused," Amaria would say. "After that, my parents threatened that I would have to get married to this man if I made any mistakes at home."

Although grateful for the escape offered by Hamida, Amaria still wanted to do things properly, to add at least a splash of romance to the affair. She asked him to come to the family apartment and announce their wedding engagement. Hamida would have none of it. He said he didn't have enough money to marry her and would come back and meet her parents when he did. So they waited for Amaria's parents to go out shopping and then snuck into the apartment and packed her bag. Amaria didn't even leave a note.

After the five-hour drive back to Marseille, Amaria saw the apartment for the first time. It was cramped—one main room with a bed, a table and some shelves, a small kitchen, and a toilet. Still, it was a home to call her own. She didn't ask questions when Hamida took her identification papers for "safekeeping."

"The perfect love" was how Amaria described it.

Life settled into a routine. Hamida left at five o'clock every morning for the bakery and would be home in the early afternoon. Amaria found a full-time job in a shoe warehouse and worked Monday to Friday. And when Amaria was away in the afternoons, Annie would come over, and she and Hamida would make love. He always made her leave at precisely five o'clock to ensure there was no overlap between the girls.

Hamida confided in his neighbor across the hall, Marie-Claude Kervella, that it was difficult to juggle two girlfriends. He found it frustrating that he had to hide Amaria's belongings every time Annie came over.

Marie-Claude thought it was amusing at first; she'd always heard that Arab men liked to have more than one wife. Besides, she genuinely liked Hamida.

"He was big, he was charming, he was really a beautiful man," she said.

Marie-Claude wasn't much older than his girlfriends. She was twenty-one years old that winter, a single mother raising a three-year-old son, Stefan, by herself. They were good neighbors. Hamida would often babysit for Marie-Claude when she went to her job as a dental secretary. For her birthday party, he brought trays of pizza and *tarte aux pommes* from the bakery. Hamida also trusted Marie-Claude enough to ask for her help. She would go to the pharmacy for him and fill his prescription for painkillers. Once, his prosthesis got lodged behind his bed and Marie-Claude had to yank it out for him.

"He was always very kind to me, very respectful," said Marie-Claude. "I think it's because my father came to visit me every week. He saw I had somebody to protect me so I was safe."

Sadly, the same didn't go for Annie and Amaria.

16

AS GHOULISH AS CERTAIN aspects of early European capital punishment might have been, there were always at least faint contrarian voices. When Canute ascended the throne of England in 1016, for instance, he declared that Christian men not "for altogether too little be condemned to death, but rather let gentle punishments be decreed for the benefit of the people."

A half century later, William the Conqueror, fresh from Normandy, announced, "I forbid that any person be killed or hanged for any cause." True, this was pragmatic rather than compassionate; William simply saw no point in hanging men who could just as easily die for him on the battlefield. And this was, after all, a king who introduced such practices as tearing off a criminal's testicles. Still, for forty years there were no executions in England. The policy ended when William's son, William Rufus, an ardent hunter, reinstituted the death penalty for those caught poaching deer in the royal forests.

A truer movement for judicial reform began in the sixteenth century when the Dutch theologian Erasmus wrote that too many trivial crimes were punishable by death "in countries professing Christianity." Erasmus, one of the major influences on Martin Luther, argued work camps should replace the death penalty for all but the most serious crimes. "Punishments of this description are attended with a double advantage: for, while they correct, without crushing the offender, they promote the interests either of the public, or of the individual injured by his delinquency," wrote Erasmus.

This thinking was similar to that of Erasmus's close friend Thomas More. More was born in 1478, a time when women were publicly hanged for stealing table linens. Perhaps it is no surprise, then, that he described a more humane justice system in *Utopia*. "God has commanded us not to kill," he wrote in 1515, "and shall we kill so easily for a little money?"

More was also one of the first who felt resources would be better spent attacking the roots of crime. As no punishment is severe enough to stop a hungry man from stealing, he argued the state must improve the miserable living conditions. "For if you suffer your people to be ill educated, and their manners to be corrupted from their infancy, and then punish them for those crimes to which their first education disposed them, what else is to be concluded but this, that you first make thieves, and then punish them."

More ended up a victim of the capricious justice he railed against. When Henry VIII tried to manipulate Catholic law so he could divorce Catherine of Aragon and marry Anne Boleyn, More supported the pope's decision not to annul the royal marriage. In doing this, More displeased a very dangerous man: seventy thousand people were executed during the reign of Henry VIII, and he actually made it legal to boil people to death. Henry trumped up treason charges and More was decapitated in 1535. According to custom, his severed head was displayed atop London Bridge for thirty days.

Erasmus and More were voices in the wilderness. More than a century later the vast majority of thinkers, from Thomas Hobbes to John Locke, continued to see the death penalty as a logical, moral, and judicious punishment. Reform movements concentrated more on the ludicrous scope of crimes punished by death rather than quibbling with the belief that death was an appropriate punishment. The influential English jurist William Blackstone, for instance, supported the death penalty for murder and treason but in his *Commentaries on the Laws of England* (1765–69) called it a "melancholy truth" that more than 160 crimes were considered "worthy of instant death."

In France, a series of judicial reforms was initiated by Louis XIV and his trusted minister Jean-Baptiste Colbert between 1666 and 1670. But this was more of a standardization of legal procedure than any radical humanization of the system. Particularly telling was the fact that both men thought it fit to continue with "the Question"—the law that allowed an accused person to be tortured to evoke a confession. By the mid-eighteenth century, there were 115 crimes punishable by death in France, including wearing armor without authorization, fighting a duel, smuggling salt or tobacco in groups of five or more armed men, and causing a leak in a ship. The methods of execution ranged from being burned alive, broken on the wheel, hanged, beheaded, or drawn and quartered like the hapless Ravaillac.

It was Montesquieu who spurred a true debate on reform. Born to a wealthy Bordeaux family in 1689, he had a private income, including his infamous shares in a slave-trading company, which allowed him to concentrate on intellectual pursuits. His lifetime project, *The Spirit of the Laws,* was a study of legal customs throughout human history.

With the tenet "Mankind must not be governed with too much severity," Montesquieu argued for moderate justice, as he believed people obeyed laws out of love for their country, and that if the laws were too violent, people themselves would act violently. Although not an outright abolitionist, Montesquieu felt only murder or attempted murder should be capital crimes. "A man deserves death when he has violated the security of the subject so far as to deprive, or attempt to deprive, another man of his life," Montesquieu wrote.

One wonders whether the case of François Damiens would have met Montesquieu's criteria. In 1757, nine years after the publication of *The Spirit of the Laws,* a delusional Damiens rushed at Louis XV with a penknife. The king escaped with only a scratch on his forearm, but Damiens still met the gruesome fate reserved for regicides.* Like Ravaillac before him, he had his hand melted off, his flesh peeled with

---

* Damiens is often cited as the reason France clung to the law that punished the criminal's family for the criminal's misdeeds. In the midst of his torture, he is said to have asked the executioner why his children had been put in prison. "Had you known your children would meet this fate, would you have forsaken the act?" the executor asked. "Yes," came Damiens's famous reply.

red-hot pincers, boiling oil poured into his wounds, and his limbs torn off by horses. Among the many hundreds in attendance was Casanova, who'd just arrived in Paris after escaping from Venice, where he'd been imprisoned for practicing magic.

"I was several times obliged to turn away my face and stop my ears as I heard his piercing shrieks," the sensitive Casanova wrote.

Despite its brutality, Damiens's death caused barely a stir among the intellectuals of his day. Rather, it was the case of a humble cloth merchant that would resonate throughout the French legal system as it raised, for the first time, that damning specter of judicial error.

In 1761, Marc-Antoine Calas was found dead in his parents' home outside Toulouse. The young man had apparently hanged himself, a fact his father, Jean Calas, tried to conceal because of the stigma and religious repercussions associated with suicide.

It didn't take long for the gossip to start. The Calas family was Protestant but lived in a predominantly Catholic village, and the rumor began to spread that Jean Calas had killed his son to prevent him from converting to Catholicism. Charges were eventually laid, and in a highly questionable trial Calas was found guilty by a vote of 8 to 5. On March 10, 1762, he was broken on the wheel and then burned at the stake.

The case caught the attention of Voltaire, the essayist and author of *Candide,* who was himself all too familiar with the foibles of eighteenth-century justice. Voltaire had been thrown in a dank cell in the Bastille prison for satirizing the duke of Orléans and was publicly whipped on a visit to Berlin for a poem mocking the king of Prussia. Voltaire was even forced to write a receipt for the latter punishment: "Received from the right hand of Conrad Bochoffner, thirty lashes on my bare back, being in full for an epigram on Frederick the Great, King of Prussia."

After meeting the widow of Jean Calas, Voltaire investigated the case, and his resulting essay, *Traité sur la tolérance,* led to the case being reopened. "The sword of justice is in our hands," wrote Voltaire, "but we must make it more blunt rather than more cutting."

Three years later Jean Calas was exonerated, and his case gave birth to one of the most poignant arguments against the death penalty, the fact that innocent men and women could well be put to death by error or prejudice. For Calas, whose charred remains were already in the grave, this was likely of little solace.

17

FOR ELISABETH, THAT NIGHT of prostitution was the beginning of a long year of pain.

She spent the month of June in a psychiatric ward undergoing a "sleep cure" and then was transferred to a sanatorium in the Alps for two more months of rest and isolation. She found a semblance of peace in the mountains. It was quiet, the nature walks were breathtaking, and she enjoyed the sense of community between patients. Her best friend there was Martine Guiraud, a gas station employee who was also recovering from an attack of nerves.

Martine remembered Elisabeth as a sweet girl who was extremely anxious. "She was really pretty sick," she said.

Elisabeth mostly talked about two things: her family and her ex-boyfriend. Elisabeth said her parents had just divorced and she didn't get along with her mother. She also said she had escaped a boyfriend who had forced her into prostitution.

"She didn't want to go back to Marseille," Martine would tell the police. "She thought the boy she went out with would find her. She even said she was scared he was going to kill her."

Martine never knew the name of the boyfriend.

Elisabeth's stay at the sanatorium ended in August 1973, the same month Hamida Djandoubi was in Lodève with his two new girl-friends. Elisabeth's brother Jean-Pierre came and took her back to Marseille, where she spent several more weeks at the Hôpital Édouard Toulouse.

Jean-Pierre Bousquet often helped Elisabeth during this difficult time. He drove her to appointments, he arranged for her to stay with friends of the family, he offered her small loans. "She was always complaining that she didn't have any money, and she got a little from everyone in the family," he told the police. "Personally, I gave her some on two occasions, fifty or sixty francs each time. I knew she was a real spendthrift."

Still, some people thought the family wasn't doing enough. Her former employer, François Ceccaldi, watched Elisabeth's downward spiral with a despair that bordered on disgust.

"What were her father and brother doing?" he asked. "If she had another family, it wouldn't have come to this."

Indeed, once out of the hospitals, Elisabeth was back to bouncing around the women's shelters. They weren't uplifting times. She came down with the scabies and was banned from one shelter for fear she would infect the other women. She began to idealize her earlier lives, talking endlessly of growing up in Langogne or how happy she'd been with the Ceccaldi family. When she stayed at the Foyer Ariane, the counselors wrote letters encouraging those who knew Elisabeth to get more involved in her life.

"It was like people decided to wash their hands of her after she was connected to prostitution," recalled Marie-Solange Guiard.

Despite such efforts, whatever tranquillity Elisabeth had found in the mountains steadily evaporated. In January 1974, she attempted suicide by cutting open her wrists with a razor blade. She spent the next three months in the hospital under observation.

*

* *

AS ELISABETH'S PERSONAL troubles mounted, a national tragedy was playing out. In April 1974, after months of rumored illness, President Georges Pompidou died of Kahler's disease, a cancer of the plasma cells. He was just sixty-two years old.

An emergency election was called, and two major candidates emerged: Valéry Giscard d'Estaing on the right and François Mitterrand on the left. Giscard was an aristocrat, a member of the same family that owned the massive castle in Estaing, the village where Pierre

Bousquet was raised. He was a familiar face in government, having held several cabinet positions in the 1960s and early 1970s, including minister of finance under both de Gaulle and Pompidou.

Mitterrand had been a member of the right-wing Croix-de-Feu as a young man before ultimately embracing socialism. He was savaged for his role in the Vichy government during World War II until it emerged that he was actually a spy for the Resistance who had operated under the cover name Morland. After the war, he feuded incessantly with de Gaulle, even referring to him as the "new dictator." Mitterrand challenged de Gaulle for the presidency in 1965 and lost. The 1974 elections were seen as his chance at political redemption.

It was a battle between two grand actors on the French political stage, but whatever the outcome, France would take its first step away from the socially conservative politics of de Gaulle and Pompidou. Among the issues on the table were the legalization of abortion, the relaxing of divorce laws, easier access to contraception, the lowering of the age of majority, and the abolition of the death penalty.

As the election neared, the polls had the two men equal. In the second-round runoff on May 19, 1974, Giscard defeated Mitterrand by the narrowest of margins, winning 50.8 percent of the vote.

And so everyone awaited the promised social changes. By all accounts, Giscard was a progressive politician. He appointed Simone Veil, a strong feminist, as minister of health to move the abortion dossier forward, and he had told his friends that he held a "profound aversion to capital punishment." And the early efforts of the new government testified to the president's sensitivity. He lightened the shade of blue in the French flag because he considered it too aggressive, and then ordered the rhythm of the national anthem, "*La Marseillaise,*" slowed because he thought it too warlike.

On the latter issue, the new president had just cause. "*La Marseillaise*" was, in fact, born a battle song. In the midst of the French Revolution, the mayor of Strasbourg asked an army officer, Rouget de Lisle, to write a song that would stir the troops. On the night of April 25, 1792, de Lisle produced a strident anthem he titled "War Song for the Rhine Army." It quickly became the theme of the revolution and was forever baptized "*La Marseillaise*" because it resounded from the lips of the revolutionaries from Marseille when they marched into Paris in the summer of 1792.

Rare is the national anthem that evokes such violence. The first stanza warns that the enemies of the new French Republic are coming to cut the throats of women and children, while the chorus hopes these same enemies will be slaughtered and their "impure blood water our fields."

Considering the violence of the Reign of Terror that accompanied the French Revolution, Rouget de Lisle's macabre lyrics proved rather prescient.

*

*　　*

JUST BEFORE HER BIRTHDAY, Elisabeth found new love.

She met Jean-Louis Azzarello late in the spring of 1974. On the surface, he wasn't the most desirable of partners for a woman on the cusp of her twenty-first birthday. He was thirty-four years old, he had six children, he was an alcoholic, and he was on a permanent disability pension because of what he claimed was a war wound from Algeria. But when they met in a Marseille café and Azzarello asked her out, Elisabeth, as always, could only say yes.

Azzarello lived in La Roque d'Anthéron, a Provençal town about an hour from Marseille. He was in the midst of a stint at a rehabilitation center called La Méditerranée, where he boasted to other residents that he'd served in the French Foreign Legion. At the time, to be a legionnaire was a romantic thing indeed. The Foreign Legion was founded in the 1830s to raise troops for the invasion of Algeria, and its reputation for bravery was earned in 1863 when sixty-five legionnaires held out against more than two thousand Mexican soldiers. In the 1970s, the

Foreign Legion still accepted recruits without a background check and allowed them to choose the name on the French passport they were given after completing their service.

Few doubted Azzarello's claim to be a legionnaire. The south of France was full of them, as the Foreign Legion had a recruitment office in Marseille, a training center overlooking the Mediterranean, and its main headquarters was in the nearby city of Aubagne. One could hardly enter a bar or café without stumbling across someone who had served under the Legion's colors.

Elisabeth took the train to visit Azzarello every Saturday afternoon. She would stay with him in his room at La Méditerranée, sometimes for two or three days at a time. Azzarello put aside part of his food ration from the week so he would have something to share with her.

Azzarello spun big dreams for the couple. He said he had money saved and he was going to buy a restaurant for them in Marseille. After a few weeks, he asked Elisabeth to marry him. Again, she said yes. Again, she was so desperate for love she was blinded by any man who promised it to her.

Those who knew Azzarello, however, were skeptical. "He was a gasbag," said Émile Izoret, who worked as a handyman at La Méditerranée. "And he was always drunk."

But Elisabeth forgave Azzarello's faults. And she liked the way he called her Betty. It was a new name for a new beginning.

Wanting to be closer to her new fiancé, "Betty" left Marseille and found work as a chambermaid at a hotel in La Roque d'Anthéron called Le Silvacane. It was named after the nearby Silvacane Abbey, an 850-year-old structure that was one of the few traces of the austere Cistercians in Provence and the town's main attraction. Along with a small salary, Elisabeth was given a room and meals. Her first day on the job was June 13, 1974. She was fired four days later.

"She tried hard," said Carmelo Cascio, the hotel owner, "but just wasn't cut out for the hotel business."

Back in Marseille, Elisabeth became carried away when describing her new relationship. On a visit to her sister, Marie-Josée, at the end of June 1974, she announced she was already married to Azzarello. She also told her mother, Alphonsine, about her "husband."

"She wanted me to meet him but I refused," Alphonsine told the police. "Let's just say he was thirty-six or something and was already the father of six children."

Her father was nonplussed by the development. "All I can say is she really liked men," Pierre said.

Considering she'd known the man for a little more than two months, Elisabeth had invested a dangerous amount of emotion in Azzarello. It was understandably devastating when, in the first week of July 1974, he broke off their engagement.

They'd gotten into a fight over the lack of serious wedding plans. Azzarello told her she was no good and he never wanted to see her again. Elisabeth ran from his room. Several people heard her scream back at him: "*Je vais faire le trottoir.*"

I'm going to go work the street.

18

ON MAY 27, 1738, Catherine Guillotin, in the late stages of pregnancy, went shopping in Saintes, a town near Bordeaux. By chance, a public execution was being staged that afternoon in the main square.

The condemned man had robbed a carriage, and the punishment for highwaymen was the dreaded wheel. Hence, the man was belted onto a wooden wheel roughly four feet in diameter, and the bones in his arms and legs were pulverized with a metal club so they could be bent around the rim of the wheel. Then he was rolled around the town so all could see that justice was truly being served. Finally, the executioner caved in his chest. This method of execution was also known as the Catherine wheel in honor of Saint Catherine, who was executed in Alexandria in 310. According to Christian tradition, when the eighteen-year-old girl was lowered onto a similar wheel device, it broke in two; flummoxed, her executioners beheaded the girl, but instead of blood, milk spurted from her neck.

Even amid the pantheon of deliriously painful tortures, the wheel stands out. The official executioner of France, Charles Henri Sanson, described it as "the most atrocious sufferings ever devised by human cruelty." And, sure enough, that day in the village Madame Guillotin was so horrified by the spectacle that she fainted on the spot. Due to resulting shock, the next day her son, Joseph-Ignace, was born several weeks prematurely.

Eighteenth-century France was a morbid place for a little boy. In Bordeaux, witches were still being burned as late as 1718. In 1740 a cow judged to be under the influence of the devil was executed. And even the bedtime stories were ruthless. According to the scholar Robert Darnton, the eighteenth-century version of *Little Red Riding Hood* went something like this:

Little Red Riding Hood meets the Wolf in the forest. The Wolf races ahead to the Grandmother's house, kills the old woman, slices up her flesh and pours her blood into a bottle. Then he puts on the Grandmother's nightdress, gets into bed and waits.

When Little Red Riding Hood arrives, the Wolf makes her eat and drink. A little cat tells her: "Slut! To eat the flesh and drink the blood of your Grandmother!"

Then, the Wolf orders her to strip naked and get into bed with him

"Oh Grandmother. What big teeth you have!"

"It's for eating you better my dear!"

Then the Wolf ate her.

Judging by what transpired, this sanguinary atmosphere had its effect on Guillotin. But so too did the fact that he grew up among the first flares of the Enlightenment. Among those who influenced the young man were Montesquieu, Voltaire, and a soon-to-be-famous fellow by the name of Beccaria.

*

* *

BECCARIA, ALSO KNOWN AS Cesare Bonesana, was a member of the Milan Enlightenment, a boisterous group of Italian intellectuals who congregated around the journal *Il Caffè*. In 1764, at the age of twenty-six, he published his signature work, *Dei delitti e delle pene* (On Crimes and Punishments), a manifesto arguing civilized communities should not kill their own people. "Is it not absurd that the laws, which detest and punish homicide, should, in order to prevent murder, publicly commit murder themselves?" he wrote.

As banal as this assertion might seem in the context of contemporary debates, it was utterly groundbreaking at the time. While there had been various religious initiatives to abolish the death penalty—under the Royal Charter for South Jersey, for instance, the Quakers outlawed the death penalty in 1646, and there were no executions until 1691—this young Italian became the first person to publicly argue that the death penalty was not an appropriate tool of government.

In Italy, the grandduke of Tuscany was so impressed by Beccaria's proposition that his territory became the first in Europe to constitutionally ban the death penalty. In France, Abbé Morellet, Diderot's collaborator on the *Encyclopédie,* translated *Dei delitti e delle pene* into French in 1765. The following year, Voltaire wrote a commentary endorsing Beccaria's ideas.

It was part of the explosion of intellectual ferment that culminated in the French Revolution. This wasn't the only factor, of course. There was a clamor for an elected parliament to balance the royal powers. An expanding middle class resented having no say in the government. The Church was considered too rich and too corrupt. Louis XVI introduced unpopular new taxes. An economic crisis resulted in a brief famine in Paris. The gutter newspapers published drawings of Marie-Antoinette in pornographic positions. In short, there were a dozen fuses lit on this particular social bombshell.

Sensing catastrophe, in May 1789, Louis XVI called a meeting of the États Généraux, the political assembly of representatives from the three French "estates": the nobility, the Church, and the people. Much to the king's alarm, the representatives occupied his handball court and swore their famous Tennis Court Oath demanding a constitution.

On July 14, 1789, there came the event that symbolized the revolution: the storming of the Bastille. Some blame the Marquis de Sade. Having finally been captured by French authorities, he was serving time for the Marseille rape charges. Witnesses say he enjoyed yelling out to the crowds beneath his cell window that prisoners were being tortured. In the end, he was transferred to another prison days before the siege.

Suitably chastened, Louis XVI eventually agreed to an elected National Assembly. In August 1789, using America's Declaration of Independence as a model, a French constitution, the *Déclaration des droits de l'homme et du citoyen*, was proclaimed. One of the grand projects yet to come was a reform of the justice system to meet the new Enlightenment ideals.

*

* *

YOUNG JOSEPH-IGNACE Guillotin found himself plumb in the middle of it all. After receiving a humanities degree from the University of Bordeaux, he went to Paris in 1763 to study medicine. Once he'd defended his thesis on rabies, Dr. Guillotin was named a professor of anatomy at the Faculté de Paris in 1770.

The crusade for reform captivated Dr. Guillotin. He published pamphlets urging the end of the vinegar tax. He led an investigation into the charlatan Franz Mesmer, who was charging wealthy Parisians enormous sums to be healed by magnets. And in the 1780s, he earned his revolutionary credentials by writing the *Pétition des citoyens domiciliés à Paris*, which argued for an elected government of the people. Dr. Guillotin was also one of the delegates at the meeting of the États Généraux, and some say he was the one who suggested they retire to the handball court.

Once the National Assembly was formed, Dr. Guillotin was elected and took an interest in judicial reform. At the head of the movement was the representative Le Peletier de Saint-Fargeau, who denounced the "tortures imagined during the centuries of barbarism that have been conserved during the centuries of light." Quickly, practices such as the branding of prisoners were outlawed while the number of capital crimes was reduced from 115 to 33. Saint-Fargeau also became the first French politician to demand the abolition of the death penalty on the floor of the National Assembly.

Dr. Guillotin took a unique perspective on this debate, deploring the elitism of the death penalty. At the time, commoners were hanged, burned, or broken on the wheel, while nobles had the luxury of being beheaded. In October 1789, he submitted a watershed proposal to the Assembly: all condemned criminals should be decapitated, as it was both egalitarian and humane. The National Assembly debated the idea, but no conclusion was reached. Two months later, Dr. Guillotin again raised the subject, this time bulwarking his case with a six-clause proposal:

Article 1: All offenses of the same kind shall be punished the same way, regardless of rank or status.

Article 2: When the death penalty is imposed, it shall be by decapitation effected by a simple mechanism.

Article 3: The punishment shall not bring discrimination to the guilty party's family.

Article 4: Nobody will be reproached for the acts of their relatives.

Article 5: The condemned person's property will not be confiscated.

Article 6: If requested, the corpse will be returned to the family and no reference to the nature of death will be cited.

Dr. Guillotin spoke for more than an hour. Although there are no records of his speech, journalists took special note of his imagined decapitating machine. One newspaper, the *Journal des États Généraux,* quoted him as saying, "The mechanism falls like thunder—the head flies—the blood spurts—the man is no more."

Another newspaper, *Les Actes des Apôtres,* raised a pertinent question. With more than a hint of irony, it praised the "decapitating machine that will extend the glory of the French name to the shores of the

Bosporus," but wondered: "A grand difficulty now raised is what to call this instrument. Should we take, to enrich our language, the name of the inventor?"

Then a poem appeared. Particularly telling was the final verse:

La machine
Qui simplement nous tuera
Et que l'on nommera
Guillotine.

The machine
Will kill us simply
And we will name it
Guillotine.

The poet, the Chevalier de Champcenetz, made full use of his artistic license and added the "e" to Guillotin because "Guillotine" rhymed with "machine."*

The name stuck.

---

* In that time of revolutionary extremes, Champcenetz was eventually charged with conspiracy for his parodies of the new government and on July 23, 1794, ended up under the very guillotine he named. This esteemed man of letters could actually have avoided death as he'd found sanctuary in the countryside, but he insisted on returning to Paris to collect his beloved library of books and was arrested while in the city.

19

HAMIDA DJANDOUBI DOMINATED the lives of his two young girl-friends. In his mind, he was the master, they were his harem.

Money was one of his more conventional methods of control. At the end of every week at the shoe warehouse, Amaria gave her entire salary of 250 francs directly to him. He did the shopping, he paid the rent, he bought the drinks when they went to his favorite bar in Cassis. She never even had enough change in her pocket for a bar of chocolate.

At first, Amaria didn't mind. "He was nice to me," she said. "I was happy to live with him."

One month after Amaria moved in, Hamida left the bakery. The man he replaced had returned from military service, and the owner had no desire to keep the petulant Hamida on staff. He eventually got another job as a busboy and dishwasher at a restaurant called Le Petit Port in Les Goudes, an idyllic seafront village at the southern extreme of Marseille. With its small port, wooden fishing boats, and bleached rock cliffs, it was the perfect spot for a romantic dinner, and several restaurants catered to this crowd.

Hamida told the owner of Le Petit Port, Ohannès Medjikian, that he wanted to learn the business. He inexplicably lied and said he lost his leg in a car accident in Nice. "He was flexible, friendly, and very polite," Medjikian recalled. "I was very surprised when I read about him in the newspaper."

It was also a surprise for Marie-Solange Guiard, the counselor from Foyer Ariane, when she arrived for a quiet dinner at Le Petit Port and found Hamida staring evilly at her. It was such a disturbing situation, she and her companion left the restaurant before the menus arrived.

Hamida's other means of controlling his girls was violence. In March 1974, he began beating Amaria. The first time, he used his belt.

He accused her of flirting with other men, so he forced her to strip naked and then interrogated her. "He would hit me for a yes or a no," she said.

The next time, he beat her because he wanted to "correct" her. She didn't know how to cook. She burned things in the kitchen. "I didn't hit her in a mean way," Hamida would say. "I only used my little stick."

This "little stick" was a solid wood club that was sixteen inches long and one and a half inches thick. Hamida normally used it to roll pastry dough.

Prostitution once again cast its toxic shadow across the case. Hamida forced Amaria to quit her job because he thought she was meeting too many men at the warehouse. To replace the lost income, he apparently decided he could sell Amaria.

Amaria told police that Hamida took her to his old Sonacotra residence every Saturday night for month. He called it "The Chicago." Amaria said Hamida brought her from room to room while he collected the money at the door. There were as many as ten or twelve men every Saturday night.

"I was too scared to cry for help or to run away, because when he's mad, he's like a wild animal," Amaria said. "He told me, 'If one day any of the men I send to you isn't happy, you know what's waiting for you: I'll kill you.' "

Amaria said this went on for four or five weeks. Then she became so racked with stomach pain and sobbing fits that Hamida let her go back to working at the shoe warehouse.

In May 1974, Annie moved into the apartment on rue Villa Paradis. At Hamida's request, she too had run away from home. He had collected her suitcases when her parents were away. On his advice, she also quit her job as a saleswoman at a hardware store on rue Longue des Capucins so she couldn't be traced.

Her parents filed a missing person report with the Marseille police. Nothing came of it.

Arriving at the apartment on rue Villa Paradis, Annie was stunned to find Amaria already living there. Hamida had managed to keep his two girlfriends in the dark until that moment. Annie moved in anyway.

"He acted all hopeless and I had pity on him," Annie said.

Of course, Amaria wasn't pleased to discover her "fiancé" had another lover, but she didn't see any other options. She was too embarrassed to return to her parents. And she'd boasted so much to her friends about her handsome new boyfriend, she couldn't face up to the awful truth. She saw no place else to go.

The apartment had only one large bed. The first night, Hamida had sex with Annie while Amaria lay beside them. It didn't take too long before they were having group sex. Hamida sometimes took out his collection of Swedish pornography. He liked to re-create the scenes from the pictorials.

"He forced us to caress each other in front of him while he watched," Amaria would tell police.

At Hamida's urging, Annie quickly found another job in an atelier that made leather goods on rue de la République. Like Amaria, she turned all her money over to him at the end of every week.

Three weeks after Annie moved in, Hamida became violent with her too. It was a Saturday morning. He asked her to kneel in front of him. When she said no, he slapped her. She got down on her knees and he went at her with his belt.

The hidden girlfriend, the group sex, and the beatings were enough for Annie. She decided she was going to escape.

*

*   *

AS ANNIE AND AMARIA lived their private misery, a more public nightmare was playing out in Marseille.

On the morning of June 3, an eight-year-old girl by the name of Marie-Dolorès Rambla was abducted from an apartment complex.

Police were quickly notified, and newspapers and television channels began blaring her photograph. Teams of officers and volunteers scoured the city and its surroundings. Two days later, the body of Marie-Dolorès was found wedged beneath a bush on a mushroom farm outside Marseille.

The murder of a child is a parent's worst agony. It's also a guaranteed blockbuster for the media, and reporters from across France descended. The story became even more curious because it wasn't a typical pedophile killing: Marie-Dolorès hadn't been sexually abused in any way.

Acting on a tip, the police eventually arrested a befuddled young man by the name of Christian Ranucci. He was just twenty years old that summer and still lived at home with his mother in Nice. Earlier that year, his mother had given him a car for his birthday, a gray Peugeot, and he had taken it for a drive through Provence. On the afternoon that Marie-Dolorès disappeared, Ranucci's car became mired on a muddy road on the mushroom farm where the body was found. One of the men at the farm helped tow Ranucci out and would later identify him for the police.

Once at the police station, and after a sleepless night and more than a dozen hours of questioning, Ranucci confessed to the murder. Then he retracted his statement.

It would become one of the most controversial criminal cases in French history, and it would be at the heart of the debate over the country's use of the death penalty. Other murder cases wouldn't cause quite so much political commotion.

*

*   *

THE GIRLS WERE beginning to show signs of their distress. Amaria, always thin, lost more weight while Annie became increasingly lethargic. Hamida became paranoid that they were plotting against him. So he threatened them. He played one girl off the other, playing nice with

Amaria one day, then Annie the next. He kept the doors locked and the windows shuttered.

"I never got to really talk to Annie because Djandoubi didn't allow it," Amaria said.

Finally, while Hamida was sleeping one morning, Annie mustered her courage and snuck the keys out of his pocket. After she woke up Amaria, the two girls crept away. The plan was to go to the post office, where Annie's mother worked. But only a few blocks away, Amaria realized she'd forgotten her wallet and insisted on going back to the apartment.

Hamida was already awake. He locked Amaria in the apartment and went to fetch Annie. Then the real violence began.

He forced Amaria to sit on the bed and watch. Annie was to be punished for planning the escape.

He beat her with his "little stick," he whipped her with his belt, he burned her with a cigarette, he sliced her thighs with a Gillette razor blade. He also invented a special device just for Annie. He cut the cord from a table lamp and peeled back the protective covering on the electrical wires. Then he plugged it into the wall and used it to torture the adolescent girl with electric shocks to the arms, legs, and genitals.

The beatings went on for three days. Once, while Hamida was checking the mailbox, Annie made a run for it and got as far as the street. Covered in bruises and cuts, and wearing only her bra and underwear, she stopped an elderly woman and begged for help.

The woman only said, "*Mon Dieu! Mon Dieu!*" and backed away. Then Hamida was on the street, pulling Annie back into the apartment.

The tortures became more perverse. Hamida made the girls drink his urine. He filled a hypodermic needle with water and injected them. One night, the girls screamed so much they woke up Marie-Claude Kervella and her son. Kervella called her father for advice; he told her that, as a single mother, she couldn't risk getting involved. Still, one morning she tapped on Hamida's door and complained.

"I was tempted to call the police, but Hamida was really apologetic," she remembered. "He told me the girls didn't know how to cook. That was his excuse. He promised it wouldn't happen again."

Hamida began behaving more and more erratically. He bought two starter pistols and told Annie and Amaria they were real guns. He would walk around his neighborhood at night and steal car stereos, rearview mirrors, whatever he found inside the glove boxes.

His friends from before the amputation had completely lost track of him. The Bugias hadn't seen him for almost a year. He stopped by the Comandés once with Annie. He left her in the car and made strange claims about the restaurant he was going to open.

"He refused to introduce me to the girl in the car even though he said it was his fiancée," said Bruno Comandé. "It was troubling, almost oppressive."

As he no longer trusted Annie and Amaria alone together in the apartment, he always took one girl with him when he went to the Sonacotra or his favorite café, Le Mistral at Pointe-Rouge. He would park within sight of his table. Then he would leave the girl in the car and keep watch over her while he sat and played cards with his friends. Like for a pet dog, he would leave the car window open a crack so there would be a little air.

And the more irrational Hamida Djandoubi became, the more his obsession with Elisabeth Bousquet deepened.

Annie and Amaria knew all about her. They'd found a dozen records in the apartment with the name "Elisabeth Bousquet" written neatly in blue pen on the inside of the album cover. Hamida told the girls she used to prostitute for him. He said he'd bought the Simca 1000 with money Elisabeth had earned working the street.

Whenever Hamida went to the Sonacotra, he asked after her. In mid-June, his brother, Ali, reported seeing her with a group of Arabs at the market. Elisabeth had said she was married. Hamida was furious.

He ran into his friend Mohamed Kanzari a week later. Kanzari told him Elisabeth had been with a man named Azzarello at a carnival. Elisabeth had said they were engaged. Again, Hamida raged.

Toward the end of June 1974, Ali came over to the apartment on rue Villa Paradis to borrow money. Annie and Amaria were there, but Hamida didn't bother to introduce them. Hamida gave him two hundred francs, the bulk of Amaria's pay for the week. Ali promised to keep an eye out for Elisabeth.

On the afternoon of July 3, 1974, Ali returned to the apartment. Annie, Amaria, and Hamida were preparing lunch. Ali took his brother aside.

Elisabeth had turned up.

20

THERE IS NO BETTER ARGUMENT for mechanized decapitation than the case of Count Calais. Convicted of treason in Normandy in 1626, he was ordered to be executed by his coconspirator, who, unsurprisingly, was inexperienced in such tasks. It took twenty-nine blows of the sword before the count's head fell and, according to witnesses, he was still alive after the twentieth stroke.

It wasn't just amateurs who botched the job. Official executioners routinely required multiple attempts to complete the chore. Dull swords, squirming convicts, pre-execution brandies—the pitfalls were plenty. For the wealthy, it even became custom to slip the executioner a piece of gold in the hope that it would improve his concentration.

With such obvious room for improvement, Dr. Guillotin began his quest for a humane means of decapitation. He was inspired by two events: a puppet show in the Jardin du Luxembourg, *Les Quatres Fils Aymon*, in which a character is beheaded by a device with a plunging blade; and bridge builders who were using a pulley system to drive piles into the Seine. But the doctor was no visionary. Human ingenuity and medieval engineering being what they were, head-cutting machines had been around for centuries.

There are multiple pretenders to the mantle of "original" guillotine. There is the Ligurian stone blade questionably described as a "Stone Age guillotine." There are accounts from the thirteenth century of decapitating machines used in Naples and Germany. There is also a wood-carving in the British Museum collection that shows what appears to be an Irish head-cutting machine dating from 1307.

The most authoritative claim comes from England, where the Halifax Gibbet was used in the late fourteenth century. According to *Chronicles of England, Scotland and Irelande*, the gibbet was a

wooden structure with a blade held in place by a pin that was attached to a rope. After the convict was placed beneath the blade, all
of the men in the community grabbed hold of the rope and pulled
out the pin together. It was so effective that "if the neck of the trans-
gressor were so big as that of a bull, it should be cut in sunder at a
stroke."

In Scotland, the earl of Morton introduced a similar device, the
"Scottish Maiden," in 1561. In an episode of Ciceronian judicial irony,
Morton was decapitated by his own invention after being convicted of
treason in 1581. That machine, the oldest extant version of a guillotine, is on display at the antiquities museum in Edinburgh.

By far the most romanticized device was the *mannaia* used in Italy
starting in the fifteenth century. Its most famous victim was, according
to tradition, a sixteen-year-old girl, Beatrice Cenci, who plotted to have
her father killed, most likely in revenge for raping her. Beatrice's story
has been told by Shelley, Stendhal, and Marseille's own Antonin Artaud,
but it was Alexandre Dumas who gave the most graphic account. After
the executioner raised Beatrice's head, the crowd became so excited that
the coffin was knocked over. "In the fall, the entire torso came out of its
clothes," Dumas wrote, "so that now being totally covered with dust and
blood, a good deal of time had to be spent washing it."

According to *Mémoires de messire Jacques de Chastenet,* the first authentic mechanical decapitation in France was used on a man named
Henri de Montmorency. The beheading occurred in Toulouse in 1632
using a system in which a hatchet was suspended by a cord between
two poles. When the cord was cut, "the head was separated clean from
the body."

There have also been shrewd improvisations. Most impressive was
the clock tower in Schaumburg. A hole was drilled in the clock face,
the heavy steel hands sharpened to a razor's edge, and the convict's
head thrust through the hole. Spectators could literally watch the last
minutes of the man's life tick away.

*

*   *

ALTHOUGH DR. GUILLOTIN'S proposed decapitating machine captivated the popular imagination, there remained political opposition.

In one camp, there were those who wanted nothing short of immediate abolition. In May 1791 the representative Duport told the National Assembly the death penalty was neither morally acceptable nor
a sufficient punishment. He argued that, like soldiers who grow comfortable with the idea of dying at war, criminals learn to accept the
prospect of execution and actually take a certain glory in it.

"Their soul becomes reconciled to the idea, and, alas, your tortures
cease to have any effect," Duport told the Assembly. (He would prove
prophetic; once the guillotine was implemented, the most audacious
of criminals prepared for their possible destiny by having dotted lines
tattooed around their neck.)

Duport proposed lifetime imprisonment in a dungeon to replace
the death penalty. One of the more vocal supporters of the plan was
the political upstart Maximilien Robespierre. "The death penalty is essentially unjust," he declared, "and secondly, it is not the most dissuasive sentence."

In the other camp was the influential doctrine that the death
penalty was a morally just and essential punishment. It was Immanuel
Kant who embodied this movement, and nobody was as quick to
savage Beccaria. Accusing Beccaria of sophistry, Kant claimed that *On
Crimes and Punishments* was the result of "sympathetic sentimentality
and an affectation of humanity."

This first French death penalty debate occurred a decade after
the publication of Kant's masterwork, *Critique of Pure Reason.* His
views on capital punishment are found in *Metaphysical Elements
of Justice,* in which he endorses the *lex talionis* school of thought:
the punishment should fit the crime, and thus murder must be punished by death. "There is no sameness of kind between death and re-

maining alive even under the most miserable conditions, and consequently there is also no equality between the crime and the retribution unless the criminal is judicially condemned and put to death," wrote Kant.

For Kant, death was the perfect punishment: if a decent man commits murder, then the execution is merciful because the man isn't forced to live with his guilt and he can die with honor, having paid his debt to society; but if a corrupt man commits murder and refuses to repent and accept his punishment, then the execution becomes even more severe because the man wants to live, even a life "covered in disgrace."

Kant also dismissed the notions of rehabilitation and deterrence. Judicial punishment should not be concerned with the common good; it should simply redress the original wrong in order to restore the balance of the scales of justice. According to Kant, what society needed to follow was the principle of equality, that is, "If you vilify him, you vilify yourself; if you steal from him, you steal from yourself; if you kill him, you kill yourself."

*

*   *

ONCE THE DEBATES were exhausted and the votes counted, the National Assembly retained the death penalty but approved Dr. Guillotin's proposal. In the words of the representative Tuant de la Bouverie, "It takes a terrifying spectacle to hold the people in check." And what could be a more terrifying spectacle than Guillotin's machine?

But this led to something of a judicial quagmire. With the law stipulating that all condemned prisoners be beheaded, but no beheading protocol in place, there was a backlog of executions. Some suggested that Charles Henri Sanson, the official executioner, start manually beheading until Dr. Guillotin's machine could be built, but he would have no part of it. Sanson told the minister of justice that his sword became dull and nicked after a single beheading, so he couldn't possibly carry out the required number of executions. Worse, he feared common criminals wouldn't hold still; one reason decapitation had been reserved for aristocrats was that only nobles were thought to have the internal fortitude to keep steady in the face of the blade.

The pivotal case turned out to be that of Nicolas-Jacques Pelletier, who was condemned to death for robbery in December 1791. For months he waited in vain to be executed, prompting Judge Moreau to write the minister of justice, asking that "in the name of humanity" the machine be built quickly. "In prison there is an unfortunate man condemned to death, who realizes his fate and for whom each moment that prolongs his life must be a death for him," wrote the judge.

As Dr. Guillotin had no engineering experience, the matter was left to Dr. Antoine Louis, the secretary of the Académie Chirurgicale. Not only did he invent surgical instruments as a hobby, but he was also fluent in the language of official death. After the scandal surrounding the unjust execution of Jean Calas, Dr. Louis was commissioned to find out if a hanging could be differentiated from a suicide, and as a result traveled the countryside to witness dozens of executions. In March 1792, Dr. Louis submitted his *Avis motivé sur le mode de décollation,* which outlined his proposed mechanism:

- two parallel uprights in oak ten feet high, joined at the top by a crosspiece

- a well-tempered blade with the solidity of the best cleavers with openings so that a weight of at least 30 pounds can be attached to the top; the blade must slide down grooves in the two uprights

- a sufficiently long and strong rope to keep the blade held to the crossbar

- a wooden block, slightly scooped out, for the victim's neck

- an iron crescent, like a horseshoe, to hold the head down and ensure that it is not lifted at the moment of execution

The plans were submitted to a carpenter named Guidon, who built the hanging scaffolds for the government. Claiming such an assignment would besmirch his workers' reputations, he demanded the exorbitant sum of 5,660 livres. The government balked. Hearing of the stalemate, a German harpsichord maker, Tobias Schmidt, submitted a rival bid. His quote was only 960 livres and included a leather bag for storing the severed heads. A rush order was placed.

The week of April 15, 1792, the tests began. The Bicêtre, a combination prison, hospital, and old-age home outside Paris, saved its corpses, and a crowd that included Dr. Guillotin, Dr. Louis, and the executioner Sanson gathered in the building's courtyard. They started with a child and a young woman. The heads came off so quickly that Sanson declared it "a fine machine."

Then, frustration. When it came to an adult male, the blade couldn't cut through the last strings of cartilage, and the head was left dangling. When they tried a particularly mammoth-necked cadaver, the blade didn't make it halfway through.

A redesign was in order, and, according to Alexandre Dumas's version of events, none other than Louis XVI, known for his royal fascination with mechanics, was consulted. In *The Tragedies of 1793*, after hearing of the failed tests, Louis XVI asked to see the original sketches. "The King examined the drawing carefully and when he came to the blade said: 'The fault lies there, instead of being shaped as a crescent, the blade should be triangular in form and cut obliquely like a saw.'"

Whether the modified blade was inspired by the king is of historical question, but regardless, the redesigned machine was ready within days. This time, they asked a military hospital for the corpses of strong young men. By luck, in the space of a week one soldier died in a duel, another died from alcohol poisoning, and a third committed suicide. These three sturdy heads fell without a whisper.

The latest tests were almost too successful for Dr. Louis's taste. He complained to a friend: "My enemies are trying, by the channels of the most licentious newspapers, to give this fatal machine the name the Petit-Louison."

He needn't have worried. As Victor Hugo would later write, "There are those who have no luck. Christopher Columbus cannot attach his name to his discovery; Dr. Guillotin cannot detach his from his invention."

*

*   *

IT WAS THE ROBBER Nicolas-Jacques Pelletier who was the true test. On the morning of April 25, 1792, the same day Rouget de Lisle introduced the song that would become the French national anthem, the guillotine was officially unveiled. Erected on a platform at la place de Grève, which is today the esplanade in front of Paris's Hôtel de Ville, the guillotine took two hours to assemble and was painted red for the historic occasion.

A special unit of soldiers stood guard, under the command of none other than Lafayette, who was back in France after serving in the American Revolution and who had been elected head of the Paris national guard. The orders Lafayette received that day stated: "The new method of execution will undoubtedly attract large crowds to the Grève and we must ensure adequate steps are taken to avoid damage done to the new machine."

Sure enough, with newspapers heavily promoting the event, thousands turned out. When Pelletier arrived dressed in his convict's red shirt, cheers burst from the crowd. It was too much for the condemned man. According to Sanson's memoirs, Pelletier fainted while being strapped into the guillotine.

With little fanfare, Sanson pulled the switch. With a quiet thump, the head dropped into a wicker basket. Shovelfuls of sawdust absorbed the blood.

Alas, the crowd was unmoved. Accustomed to drawn-out hangings and public torture, the guillotine was unbearably boring. The *Chronique de Paris* reported: "The people were not satisfied at all. There was nothing to be seen. Everything happened too fast. They dispersed with disappointment, consoling themselves for their disillusionment by singing, 'Give me back my wooden gallows, give me back my gallows.' "

21

THE CAR SLOWED and pulled to the side of the highway. To the right of the road was an olive grove and beyond that the still waters of the Étang de Berre. Ahead was the haze of Marseille.

It was just past three in the afternoon and the sun was remorseless. The Bartoli family—Antoine, his wife, Yvette, and their son, Frederick—climbed from the car. They had been on the road more than ten hours and were grateful to stretch their legs.

Every summer, the Bartolis drove across the south of France, from their home outside Bordeaux to the port in downtown Marseille. There, they caught the ferry to Corsica. Antoine had inherited property in Propriano, a fishing village south of Ajaccio, and it was the family's summer retreat. They'd already made the trip more than a dozen times.

The family always left the first weekend in July. Yvette worked as a secretary in an explosives company, and July was the month the factory shut for holidays. Antoine's vacations were more flexible, as he worked for the regional government in the roads department. This year, Antoine took a little extra care behind the wheel. After a decade of driving Fiats, he'd bought his dream car, a Mercedes. It was second-hand and a peculiar shade of apple green, but he couldn't have been happier.

They left the car parked on the shoulder of the highway, Nationale 113. They were at a spot known as the Col du Télégraphe, because the old telegraph wires used to pass by there. The family was in no hurry. It was an hour's drive at most to get to the ferry port, and the boat didn't leave until eight o'clock that night. There was time to walk, to nap, to explore.

An overgrown path descended into the fields of olive trees. Frederick lunged along it, looking for a place to empty his bladder. He would turn seventeen years old that summer and was all energy after the long hours in the car. He was an athletic type with a passion for rugby. Too small for the scrum, he played on the wing for his high school team.

A stone cabin lay just off the path. It was an overnight shelter from the previous century, used by shepherds and hunters. It had been abandoned for decades. There were chinks in the walls and broken clay shingles on the ground. Out front, the remains of a stone fence crumbled badly.

Frederick was drawn to the cabin. He cut between a half dozen olive trees and came to the stone fence. There were dry scrubs of rosemary and the scent of pine. The cicadas were humming. The sun was bright overhead. Summer in Provence, he thought.

He moved closer. There were no windows in the cabin. The wooden door was closed, but he could see it had only been pulled shut. He gave it a push. It took a moment for his eyes to adjust to the dim light. Then he saw it. In the corner. Something. A woman. Lying on her back. Matted hair. Eyes closed. Dead.

Frederick backed out of the cabin and called for his mother.*

*

*   *

BODIES WERE A REGULAR phenomena in the hills and fields outside Marseille. The city was renowned for its crime. A. J. Liebling compared Marseille to New Orleans for its rough and violent port. It was more commonly known as the Chicago of France because of its gangster mythology. It was an accurate nickname.

Part of the city's criminal reputation was due to the port that facilitated such traditional illegal enterprises as cigarette smuggling and

---

*Interviewed at his home in Bordeaux in January 2006, Frederick Bartoli retained amazingly precise memories of the afternoon. "Even today, if I am walking in the countryside and I see a little cabin in the distance, I am overcome by dread," he said. "For an instant, I am convinced that if I were to go and look inside I would see another dead woman."

drug running. And part of it was the fact that Marseille was a city that embraced a good outlaw. Just as aspiring painters might head north to Paris, if you wanted to make a name for yourself in crime, Marseille was the city for you. If you pulled the right heist or one-upped the police with enough aplomb, the newspapers would run breathless accounts of your exploits and heads would swivel in admiration and fear the moment you walked into a bar.

The tradition began in the 1920s and '30s with François Spirito and Paul Carbone. They were the first *parrains,* the godfathers of Marseille, and they ran the prostitution, the gambling, and even the city hall. For Spirito and Carbone, their run came to an end when they made the mistake of cozying up with the Nazis and the local Gestapo chief Ernst Dunkel during World War II. After the war, the mantle passed to the brothers Antoine and Mémé Guérini, who worked out a deal with the local politicians to take over the nightclubs that had been run by collaborators. Then came the likes of François le Belge and Tany Zampa and Jacky le Mat and the unending string of violence as their gangs jostled for market share. The local papers gave the impression that the city was constantly in the crossfire of gang warfare. And when it was time to *prendre une belle* (take a rival gang member for that last walk), the bodies usually turned up in the hills that surrounded Marseille.

Indeed, in the past couple of years, three other bodies had turned up in that same cabin that Frederick Bartoli stumbled into that July day. But those bodies were clear Mafia kills: they came with a bullet in the skull, the teeth smashed, and the head burned beyond recognition. The body Frederick found didn't look anything like this. The body Frederick found looked like the work of a pervert.

*

*   *

FREDERICK'S MOTHER, Yvette, went into the cabin to confirm what her son had seen. She was out in a flash, grim and pale. His father refused to look. Instead, Antoine took them back to the car. They would drive toward Marseille and stop at the first phone booth they saw. By chance, at that moment two officers on motorcycles came up the hill. Antoine waved them down.

Within a half hour, there were police from three forces at the crime scene. The motorcycle officers were a highway patrol from the CRS, the French national security force. A dead body wasn't their mandate. Officers from the Berre-l'Étang division arrived next. One of the constables pushed up the dead woman's T-shirt and unzipped her jeans to see how far the torture went. It went far.

Finally, a team from the *brigade des recherches* in Salon-de-Provence arrived. The brigade is the major crimes unit of the gendarmes. The group consisted of three constables and a lead officer by the name of Captain Jacques Chauley. They wore their summer khaki uniforms with short-sleeved shirts and carried 9mm handguns.

The body was officially in Salon's jurisdiction, but the local prosecutor's office often handed murder cases to the police in Marseille. This one might be different, though. The head of the Salon brigade, Commandant Yves Salendre, had a reputation for solving tough cases. They called him Columbo because of his instincts, and if a body dropped on Salon territory, "Columbo" had the influence to make sure his team got the case.

That July, Commandant Salendre was on vacation, but his colleagues knew he was doing some construction work not far from the stone cabin. Chauley sent one of the constables to run down the case for him. Salendre sent word back that the Salon brigade would take it.

The decision made, the officers alerted the regional police commander for the Bouches-du-Rhône, then radioed the Service Régional de Police Judiciaire in Marseille. Finally, they contacted the prosecutor's office in Aix-en-Provence. The case was to be treated, in French judicial terminology, as a flagrant crime. This designation was reserved for the most serious cases, and for up to sixteen days the police would have extra powers to seize evidence and hold witnesses.

France operates under the civil law that descended from the Romans, the *Corpus Iuris Civilis*. Unlike in America or Britain, where police handle the investigations, under the French civil law system, criminal investigations are overseen by an independent judge, the *juge d'instruction*. This serves as an additional check on the powers of the police. For this case, Judge Jean-Claude Girousse of Aix-en-Provence was assigned to the file, while Captain Chauley organized the physical police work.

It was July 6, 1974. The investigation was officially under way.

Constable Pierre Vidou searched the cabin for evidence. The dirt floor was covered with debris: crushed cardboard boxes, empty tins of food, traces of human feces. One item demanded attention. An empty wine bottle was near the legs of the dead woman. It was the cheapest of wines, a plastic bottle with a screw top. According to the label, it was the house brand sold by the Casino chain of grocery stores and had contained one liter of rosé. Vidou bagged the evidence.

The officers also noted what wasn't found. First, there were no personal papers. Nothing in the pockets and no purse or handbag in the vicinity. And second, there was no blood. The woman had obviously been beaten, yet there was no sign of struggle or bloodstains. It looked as if she had been killed somewhere else and dumped in the cabin.

Photographs were taken by Constable Gaston Morant. The view from the highway, the olive grove, the cabin, the interior, and then the body, both full-length and close-up. There was a photography lab back at the Salon headquarters, and the film would be developed on-site that evening.

The job of mapping the hut went to Captain Chauley. The structure was thirteen feet by sixteen feet, with walls more than a foot and a half thick. The dead woman was in the southeast corner. She lay on her back, legs slightly bent, her right arm splayed out, her left arm partially lodged under her body. She wore a light blue tank top, blue jeans, and light purple underwear. There was a silver ring on each of her hands.

When Chauley learned that one of the officers from Berre-l'Étang had unzipped the woman's pants, he was profoundly irritated. Basic police procedure dictated that the crime scene should be left untouched. He noted the violation of protocol in his report.

A body van was called, and the cadaver was transported to the morgue at the Salon-de-Provence hospital. The police would know more after an autopsy, but at first glance, it looked as if the woman hadn't been dead long. Even with the July heat, the body didn't smell. They guessed it had been forty-eight hours.

Meanwhile, the Bartoli family waited. And waited. It had been simple happenstance that Frederick found the body, but even happenstance requires bundles of paperwork in France. Frederick told and retold his story. An hour passed, then another, then another. Finally, Antoine reminded the police officers the family had to catch the ferry at eight o'clock. During the summer peak, if you missed your booking, you might have to wait for days for a cancellation. Antoine thought his vacation had gotten off to a miserable enough start already.

The police agreed and let the family go on their way. The Bartolis climbed back into their apple green Mercedes and hurried to Marseille. They made their ferry.

Frederick didn't sleep well that night on the boat, nor the next night at the family house in Propriano. Thoughts of the body, of death, plagued his sleep. But then summer and sea took over. He was young, and the horrors passed. For his mother, Yvette, it took longer. She suffered a week of nightmares. Antoine was happy he'd refused to look.

22

THREE DAYS AFTER NICOLAS-JACQUES Pelletier became the first person guillotined in French history, three more men were beheaded for killing a lemonade seller. A few days later, it was a trio of forgers who met the blade. The new machine proved so efficient and easy to operate that officials across France hungered for their own guillotines. And then the blood truly began to flow.

France was, after all, in the midst of a revolution, and even without the introduction of such a wondrously proficient killing machine, a revolution tends to be a violent affair. The Marquis de Sade had a prime view of the carnage. After being removed from the Bastille, he occupied a new prison cell overlooking a courtyard where a guillotine had been installed. According to his running tally, during the height of the Reign of Terror, 1,800 prisoners were guillotined in thirty-five days. He regretted that the streams of blood killed the plants in the garden.

Sade's own blood was almost spilt as well. He had been sentenced to death for speaking out against the new regime, but a clerical error saved his head, and a man named Salle was executed in his place. To no great shock, Sade became a determined opponent of the death penalty. In his treatise *Frenchmen: One More Effort If You Wish to Be Republicans,* he echoed the sentiments of Beccaria: "Either murder is a crime, or it is not. . . . If it is, then by what perverse logic do you punish it by the same crime?"

As impressive as Sade's count of fallen heads may have been, it was nothing compared to the efficacy of the main Paris guillotine. On one record-setting day, October 31, 1793, twenty-one people were guillotined in just thirty-eight minutes. And the guillotine was as indiscriminating as it was relentless. Among the twenty-four people guillotined in Nantes on December 17, 1793, were two boys aged fourteen and thirteen. The holy weren't exempt: in July 1794, sixteen Carmelite nuns went to the guillotine singing "*Veni Creator Spiritus.*" Nor were the dead: a man by the name of Valazé committed suicide on the eve of his execution, but his corpse was nonetheless strapped into the guillotine the following morning. Even animals found a place beneath the blade. According to newspapers of the day, an unrepentant monarchist taught his dog to howl at the word *Republican.* Both man and beast were guillotined.*

Amazingly, the government sought to improve the guillotine. When the inventor John Fitch came to Paris seeking investors for his steam engine, there were inquiries as to whether it could be attached to the guillotine. It was rumored Dr. Guillotin was asked if a three-bladed guillotine was possible. A four-bladed guillotine was actually commissioned in Bordeaux, though never put to use. And in July 1794, a mechanic named Guillot invented a nine-bladed machine. However, before this device could be tested, Guillot was arrested for counterfeiting and executed on the traditional guillotine.

*

* *

MUCH OF THE BLOOD spilled by the guillotine was a result of the battle to control the new French Republic. First to go were the monarchists and those interested in maintaining the religious order. Then, once the various factions began squabbling, it was political undesirables who were fed to the guillotine.

This epidemic of violence was personified by Maximilien Robespierre, the head of the benignly named yet dictatorial Committee of Public Safety. In 1792 it was Robespierre who denounced the death

---

*Many of these incidents are found in the book *A History of the Guillotine* by Alister Kershaw. I mention this because Kershaw was part of a curiously friendly literary divorce. In the 1950s, Kershaw and his colleague Jacques Delarue embarked on a joint project on the death penalty in France. After a year of work, one man found himself fascinated with the death machine, the other with the men behind the machine. As a result, they wrote separate books, Kershaw's *Guillotine* and Delarue's *Le Métier de bourreau.*

penalty as "essentially unjust" before the National Assembly; two years later, the same man was delirious with power and paranoia and was having people killed by the thousands.

"Terror," he famously announced, "is nothing other than prompt, severe, inflexible justice."

Robespierre relied upon the arguments of Jean-Jacques Rousseau to justify his policy of eliminating his political enemies. In *The Social Contract*, Rousseau argued the death penalty was a valid element of the unspoken agreement that binds together a community. "To preserve our lives from the knife of the murderer, we consent to die if we should ever commit murder ourselves," he wrote. "In this agreement, far from disposing of our lives, we are only providing for their protection." Rousseau also insisted that any person who attacks the rights of society becomes a traitor and thus should die "less as a citizen than as an enemy."

This was the fig of logic that Robespierre clung to when it came to the two most famous guillotinings in French history. When the monarchy was officially abolished in September 1792, the mere existence of Louis XVI and Marie-Antoinette was a menace to the Republic, as they were a rallying point for monarchists across Europe.

"It is with regret that I pronounce the fatal truth," Robespierre said in arguing for the royal executions. "Louis ought to perish rather than a hundred thousand virtuous citizens; Louis must die that the country may live."

The National Assembly was convinced and found Louis guilty of treason by a vote of 721 to 0. The decision to execute was much closer: 387 to 334.

On January 21, 1793, Louis mounted the scaffold. It was the first execution to be held at la place de la Révolution, now la place de la Concorde, and the crowd stretched for miles. There were more than sixty thousand soldiers alone.

Antimonarchist newspapers reported that a sobbing Louis begged for his life. The executioner testified otherwise. "He bore it all with a sangfroid and a firmness which astonished us," wrote Charles Henri Sanson. Once strapped into the guillotine, the king's last words were "I hope that my blood may cement the happiness of the French people."

At the very least, it cemented an afternoon of fun. One newspaper described the execution as a "fête," with gales of laughter and hats thrown in the air. "His blood flowed and some dipped their fingers in it, or a pen or a piece of paper," wrote the journalist Louis-Sébastien Mercier. "One tasted it and it was well salted."

Marie-Antoinette was escorted to the guillotine the following October. Along with treason, prosecutors accused her of sexually abusing her own son. Yet she also remained dignified to the end. After stepping on Sanson's foot, she exclaimed, "I beg your pardon, Monsieur, I did not mean to do that."

And then she too lost her head.

*

*   *

THERE WAS SOME opposition to this rampant bloodletting. The citizens of Arras, for instance, were upset because the city guillotine stank of fetid blood. In Paris, the guillotine had to be moved from the Barrière du Trône because the sinkhole where the blood collected overflowed onto the street. According to the official report, it emitted "a pestiferous odor of which the neighboring inhabitants complain bitterly." Then there were the stray dogs. The public prosecutor reported: "After public performances of criminal sentences, the victims' blood remains where it is spilt and dogs come to drink it."

But mostly the guillotine delighted and intrigued. Stores sold earrings with dangling miniature guillotines. There were guillotine parties during which people wore red ribbons around their neck. And a popular table decoration was a replica guillotine that severed the heads of special dolls, releasing a red-colored perfume so guests could dip their handkerchiefs into the "blood."

Guillotines were even considered appropriate playthings. Children used two-foot-high models to decapitate birds, mice, and toy soldiers. Goethe, regarded by some as Germany's greatest author, asked his mother to buy one for his son when she visited Paris in 1793. She refused, writing:

Dear Son,

I'll do anything you please and do it with great pleasure, but to buy a miniature model of the infamous guillotine as a plaything for the baby—no, I won't do that at any price. If I had a say in the government, the manufacturers of this toy would themselves be put under the guillotine and I would have the machine itself publicly burned.

The guillotine was even co-opted by opponents of the new regime. Ingenious priests rubbed rope around their necks, leaving a ring of red swollen skin. They would then present themselves to the gullible masses and proclaim they'd been guillotined, but God had replaced their heads so they could continue their divine mission to restore the Church.

*

* *

SLOWLY, THE MADNESS of the butchery dawned on at least some of the Revolution's leading figures. Robespierre's cohorts on the Committee of Public Safety, Georges-Jacques Danton and Camille Desmoulins, issued a pamphlet asking: "Where is this system of terror to end? What is the good of a tyranny comparable only to that of the Roman emperors as described by Tacitus?"

Robespierre had both men guillotined.

This would be his ultimate undoing. In July 1794, he was arrested, suffering a mysterious gunshot wound to the face in the process. One story has it that he was shot by a guard; more likely, it was a bungled suicide. Whatever the case, Robespierre became the first man guillotined while lying on his back because his jaw injury made it too painful to be strapped facedown.

After three years of Terror, between 35,000 and 40,000 people had met their death at the guillotine, including an officially estimated 2,627 in Paris. Out of the blood emerged one hopeful sign. In the fall of 1795, under the Act of 4 Brumaire, Year IV, the death penalty was actually abolished in France. In the National Assembly, Boulay de la Meurthe promised that the new government "wouldn't be dirtied by a single drop of blood."

There was just one minor catch: abolition would come into effect only when there was "general peace" in France.

And as Napoleon was about to come to power, that clause wouldn't be met anytime soon.

*

*   *

FOR THE FATHERS of the guillotine, their stories do not end happily.

Tobias Schmidt, the German harpsichord maker who built the machine, looked to get rich. France was divided into eighty-three political *départements* at the time, and each needed at least one guillotine. He generously offered a bulk rate of 920 livres each. But a government official argued guillotines could be made for just 500 livres, and within days less expensive bids were submitted.

Schmidt's chances appeared bleak until he played his trump card. With Dr. Guillotin and Dr. Louis shirking responsibility for their creation, Schmidt filed a patent claiming it was his invention. The government refused to recognize his claim, but to avoid an unpleasant legal process, Schmidt won the lucrative contract.

In all, he earned a fortune of more than seventy thousand livres. Alas, he fell in love with a wanton showgirl in one of the Montmartre cabarets. Her name was Chameroi, and Schmidt spent his entire fortune wooing her. When his money ran out, so did she. Schmidt died an alcoholic's death.

Things weren't much better for Dr. Louis. He died of a chest infection the month after the guillotine's inauguration. On his deathbed, he told a friend: "I was only happy when I was young, when my success hadn't yet awakened the envy which will very likely pursue me beyond the tomb."

And Guillotin himself was tormented by his notoriety. When he walked the streets of Paris, those who recognized him tapped the back of their necks. He developed a fathomless hatred for Robespierre, whom he described as having "hell in his face, in his temperament, and in his future." Guillotin joined a secret society that opposed the Reign of Terror, and he furnished members with laudanum pills so they could commit suicide if faced with the machine he once so lovingly promoted.

In the end, Guillotin spent twenty-seven days in jail for his seditious activities. From this, the legend was born that he met his death on the guillotine. In truth, after being released from prison, Guillotin faded into obscurity. He died in 1812 at his home on rue Saint-Honoré after complications from a carbuncle on his shoulder.

"Sadly for our colleague, his philanthropic movement welcomed and gave a place to an instrument that the vulgar attached his name to," wrote a certain Dr. Bourru in eulogy. "So it is true that it is difficult to do good for men without it resulting in some unpleasantness."

23

A WOMAN BRUTALLY TORTURED and killed, then dumped in an abandoned cabin. The local papers were all over it.

In France, there are two very different journalistic traditions. There are the intellectual newspapers published in Paris: *Le Monde, Le Figaro, Libération,* and their ilk, filled with political essays and cultural analysis and distributed to concerned readers across the country. Then there are the "popular" papers. Some, like *Le Parisien,* are based in the capital, but most come from places like Bordeaux and Nice and have names like *Sud-Ouest* and *Nice-Matin.* This is a bawdy collection of tabloids and broadsheets that devote more space to photos than words and, as a rule, pay more attention to the feats of their soccer team than the politics at the Élysée.*

In Marseille, sports and crime are the staples of the local papers, if not their raison d'être. And since the World Cup had finished the same July weekend the body was found—West Germany beat Holland 2–1 after the chain-smoking Dutch striker Johan Cruyff played a sub-par match—editors were thrilled to have an atrocity for their pages.

In 1974 there were four dailies in the city. *La Marseillaise* was the left-wing paper with links to the Communist Party and the unions. It ran the story on the front page, below a piece about the Tour de France and above an article about two actresses hurt in a car accident in Saint-Tropez. The article detailed the injuries to the body and noted that identification was impossible at the time. There was also one small error: *La Marseillaise* stated the body was found on Sunday, not Saturday.

---

* Located on rue du Faubourg-Saint-Honoré near the Champs-Élysées, the Palais d'Élysée is home to the French president, and the term the *Élysée* is used as a synonym for the center of political power, much as *White House* is used in the United States.

Next were the three papers that were part of the mayor Gaston Defferre's publishing empire: *Le Méridional, Le Provençal,* and *Le Soir.* On the extreme right was *Le Méridional.* It ran the most crime articles of all the papers, trumpeting the rise in break-ins and murders, and editorializing in favor of tough-on-crime politicians. In an article titled "The Mysterious Crime in Lançon," the editors made a strained leap in logic: after learning from the police that the dead woman had shaved legs and trimmed pubic hair, they declared it likely that she was of North African descent.

Next was the largest newspaper in the region, *Le Provençal,* which ran a banner headline about the body across the top of the front page, trumping stories about the World Cup, a matador being gored in Arles, and a disturbing poll revealing one in two French people wouldn't be able to take a summer vacation in 1974. A story about Pierre Trudeau and the Canadian elections was relegated to the bottom of the page.

The Defferre group also put out an afternoon tabloid, *Le Soir.* All three of the newspapers went heavy on the details, and all three included certain inaccuracies. *Le Provençal* reported that the body was found by two children, *Le Méridional* that the woman was found completely naked.

In one of the quirks of French law, strict measures are taken to protect the identities of those involved in the criminal justice system. It is, for example, illegal to publish a photograph of certain ranks of French officers without first covering their eyes with a black bar or some other photo-altering technique to mask identity. For this reason, none of the media referred to the unfortunate Bartolis. Police assigned the family the name Mercier to ward off any unwelcome attention.

Over the next days, the papers did their best to keep the story alive. They publicized the police's request for help from the public. They put forward their own theories, *Le Méridional* guessing it was a settling of accounts, *La Marseillaise* suggesting the woman was tortured to death by "*individus appartenant au milieu des proxénètes*"—individuals from the world of pimps. But with no identification and no suspects, the papers could only report the obvious. As *Le Provençal* declared, it was to be an "*enquête difficile.*" A difficult investigation.

*

* *

THREE DAYS AFTER the body was discovered, the autopsy was conducted in Salon-de-Provence. The town is twelve miles north of the stone cabin where the body was discovered and is best known for being home to Nostradamus from 1547 until he died of gout, in 1566.

Two doctors from the police laboratory in Marseille, Gabriel Thiroux and François Vuillet, were assigned the case. Vuillet was highly regarded by the police but somewhat eccentric. He was known to sing French folk songs while sawing open skulls.

Thiroux and Vuillet started by cataloging the dead woman's clothes. They removed the jeans, noting they were made by Creation Handa and were a European size 44; they removed the tank top, made from a light blue fabric with a pattern of white anchors and navy blue sailboats; they removed the purple underwear; and, finally, the two silver rings. They were ready to begin.

The woman measured five feet six inches in height. She had blue eyes. Her hair was brown and curly and cut short, barely reaching her shoulders. She regularly plucked her eyebrows, and her legs were shaved. Her nails were painted translucent mother-of-pearl. She had a scar on her lower stomach from an appendectomy. The doctors estimated she was twenty-four years old.

A surface examination of the body revealed multiple traumas. There was a two-and-a-half-inch wound on her forehead. There was a circular burn mark on her left temple. There were cuts and bruises on her chin, eyelids, and lips. There was a deep furrow in the skin of her neck, three inches below the earlobes.

On her left breast there was another deep circular burn. On her back were more than a dozen cuts and bruises, some long and thin, others square with indentations.

The woman's arms were bruised. Her hand was burned. Her thighs and calves were bruised and cut.

Her pubic region was burned in two different ways. Light burns on her inner thighs where the skin was blistered, and more intense first-degree burns around her vagina. Traces of candle wax were found.

The doctors made a horizontal incision at the rear of the scalp to access the dead woman's skull. They found multiple bruises, each between one and a half and two inches in width. The nerve centers of her brain were swollen.

On the woman's neck there was deep bruising on the sternocleida mastoid muscles. The pharynx had been pushed back into the vertebrae of the upper spine. The lungs were bruised and filled with a dark liquid.

There was bruising around the anus, and traces of candle wax were found in the woman's rectum. In her vagina, they found residue of harissa pepper sauce.

The official conclusion of the autopsy was that the woman died of forcible asphyxiation. The hard truth was she had been brutally tortured and suffered a horrendously painful death.

*

*   *

THE LEAD INVESTIGATOR watched the autopsy with the resigned horror of an experienced police officer. Captain Jacques Chauley had plenty of experience with brutal death. He was forty years old that summer and had served with the French military in Algeria before entering the *gendarmerie*. He saw bad things during the war, but nothing marked him like a case he handled while with the Nice brigade.

Chauley had worked on the sordid murders that were committed in Nice in September 1971, just a few weeks before Hamida Djandoubi's tractor accident. Four seasonal laborers had robbed a farmhouse owned by the Marra family. There was a rumor the family was saving money to buy land and had thirty thousand francs in the house.

Two men waited outside the farmhouse, while two more went inside. The husband, Francesco Marra, had gone to the market. His wife, Catina Marra, who was eight and a half months pregnant, was alone with her seven-year-old daughter, Danièle.

One of the men, Ali Benyanès, was armed with a knife. He demanded the money. Catina Marra gave him two thousand francs. Benyanès wanted the full thirty thousand, but Catina insisted that was all there was. He threatened her and she started screaming. Danièle ran down the hall.

Benyanès chased the little girl down and slit her throat. Danièle died instantly. He then returned and stabbed Catina repeatedly in the stomach. Three blows pierced the womb and struck the fetus.

The men fled. A passing neighbor heard the screams and called the police. At the hospital, emergency surgery saved Catina's life. The baby, a little girl, was delivered prematurely but alive. The couple called her Danièle to replace the daughter they'd lost.

Benyanès and his accomplices were arrested one hour after the robbery at the farm barracks where they lived. Benyanès was convicted of murder and sentenced to death. He was guillotined at the Baumettes prison in Marseille in May 1973.

Chauley couldn't forget the case. He was a devout Christian and had been morally opposed to the death penalty. He'd always thought it should be abolished and replaced with true lifetime imprisonment. "Put them in a cell and let them know the only way they'll be leaving is in a coffin," he said. The Benyanès case shook his beliefs.

"When you see the mother, who is pregnant, leaving on a stretcher after being stabbed in the stomach, and you see the little kid with her throat slit lying on the floor, you start to think maybe the death penalty is a good idea," said Chauley.

He still had no clear answer to the ethical dilemma of capital punishment. But he did understand one thing as he watched the autopsy conducted before him. As the doctors revealed one atrocity after another, Chauley knew he had another death penalty case on his hands.

*

* *

THE POLICE BEGAN with the basics. Constable Morant had taken a close-up of the victim's face. They made several copies at the police photo lab and, radiating out from the stone cabin where the body was found, the police stopped at every farmhouse and village. The officers knocked on doors, stood outside churches, and interrupted morning coffees. Nothing.

On the Monday following the discovery, Constable Vidou took copies of the woman's fingerprints and headed to the police laboratory in Marseille. There were files with tens of thousands of prints, pasted onto cardboard cards and filed according to the person's sex, age, skin color, and hair color. The comparison process was eye-straining work that took days. Nothing matched.

They ran through the missing-person files in Marseille and the surrounding jurisdictions, hoping to find a report on a young woman with dark curly hair. Again, nothing. They sent a request to the Ministry of the Interior so that the national files could be searched for a woman fitting the profile. In the age before computers, the results would take up to a week.

The entire time, they canvassed. Day after day, village after village. The temperatures pushed 100 degrees Fahrenheit. Nothing turned up. The officers grew frustrated.

"You go into every case knowing you might not solve it," says Captain Chauley. "We felt some pressure, but we kept believing something was going to happen."

In one way, the investigators were protected because of the tempest surrounding the Christian Ranucci case. So much attention was focused on the young man, the body in the stone cabin took a distant second billing. In the Ranucci case, the victim had been an innocent young girl, and nothing stokes the public fury like a crime against a child. In comparison, an unidentified woman who was suspected of being a prostitute raised a minimum of alarm. The public always breathed a little easier when they could put moral distance between themselves and the victim. If it was a middle-class teacher or helpless child, the calls for expedited justice rang forth. If it was a drug user or a mafioso or a prostitute, the victim's background helped to quell the outrage. In the shadowy corners of their hearts, people couldn't help but feel these were victims who were asking for it.

Still, the police pressed on. With the door-to-door search in the villages turning up empty, the police in Marseille began questioning informants. Had any of the local prostitutes gone missing? Any rumors of a girl being "punished"? The investigators kept hoping the phone would ring with a tip. Yet nearly a week after the body had been found, there was still nothing.

Then, on the morning of Friday, July 12, officers were re-canvassing the village of Grans, about six miles northwest of where the body had been found. At a house on the chemin de Moulin, a woman opened the door. Inside, the officers could hear the cacophony of young children. The woman glanced at the photograph. And nodded.

"I know that woman."

24

HIS EVISCERATING CONTINENTAL wars and incessant self-aggrandizement aside, Napoleon generally had his heart in the right place when it came to the advancement of French society. To appreciate this, one need only admire his transformation of the justice system, a feat Napoleon himself admitted would outshine his military accomplishments and "live forever."

With the turbulent transition from monarchy to republic to empire, France was a hopeless muddle of laws at the dawn of the nineteenth century. As an antidote, in 1804 Napoleon introduced the *Code civil des français*, soon known as the Napoleonic Code, to regulate all civil and property law. This landmark work, incorporating both French legal traditions and the *Corpus Iuris Civilis,* was one of Europe's first complete legal codes. Four years later, Napoleon redressed the baffling olio of criminal laws with the *Code d'instruction criminelle*. Court procedures were standardized across the country, and offenses such as witchcraft, blasphemy, and heresy were decriminalized. Napoleon also enshrined the principle that an accused was innocent until proven guilty, gave the accused the right to a lawyer, and even ordered a lawyer appointed at state cost for those who couldn't afford the fees.

Of course, Napoleon also eradicated one troublesome law: the Act of 4 Brumaire, Year IV, promising the abolition of the death penalty when "general peace" arrived in France, was struck from the books.

*

* *

FRANÇOIS GUIZOT WAS eight years old when his father was guillotined for the heinous offense of "federalism." Small wonder, then, that as an adult Guizot dedicated himself to fighting abuses of the death penalty.

In 1822 he published *De la peine de mort en matière politique,* a polemic against using the guillotine to settle political differences. "In political matters, even the reality of the crime, as we've seen, is often in question," wrote Guizot.

Like the Greek general Diodotus before him, Guizot was convinced executions didn't deter political insurgents. "One can kill one, two, several individuals, one can violently repress one, two, several political plots," he wrote. "But what one doesn't realize is that you will always face the same enemies, the same perils."

His arguments would soon be adopted by the French government, but for the most jaded of purposes. After Napoleon's definitive fall and exile to the island of Saint Helena in 1815, France reverted to a constitutional monarchy, first under Louis XVIII, then under his brother Charles X. This new royal regime lustily embraced the guillotine, with Charles X even introducing the Anti-Sacrilege Act, which briefly restored the death penalty for vandalizing holy items. But once Charles X fell during the July Revolution of 1830 and four popular ministers were sentenced to die for treason, the government engineered a volte-face on capital punishment. The National Assembly decided the most diplomatic way to save the ministers' lives was to follow Guizot's advice and abolish the death penalty for political matters.

Guizot greeted the development with cynicism. And for good reason. A few months later, abolition was repealed and the guillotine was once again chopping away.

*

*   *

WHAT DISMAYED ALPHONSE de Lamartine was not so much the overt governmental hypocrisy involved in the temporary abolition of 1830, but the people's reaction to it.

A poet and politician, Lamartine is most famous for "*Le Lac,*" a poem memorized by French schoolchildren to this day. After the ministers were spared in October 1830, he was galled to see crowds marching on the street to demand their death. His response was the poem "*Contre la peine de mort (Au peuple du 19 octobre 1830)*." In it, he implores the French people to adopt Enlightenment ideals.

> *Here France has closed the blood-stained book*
> *Of her savage laws;*
> *Here a great people, on the day of justice,*
> *Onto the scales of humanity, in place of foul torture,*
> *Cast its magnanimity.*

Another man of letters inflamed by the gruesome extravagance of the death penalty was Victor Hugo, the author of *Les Misérables* and *The Hunchback of Notre Dame*. Sanctioned death had been seared into Hugo's mind as a young boy. While traveling to Spain with his mother, he saw the heads of highwaymen hammered into the roadside trees. He was particularly distraught by the sight of one criminal who'd been dismembered and then reassembled into the shape of a crucifix.

In 1829, at the age of twenty-seven, Hugo anonymously published *The Last Days of a Condemned Man*, claiming he found the idea "lying in a pool of blood under the red stumps of the guillotine." The book is the fictional journal of a man waiting at the Bicêtre prison for his execution date. The crime is never revealed, but Hugo doesn't raise the shadow of innocence. Instead, he asserts the death penalty has no place in Christian society. *The Last Days of a Condemned Man* is the first book that attempts to humanize the criminal, and it introduced the idea that the wait to be executed was in itself excessively cruel.

> *They say there is nothing to it, that you don't feel the pain, that it's a merciful release, and that in this way death is made easy.*
>
> *Is that so? Then what about this six-week death agony and this day-long death rattle? What about the mental torment endured through this fateful day that passes so slowly and so fast?*

For Hugo, who so famously declared, "Blood doesn't wash away blood, tears wash away blood," the book would be his first volley in a lifetime campaign against the guillotine.

*

* *

IT SO HAPPENED that these literary appeals by Lamartine and Hugo coincided with the emergence of compelling alternatives to the death penalty.

One reason ancient societies relied on executions was the lack of an infrastructure to deal safely with violent criminals. With the advent of the modern prison, there was the possibility of long-term incarceration with little chance of escape. In France, there were institutions like Bicêtre in Paris or Château d'If, the very real island prison off the coast of Marseille where the fictional count of Monte Cristo was held.

In America, the art of the penitentiary—a place of penance—was reaching even greater heights. It made sense, in a country that so valued the notion of liberty, that the total loss of it would be seen as the ultimate punishment. At the behest of Dr. Benjamin Rush, often called the father of the American abolitionist movement, the city of Philadelphia became one of the first communities in the world to attempt to reform its prisoners. Aided by Benjamin Franklin,* Rush created the Walnut Street Jail in 1790, the first prison that tried to correct inmates' antisocial behavior. More curious was the Eastern State Penitentiary, also in Philadelphia; it opened in 1829 and was based on the principle that silence would reform sinners. Guards would actually wear socks over their shoes to dampen their footfalls.

---

* One of my more enriching library finds was the two-volume *Opinions of Different Authors upon the Punishment of Death*, compiled by Basil Montagu in 1809 (vol. 1) and 1812 (vol. 2). Montagu, the illegitimate son of the earl of Sandwich (yes, the inventor of the sandwich) and his mistress, the opera singer Martha Ray, collected work by a host of authors, including Benjamin Franklin. Franklin railed against the death penalty for theft, rhapsodizing the time when all a savage needed was "his bow, his hatchet, and his coat of skins" and pillorying those who "protect their property at the expense of humanity." Franklin concluded, "To put a man to death for a crime which does not deserve death, is it not murder?"

The birth of the penitentiary coincided with a revival of the very first punishment. Just as God banished Cain for murder, the governments of Europe realized there were alternatives to hanging criminals by the neck or severing their heads. The offenders could fill distant colonies and toil for the good of their motherland.

Australia is perhaps the most famous of the penal colonies, and Russia made abundant use of Siberia. It was in fact while in exile in Omsk that another committed abolitionist, Fyodor Dostoyevsky, embraced the ideal of redemption that so influenced his work. Imprisoned for revolutionary activities, Dostoyevsky actually stood in front of the firing squad before his death sentence was commuted, at the last instant, to four years of hard labor. The experience prompted Dostoyevsky to declare society should be "judged not by how it treats its outstanding citizens but by how it treats its criminals."

"Because it is said 'Thou Shalt Not Kill,' is he to be killed because he murdered someone else? No—it's not right—it's an impossible theory," Dostoyevsky would write in *The Idiot*.

France was no slouch either when it came to exporting its undesirables. Its colony at Cayenne, French Guiana, was known as "*la guillotine sèche*"—the Dry Guillotine—and in the nineteenth century it became a repository for tens of thousands of French scoundrels, thieves, and murderers. The advantage of the Dry Guillotine was that, unlike the wet version, it was reversible. One happy beneficiary of this distinction was Alfred Dreyfus. After he was convicted on treason charges that had more to do with his Judaism than factual evidence, it was off to the prison colony.

"The glory of time is its ability to identify falseness, to bring truth into the light," Dreyfus would write after finally being absolved.

*

* *

IN FEBRUARY 1848, after yet another French revolution ushered in the Second Republic and sent Louis-Philippe scurrying to England, one of the first acts of the new National Assembly was to winnow the list of capital crimes and, à la Guizot, permanently ban the guillotine for political crimes.

From the abolitionist perspective, it was progress. In 1670 there were 115 capital crimes in France; in 1791 there were 32; under Napoleon there were 27. With the new laws of 1848, just 16 offenses remained death-worthy. Still, Victor Hugo wasn't placated and continued to argue that abolition should be "pure, simple, and definitive." This same obstinacy prompted him to leave France when Napoleon III, Napoleon's supposed nephew, led a coup d'état in 1851. Hugo spent nearly two decades in exile on the Channel Islands, a dry guillotine of his own making.

Hugo's "definitive" abolition appeared possible for the first time early in the twentieth century. Across Europe, the abolitionist movement was gaining momentum, with Portugal eliminating the death penalty in 1867, Holland in 1870, and Norway in 1905. When the abolitionist Armand Fallières became president in 1906, it seemed to be France's turn. True to his beliefs, Fallières commuted the sentences of twenty-nine people who were condemned to death in the first year of his presidency.

The political maneuvering was left to the minister of justice, Aristide Briand. A superb politician—he would later win the Nobel Peace Prize for his efforts on the Locarno Treaties—Briand drafted the tentative abolition bill. "I am not going to resort to reasons of pity and humanity, reasons of sentiment or reasons of philosophy," Briand announced. "I will produce for you arguments based on numbers, on facts."

Briand showed that in Portugal and Holland there had been no rise in crime after abolition, puncturing one of the great arguments for the death penalty: deterrence. He also insisted that judicial error could lead to the execution of innocent men and women. "They say the mistakes aren't very numerous, the trials are well supervised today,"

Briand said. "Gentlemen, if you passed a few moments in the office of the Minister of Justice, you would see the problem is more unsettling."

The public was convinced, the politicians prepared to act. Abolition's time had come. Then, on January 30, 1907, little Marthe Erblinger disappeared.

A friend of Marthe's parents, Albert Soleilland, had offered to bring the twelve-year-old girl to the music hall. Instead, he took Marthe back to his apartment and raped her. When she started sobbing, he strangled her, raped her again, then cut her body into tiny pieces. Soleilland ended up putting the chunks of flesh in a suitcase and leaving it at the baggage consignment of the Gare de l'Est.

When Soleilland was condemned to death, even his wife applauded the verdict. The public demanded that Fallières, for once, refrain from using his right to grant clemency. As one popular song went:

> We hope that Fallières
> Doesn't cheat the call
> Of entire families
> Who demand one by one
> To revenge this child
> With the blood of Soleilland

Yet the president steadfastly commuted Soleilland's sentence, and the murderer was sent to Cayenne instead. The decision doomed his abolitionist dreams. Incensed, the popular press mounted a vigorous campaign to maintain the death penalty. The widely distributed *Le Petit Journal* was in the lead, running covers showing villains cowering in front of the guillotine. The headline on Sunday, July 19, 1908, was typical: "LA PRISON N'EFFRAYE PAS LES APACHES; LA GUILLOTINE LES ÉPOUVANTE." Prison doesn't scare thugs; the guillotine terrifies them.

With such a frenzy of support from the people and the media, opportunisitic politicians rushed to embrace the death penalty. A deputy named Maurice Barrès became the guillotine's leading advocate. "When we are in the presence of a criminal, we find a man in a state of decay, a man who has already fallen from humanity, not one who hasn't yet arrived at humanity," Barrès told the National Assembly. "I demand that we get rid of these desecrations and these degenerates."

The vote was held on December 8, 1908. The motion to abolish the guillotine lost, 330 to 201.

25

FRANÇOISE ACKERMANN WAS a busy, busy woman. At the age of thirty-one she had seven children to care for, she nursed her chronically ill husband, and she worked as a full-time waitress. She clearly didn't have time for small talk with the police.

"There is no chance of confusion," she repeated when Captain Jacques Chauley insisted on showing her the photograph of the dead woman again. "I know her."

According to Ackermann, she had seen the woman while working at the Virginia Club, a private bar with a questionable reputation that was located about ten miles down the highway from where the body was discovered. The woman in the photograph would appear around three in the morning, usually on Fridays or Saturdays, and usually surrounded by men, sometimes four or five, sometimes up to ten. She was regularly accompanied by another woman—smaller, thinner, blond.

From what Ackermann remembered, the woman normally wore the same clothes, blue jeans and a dark sweater with a collar high up on her neck, and she always ordered the same drink, Chivas Regal whiskey. Ackermann didn't know the name of the woman or anyone in her entourage. Nor could she say what types of cars they drove. There was only one thing: she'd heard that one of the men in the dead woman's entourage had a restaurant in Vitrolles, just past the little bridge on the old highway.

There was nothing to add. Ackermann had stopped working at the Virginia Club in April 1974 after being assaulted by a patron at the bar.

*

*   *

JUST AS THE CASE was opening up, the investigation changed hands. Captain Chauley had a vacation scheduled. He was going trout fishing, so his junior, Constable Jean Thain, took over.

Thain was another *pied-noir*. He was born near Serres, Algeria, in 1945, and returned to France with everyone else in 1962. Thain entered the *gendarmerie* in 1968, about the same time the students were overwhelming the streets of Paris. At the Salon detachment, he was known for his meticulous work ethic. That January, it allowed him to crack a string of armed robberies. Two men on a motorcycle had been holding up banks around Avignon. A witness saw them drive off and brought Thain a purple spinning top from her child's toy chest that matched the color of the motorcycle. Thain went to work, visiting every dealership in the region until he narrowed down the make and model of the bike. He then spent weeks sifting through two years of motorcycle registrations. He got his men.

This is what the body case needed. A little bit of luck and a lot of hard work. Thain hoped Ackermann's tip was the luck; he was ready for the work.

The investigators tried to track down the owner of the Virginia Club but the bar was closed for the summer. On July 15, they found the owner's daughter, Cathy Terzian, who was living with her boyfriend, Aimé Fages, in Salon-de-Provence. Terzian had worked at her father's club every Friday, Saturday, and Sunday night from January 1974 to June 1974. She too recognized the dead woman as a Virginia Club regular who normally came in with a blond woman. Her boyfriend remembered the woman too. Always with the same group of men, always drinking Chivas.

"Nothing but the expensive stuff," Fages told police.

But the trail went cold there. Neither Terzian nor Fages knew the name of the dead woman or any of the men who came to the bar.

The officers started tracking down regulars at the bar. They interviewed men with compromising backgrounds, the types who were at ease answering, or rather evading, police questions. Nobody admitted to knowing the dead woman.

That same week, the Ministry of the Interior reported there were no missing-person files matching the victim. It would circulate the woman's photo to every police station in the country, but the chances of something turning up were thin. All that was left was to find the mysterious restaurant in Vitrolles. Thain and his partner hit the old highway. They looked for the little bridge. And soon enough, they found a place called the Auberge du Vieux Moulin.

*

*   *

VITROLLES EPITOMIZED THE conflicts of modern Provence. In the 1950s, it was one of the postcard villages scattered throughout the south of France: a collection of ancient stone houses and narrow cobbled streets, perched on a hill overlooking the calm waters of the Étang de Berre and protected by a one-thousand-year-old castle.

Then Vitrolles exploded. In 1954 only 2,500 people lived in the village. But starting in the early 1960s, *pieds-noirs* and *harkis* began to arrive by the thousands. The population boom was aggravated when Vitrolles was named "a new city of France." In an attempt to revive the sagging Provençal economy, the de Gaulle government declared the region a tax-free business zone. Companies rushed in, particularly the major oil and gas firms, which built refineries and made use of the port at Fos-sur-Mer.

By 1974, the year the body was discovered, Vitrolles had quintupled in size, with an official population of more than thirteen thousand. To complicate the matter, a thousand new people were arriving every year. The accompanying construction transformed the once-quiet village. Apartment blocks, schools, and shopping centers sprawled out. Vitrolles was idyllic no more.

Vitrolles wasn't the only place in the south of France undergoing this type of metamorphosis. Throughout Provence, towns were struggling to absorb the hundreds of thousands of new people settling in the region. Unemployment was near 20 percent, and crime rates were rising. That summer, *Le Méridional* gleefully reported that 1973 had been a record year for home break-ins. It was easy to blame the new-comers for the lack of jobs and the spike in crime. And the darker the skin of the newcomer, the easier the blame fell.

One of the politicians to take advantage of this growing resentment was a man named Jean-Marie Le Pen. The son of a fisherman, Le Pen served with the French military in both Vietnam and Algeria. In an interview he gave in 1962, he acknowledged torturing Islamist rebels. "I tortured because it's what you had to do," he explained.

As his career blossomed, Le Pen attempted to retract those statements. But that and other skeletons crowded his political closet. To cite but one example, in 1971 he was convicted of apologizing for war crimes when his music company released a record titled *The Third Reich* with an adjoining essay that praised Adolf Hitler's democratic rise to power. Nonetheless, one year later, in 1972, Le Pen was named the head of the Front National, a new political party that vowed to defend the French, halt immigration, and get tough on crime. Its early slogans included: "The Immigrants Are Going to Vote . . . Are You?"

Cleverly, the new party chose Joan of Arc as its icon. It was late in the Hundred Years' War when the pubescent Joan had a vision she would lead the French troops to victory. After convincing Charles VII of the divinity of her mission, the fifteen-year-old led the army to triumph in battles at Orléans and Reims in 1429. It was a turning point in a war that would eventually see the English chased from France.

Joan was captured the next year. Among the charges brought against her by the English was heresy because she wore men's clothes into battle, and according to Deuteronomy 22:5, "The woman shall not wear that which pertaineth unto a man, neither shall a man put on a woman's garment: for all that do so are abomination unto the Lord thy God." She was subsequently condemned to die, and the English burned her body three times to ensure there were no bones left for the relic hunters.

147

For the Front National, the choice of Joan of Arc was inspired: for a party whose sacred mission was to expel foreigners, who better than the woman who drove out the English invaders?

It was in the south that the Front National and its vitriol gained the most traction. By 1974 Le Pen was already on the way to becoming a major influence in French politics. And the conflicted city of Vitrolles was on its way to becoming one of the Front National's strongholds.

*

* *

PIERRE MANIAS WAS considered part of the Milieu, the loosely organized group of men with links to the Mafia and little reluctance to perform illegal acts. He was the type the police liked to roust whenever a problem arose, just to keep him on his toes.

In the summer of 1974, Manias was twenty-eight years old and lived with his wife, Nicole, and their young son. When he was younger, he had worked odd jobs: in his parents' fish shop, at a paint store. Now he ran the Auberge du Vieux Moulin, a combination tavern and restaurant with six rooms to rent upstairs. Manias had ungentlemanly ideas on how to make money from those rooms.

Using a warrant issued by the *juge d'instruction,* the police raided the Auberge du Vieux Moulin at 8:30 A.M. on July 22, 1974. It was a considerate hour. Under French law, nonurgent house raids could be conducted starting at 6 A.M.

Manias and his assistant manager, Alain Chaillan, were made to sit while the police searched the bar, the restaurant, the kitchens, the rooms, the toilets. There was nothing suspicious. Then the investigators took a look at Manias's car, a Renault 16. They found a stain that looked like blood on the cover of one of the armrests. The police bagged it and sent it to the police laboratory in Marseille. Manias and Chaillan were taken to the police station at Salon-de-Provence.

Constable Thain questioned Manias first. He admitted to having been to the Virginia Club, but only two or three times in 1974. "I know the owner of the club," Manias told police. "Nothing more."

Thain showed him pictures of the dead woman. He shook his head. He'd never seen her, not at the Virginia Club, not at the Auberge du Vieux Moulin.

The interview was inconclusive. In the polite language of French justice, Manias "benefited from some time to rest" at the police station while Alain Chaillan was questioned.

In her statement, Ackermann said the dead woman had been accompanied by a small blond woman. Chaillan's girlfriend, Josy, was thin and blond. Chaillan admitted they'd been to the Virginia Club and that he too knew the owner. But he said he'd never seen the dead woman and hadn't even heard of the case. "I only read the sports pages in the newspaper," he stated.

Next, they brought in Manias's wife, Nicole, and Chaillan's girlfriend. Both women said they didn't know the victim.

The police decided on a confrontation. At four o'clock that afternoon, July 22, 1974, Constable Thain brought Françoise Ackermann into the interrogation room at the Salon-de-Provence police station. Pierre Manias, Nicole Manias, Alain Chaillan, and Josy Moulin were already there. The police introduced them to Ackermann one by one.

She swore she'd never seen Josy Moulin. Or Alain Chaillan. Or Nicole Manias.

But she stopped at Pierre Manias.

"That's the man I saw, maybe four or five times, with the dead woman," Ackermann told the police. "The woman gave me the impression that she was going out with this fellow."

Thain noted Manias's reaction. He looked flustered. His wife looked furious. Manias admitted to knowing Ackermann. He had seen her when she worked as a waitress at the Virginia Club. But he was adamant: he did not know the dead woman.

Ackermann couldn't be swayed. "I stand by what I said. This man came to the Virginia Club with the young girl who was murdered."

An impasse. They released Manias that evening with orders that he not leave the region until the tests on the blood from his car were conducted. Meanwhile, they tracked down everybody who had known Manias or had anything to say about him. Nobody linked him to the murder.

The first week of August, the test of the stain on the car armrest came back. They couldn't match the blood to the victim. Constable Thain came to an unpleasant conclusion. It was a case of mistaken identity. Manias was released.* It was back to square one.

---

* In August 2006, I visited the premises that had once housed the Auberge du Vieux Moulin. It was closed, but there were two men standing out front. They refused to give their names but took an interest in my research. I asked about some of the actors in the incident:

"Do you know what happened to Pierre Manias?"

"Dead. A settling of accounts."

"And Aimé Fages?"

"Dead. A settling of accounts."

"And Terzian?"

"Dead. A settling of accounts."

26

IN THE GLORY DAYS OF THE guillotine, executions were major spectacles held in front of the Hôtel de Ville or at la place de la Concorde with crowds that reached the tens of thousands. For especially titillating beheadings, windows overlooking the scaffold rented for exorbitant sums, much as landlords today rent out their apartments neighboring Wrigley Field in Chicago. Those without funds would camp out days ahead of time to secure a spot close to the scaffold.

For a while, no Paris visit was complete without seeing the guillotine. When Leo Tolstoy came in 1857, he made sure to attend an execution. He regretted the decision.

"If a man had been torn to pieces before my eyes it wouldn't have been so revolting as this ingenious and elegant machine by means of which a strong, hale, and hearty man was killed in an instant," Tolstoy wrote. "There's nothing grand about it. It is the insolent, arrogant desire to carry out the justice and the law of God."

More typical was the pandemonium surrounding the execution of two men during the Paris Exposition Universelle of 1889. Although the newly unveiled Eiffel Tower was the star of the exposition, for one afternoon at least, the guillotine eclipsed all else. The Thomas Cook and Company travel agency even included the execution on its list of "Paris Attractions" and provided seven horse-drawn buses to bring the eager tourists to watch the heralded machine at work.

Rather predictably, French officials grew squeamish about their gory reputation, and the guillotine was shuffled to the periphery of Parisian life. First, executions were held at dawn instead of midafternoon to discourage crowds; then the guillotine was moved from public squares to outside the Santé prison on the southern edge of the city; and finally the scaffolding was removed so the guillotine was literally brought down to earth. But it wasn't until the execution of a serial killer named Eugène Weidmann in 1939 that the guillotine was pushed entirely out of public view.

Weidmann, an astonishingly handsome man, had been inviting women to his garden home in the suburb of Saint-Cloud and then choking them to death. Eager to profit from his seductive appeal, newspapers gave Weidmann's trial blanket coverage, and his guillotining was hotly anticipated. Still, it should have been a standard beheading save for one tiny miscue: the execution date was set for 4:30 A.M. on June 17, 1939, without taking into account that in midsummer the sun was already rising at this hour. With the dawn light, photographers stationed in the windows of neighboring buildings captured every nuance of the decapitation.

Paris-Soir and *Match* published photo essays of the event,* and there were embroidered accounts of the crowd's behavior, including one specious story that women smitten with the "Handsome Strangler" broke through the police cordon and dipped their fingers in Weidmann's blood. Ignoring the fact that executions had been journalistic fodder for centuries, the minister of justice accused the newspapers of pandering to the base instincts of readers. One week later, Article 26 of the *Code pénal* was put into law, and henceforth all executions were to be held behind prison walls.

In France, the age of guillotine as entertainment had ended, but this didn't stop the debate over the relative merits of public executions. Some twenty years later, Albert Camus argued that hiding the guillotine impeded abolition because it allowed people to ignore the reality of their justice system. "If people are shown the machine, made to touch the wood and steel and to hear the sound of a head falling, then public imagination, suddenly awakened, will repudiate both the vocabulary

---

* Founded as a sports magazine, *Match* was reinvented as a current affairs magazine in 1939 and was eventually renamed *Paris-Match* in 1949.

and the penalty," he wrote. And thirty years after Camus, one of America's leading abolitionists, Sister Helen Prejean, echoed the opinion, writing that people "would see the violence unmasked and this would lead them to abolish executions."

Of course, public executions are still common in places like Iran and China. And sometimes, just like in ancient Rome, these executions involve public participation. Under one interpretation of Sharia law, a murder victim's closest male relative is responsible for executing the murderer. In Somalia in April 2006, a man named Omar Hussein killed a high school teacher after an argument over his grading system. The Islamic court ordered that the dead teacher's son kill Hussein. Several hundred people watched as Hussein was tied to a tree behind the high school and the sixteen-year-old boy stabbed him repeatedly in the chest and throat.

Like the newspapers in Weidmann's day, *Libération* ran a half-page photograph of the event. No government minister accused the paper of pandering.

*

*   *

MEANWHILE, ABOLITIONISTS continued an indirect assault upon the guillotine by attacking Dr. Guillotin's basic premise: that his head-cutting machine was a painless means of official death.

Arguing the inhumanity of this or that killing technique is a common abolitionist tactic, seen in the United States, where execution methods such as the electric chair and lethal injection have been challenged as cruel and unusual punishment. In France, the doubts regarding the instantaneity of guillotine-inflicted death began with the execution of Charlotte Corday in 1793. Corday had assassinated Jean-Paul Marat, one of the architects of the Reign of Terror, by sneaking into his bathroom and stabbing him in the chest while he sat soaking in his tub. After she was guillotined, one of the assistant executioners raised Corday's severed head to the crowd and gave it a mighty slap on the cheek. Witnesses claimed that both cheeks flushed in indignation, and an anatomy professor interpreted this as proof that there was life after decapitation. "This blow was only struck on one cheek, and it was remarked that the other cheek also colored," wrote one Dr. Pierre Sue.

The chief executioner himself was responsible for a similar rumor of post-decollation vitality. After executing two rival politicians in less than a minute, Charles Henri Sanson told friends he looked into the basket and found one head biting the other head so fiercely that he couldn't pull them apart.

Fabulous or not, these tales led to certain ethical hand-wringing. A German professor of anatomy, S. T. Soemmering, mounted an abolition campaign based on his belief that "feeling, the personality, the ego remain alive for some time in the head" after a guillotining. In 1879 the first actual experiment was conducted. Three doctors won the right to examine the head of Théotime Prunier, who was guillotined for killing an elderly woman and twice raping her corpse. The doctors were given Prunier's head five minutes after it had been severed and then conducted tests that included shouting in the ear, pinching the cheeks, and holding a candle to the eyeball. There was no response. The doctors decided they needed to get access to a head the moment it fell in order to come to a truly authorative conclusion.

A more ingenious experiment was conducted a year later by Dr. Dassy de Lignières. He was given the disjoined head of Louis Ménesclou, guillotined for raping and killing a child. The doctor put the head in his satchel and rushed the treasure back to his laboratory. There he attached it to a machine that pumped blood from a living dog into the head. He noted the sudden reddening of the face and the swelling of the lips. The doctor became so excited that he wrote, "This head is about to speak, for it has just become animated by the beating of a heart." As result, Dr. de Lignières called the guillotine "torture" and recommended that the executioner vigorously shake the head after it was severed in order to more quickly rid it of blood.

Perhaps the most important insights we have today are the result of work by Dr. Beaurieux, who, in June 1905, was given permission to wait at the foot of the guillotine and begin his experiments the moment the head was separated from the trunk of the body. Dr. Beaurieux was especially lucky that day, as the head, belonging to a fellow named Languille, landed square on its neck, thus partially stanching the flow of blood.

Dr. Beaurieux noted that, for the first five to six seconds, the head's eyes moved about in wonder and then slowly closed. That's when the doctor called out, "Languille." He reported: "I then saw the eyelids slowly lift up, without any spasmodic contraction—I insist advisedly on this peculiarity—but with an even movement, quite distinct and normal, such as happens in everyday life, with people awakened or torn from thought."

The doctor said the eyes focused on him, then shut. Again Dr. Beaurieux called out the dead man's name and again the eyes opened and focused on the doctor. The third time, there was no response. Dr. Beaurieux came to the conclusion that the lower brain, which was responsible for such reflexes, was still functional for between twenty-five and thirty seconds after the head was cut from the body. As to whether the cortex and higher brain still functioned, the doctor admitted it was an "insoluble" problem.

Nonetheless, this problem would continue to be addressed well into the 1950s. The final word would come from Dr. Fournier and Dr. Piedelièvre, who, without the benefit of specific experiments, determined that death by guillotine was not immediate. In a report filed with the Académie de Médecine, they stated that guillotining was a "murderous vivisection" and that "every vital element survives decapitation."

*

*   *

WITH THE ONSET OF World War II, the potential suffering of criminals and the ethical questions of the death penalty suddenly weren't quite so pressing. In times of war, death is a less philosophical matter, and in occupied France, the Vichy government was true to this form.

If anything, there was renewed enthusiasm for the death penalty. Until the 1940s, there was an unofficial moratorium on the execution of women, with the last recorded case dating back to 1893, when a Madame Bouillon was guillotined for making her son swallow sewing pins. But under the Vichy regime of Philippe Pétain, women were once again subject to the guillotine. One of the notable victims of this policy reversal was Louise Lampérière, who lost her head on July 30, 1943, for performing abortions in Cherbourg.

When the war ended, it was Pétain and his fellow collaborators who faced the penalty of death. The most prominent case involved Pierre Laval, a four-time prime minister of France and the 1931 *Time* magazine Man of the Year. Laval was condemned for high treason for his role in the Vichy administration and, as was the case with death verdicts delivered by military courts, was scheduled to die by firing squad. Somewhat timid, he arranged to have cyanide passed to him in his prison cell on the eve of his execution. Guards found Laval in convulsions and sped him to the hospital, where his stomach was pumped seventeen times and doctors injected him with a myriad of vitamins and tranquilizers.

"For two hours, this fight against death continued," wrote Laval's lawyer, Albert Naud. "The doctors seemed to forget that the success of their enterprise would be crowned at the execution post."

Barely alive, Laval was dragged to the firing range the next morning and, still vomiting, was unceremoniously shot to death.

In other European countries, such as Italy (1947) and West Germany (1949), the unpleasant wartime experiences led their new governments to adopt more humanistic policies and to abolish the death penalty for common crimes. This was not the case in France, where there was absolutely no question of abolition under the postwar regime. Like many military men, General Charles de Gaulle never considered the state's right to take life a topic for debate, even though he himself was condemned to death in absentia for his Resistance activities. He seemingly wasn't bothered by the fact that France was becoming increasingly isolated. Along with Italy, West Germany, Portugal, Holland, and Norway, the ranks of European countries where the death penalty had been abolished for common crimes included Sweden (1921), Denmark (1930), Switzerland (1942), Finland (1949), and Austria (1950).

And not only did de Gaulle dismiss the prospect of abolition, he happily turned back the clock to the days of François Damiens, when even attempted regicide merited death.

After resuming the presidency in 1958, de Gaulle made one of the great political U-turns in French history. Having proclaimed "*Vive Algérie française*" in 1958, de Gaulle ordered the withdrawal of French troops and the repatriation of French residents in 1962. There were protests throughout France and Algeria, and a splinter militia, the Organisation de l'Armée Secrète, targeted de Gaulle for assassination. The most serious attempt on his life came in August 1962, when the car he and his wife, Yvonne, were riding in was torn apart by machine gun fire. Nobody was injured.

The attempted assassination, code-named Operation Charlotte Corday in honor of her efforts during the Terror, was organized by Jean Bastien-Thiry. He claimed the writings of Thomas Aquinas justified regicide when the monarch's death would benefit the whole of the people. De Gaulle didn't agree. After Bastien-Thiry was condemned to death by a military tribunal, the president refused to commute his sentence, arguing that Bastien-Thiry had acted cowardly by putting women in danger, all the while risking nothing himself since he wasn't one of the snipers on the scene. Bastien-Thiry was shot dead on March 11, 1963, the last man in France to die by firing squad.

27

SHORTLY AFTER EIGHT O'CLOCK on the morning of Friday, August 9, 1974, a fourteen-year-old girl named Houria S. walked into the police station at la place Castellane in downtown Marseille. She was there to report hell.

Until that summer, Houria had lived with her family in the tenth arrondissement of Marseille. It was an uneasy home. Her mother was on her third marriage, and there were five children from three separate fathers. They all lived in a tiny apartment.

The situation was aggravated by the clash in cultures. Houria's parents were Algerian and had traditional ideas of how a teenage girl should behave. Houria was struggling to fit in at her school and wanted the freedom her friends enjoyed. There were fights. Things were especially difficult with her stepfather.

In June 1974, three months after Houria's fourteenth birthday, she ran away from home. She hitchhiked to Toulon, another port city about an hour east of Marseille. Houria stayed with a friend for a several days before getting into trouble for shoplifting and other nuisance crimes. The police were called, and she was sent to a Catholic group home for runaways.

A month with the nuns made her think maybe life at her parents' apartment wasn't so bad after all. At the end of July, she slipped away during a group outing to an amusement park. Houria arrived back at her parents' building the morning of August 1, 1974. Nobody answered the bell. Then she remembered: every summer, her family went back to Algeria. She'd missed them by the slightest of margins; they'd left the previous day.

Houria couldn't even get into the apartment. She didn't have a key. After trying to call some friends in Marseille, she ended up sitting on a bench on La Canebière with no money and no inkling of what to do. La Canebière was no longer the grand boulevard that Alexandre Dumas wrote about in *The Count of Monte Cristo*. Now many of the storefronts were boarded up. As the city's economy faltered, the grand cafés and luxury boutiques of the nineteenth century were replaced by cheap sandwich shops and discount clothing stores. Worse, the street was a mess. The city was finally putting in a metro system, a modest two lines, and there were stops being built along La Canebière. It was all dust and construction.

Houria told police that she sat on the bench for hours, wondering whom she could call, what she would eat, where she might sleep. That's when Hamida Djandoubi found her.

*

*   *

ALL OF THE PSYCHIATRISTS who examined Hamida noted the extraordinary effect he had on women.

"This is a subject who is very adept and very seductive in his general behavior," reported Dr. Suttel and Dr. Merlin. "His physique is attractive and harmonious. He speaks in a soft voice and we note in his vocabulary a certain depth and a certain precision that is rare to find among agricultural laborers."

It was quite the impression. A tired and hungry fourteen-year-old could understandably be swept away.

And Houria was certainly Hamida's type: young, unsure of herself, difficulties with her family, no real experience in the world. In brief, extremely vulnerable.

That afternoon, Hamida was doing some shopping on La Canebière with Annie and Amaria. When he spotted Houria, he told his two girlfriends to wait behind so he could talk to the new girl alone. He went up and offered her a cigarette. She accepted.

Hamida kept asking her to go on a walk with him. The third time, Houria said yes.

Houria sensed something eerie about the man. She tried to impro-
vise a story. She told him she'd come to Marseille to see an aunt. He
saw through the lie and pressed her with questions. When he discovered her parents were in Algeria, he insisted she come back to the
apartment on rue Villa Paradis for coffee and couscous.

Houria agreed. She was tired, she was hungry, she felt safe because
there were two other young girls there. And, in the end, where else was
there for her to go?

The four of them drove back to the apartment in Hamida's white
Simca. While Annie and Amaria prepared the meal, Hamida fed Houria
glasses of Martini Blanco mixed with lemon soda, slowly getting her
drunk. He wanted to know the exact details of how she ran away from
home and how long she'd been gone from her family.

"I only told him nonsense," Houria said to the police. "He frightened me."

Hamida told her she was pretty. He said he wanted to have sex
with her.

Houria protested. She was a virgin. And she was too young. Only
fourteen years old.

Hamida took out his wooden club and beat her.

Afterward, he gave Houria paper and a pen. He made her write two
letters, one for her father and one for her godfather. Hamida dictated
what to say. Houria wrote that she'd slept in the streets of Toulon and
ended up doing things that would bring shame to her family. "I want
you to forget about me," she wrote. "I am no longer part of the family.
I am too young, I regret a lot."

In French, there are two main ways to say good-bye. *Au revoir*
roughly translates to "see you again soon" and is used for brief part-
ings; *adieu* literally means God only knows when you will see each
other again, and is used for the longest of separations. Hamida forced
Houria to sign the two letters *adieu*.

After the letters were sealed in envelopes, Amaria and Annie set the table. Then the four of them sat down for their couscous dinner.

The second day, despite the letters, Houria tried to run away. Hamida stopped her in the staircase. First he beat her with his belt. Then he got out his electrocution kit. "That night, he told me I was good for nothing and was going to have to work as a prostitute for him," Houria told the police.

Hamida even drove her to his old Sonacotra foyer at Pointe-Rouge. He went inside but quickly reappeared. He told Houria that the men inside had no money to buy sex and they would come back later.

The third day, Hamida raped Houria. He made Annie and Amaria stay in the kitchen and then he forced her down onto the bed and pushed open her legs. Houria sobbed the entire time. Annie washed the bloodstained sheets afterward.

The next day, Hamida forced her to give him oral sex and raped her again. This time, she felt him ejaculate inside her.

The violence and rapes continued. Hamida told Houria if she ever left he would find her and kill her. The night of August 8, it got so bad Houria thought everyone was going to die. After watching a movie on television, he made the three girls strip naked and lie on the bed. He beat them and then took out his electrocution kit and tortured them one after the other. He made Amaria and Annie hold open Houria's legs so he could push harissa into her vagina.

As Houria sat in the police station giving her statement, she said she could still feel the hot pepper paste burning inside her.

It was the final indignity. That night, Houria snuck across the hall and knocked on Marie-Claude Kervella's door. She begged for help. Kervella promised to talk to a police officer she knew the next day. But Houria decided to take things into her own hands. The next morning, Hamida took Annie out to run errands. They needed to go grocery shopping, and Hamida wanted to sign up for welfare.

As soon as they were gone, Houria convinced Amaria it was their best chance to get away. Maybe it was because, unlike Annie and Amaria, she didn't love Hamida. Or maybe it was because she hadn't been demoralized by months of rape and torture. Whatever the case, young Houria had the strength the other girls lacked. With Amaria in tow, she arrived at the police station a half hour later.

After telling her story, Houria agreed to press charges against Hamida Djandoubi for rape, assault, forcible confinement, and death threats.

Of even greater interest to the police was what Amaria had to say.

*

* *

AMARIA GAVE THE POLICE an almost identical account of the previous night's torture at the hands of Hamida Djandoubi. She described how, over the past months, she'd been beaten with clubs and belts, cut with a razor, burned with cigarettes, given electric shocks, and raped. She also told the police about the prostitution and the Saturday nights at the Sonacotra residence, when she was forced to have sex with ten men in a row.

Finally, Amaria said there was something else the police might want to know.

The month before, Hamida had brought another woman back to the apartment. Her name was Elisabeth Bousquet. Things turned extremely violent. Amaria gave police precise details of the horror.

*

* *

THIS TIME, THE POLICE took the complaint against Hamida Djandoubi seriously. At 10:15 A.M., a team of four police officers from the Marseille station arrived at the apartment on rue Villa Paradis. They took Houria along with them to ensure they could identify Hamida.

The door was wide open, just as Houria and Amaria had left it when they escaped an hour and a half earlier. The officers knocked. There was no answer. They went inside the apartment and waited.

The police stationed Houria at the window to keep watch for the Simca. At 11:40 A.M., the car arrived. Minutes later, the door to the apartment swung open. Annie entered first, followed by Hamida.

Two officers blocked his escape from behind and two others took hold of his arms. They told him they were there about a domestic violence complaint.

They patted Hamida down for weapons but found nothing. He was cuffed and made to sit on the bed. The police started searching the apartment. They found a pile of car accessories in one of the kitchen cupboards. Three car stereos, one dashboard clock, one side mirror, and one rearview mirror. "I stole them from parked cars," Hamida admitted.

In another drawer, the police found two starter pistols, along with a box of ammunition for a .22 rifle. Hamida said they were his. One of the starter pistols he'd bought from a man at the street market at Porte d'Aix for 150 francs. The man had told him the pistol had been specially rigged to fire real bullets. It didn't.

"*J'avais été roulé,*" Hamida said. I was rolled, I was had.

In a drawer, they found a folder with the identification papers of Amaria and Annie. There were also the two envelopes addressed to Houria's father and godfather. Hamida said he kept the papers as insurance. He was scared the girls would leave him.

It was Amaria who directed the officers to a closet beside the bed. Inside, the police found Hamida's torture kit: the wood club, the belt, the electrical cord.

The police made one final discovery of interest. Hamida's address book. It was light blue with a spiral metal binding. On the second page was the name Elisabeth Bousquet and the address of her family's apartment on rue Consolat.

Throughout the search, Hamida remained calm and cooperative. When told he was being taken to the police station for further questioning, he didn't protest.

*

* *

INSPECTOR GEORGES TURLESQUE of the Marseille police began interviewing Hamida Djandoubi at 4:00 P.M. The strategy had been decided upon in a phone conference with the Salon brigade: the Marseille police would interrogate him only about the accusations of rape and assault on the three teenage girls.

Hamida was more than willing to talk. He admitted to using the club and the belt to hit the girls, to burning them with his cigarettes, and to putting harissa in their vaginas. And he also admitted that the previous night he had used his electrical cord to give the girls shocks to their feet and thighs.

"They kept doing stupid things so I had to correct them," he said.

When questioned about raping Houria, Hamida was equally candid. Yes, he had forced himself on her the first time. But he insisted she was consenting the second time they had sex.

"Ever since I had my accident, I haven't been normal," he tried to explain to the police. "I have these breakdowns now and it's at those times that I don't know what I'm doing."

The police were amazed at how cooperative their suspect was. He freely admitted to everything save for one minor exception. He was vehement that he never prostituted Amaria or any other girl. He said he did bring Amaria to his old foyer to meet his brother and other friends on several occasions. And he did threaten her with prostitution. But he insisted he never forced her to turn a single trick.

Hamida signed his statement at 6:15 P.M.

The police let him sit in a cell. As soon as Constable Jean Thain and other officers from Salon-de-Provence arrived, they'd drop the body on him.

28

June 1971

ALBERT CAMUS HAD A HABIT of embroiling himself in the major issues of mid-twentieth-century France. During the German occupation, he was active in the Resistance cell "Combat" and edited the group's eponymous magazine. When the affairs in Algeria turned ugly, he was one of the lone voices seeking a third path—neither full occupation nor withdrawal, but a coexistence between the French and the Arabs. And then there was his stand against the death penalty.

It began with his most renowned book, *The Stranger*. Published in 1942, it tells the story of Meursault, who shoots a man dead one scalding afternoon at the beach. Assigned a barely competent lawyer and unable to summon even a façade of remorse, Meursault dies beneath the guillotine. The senselessness of both killings was an allegory for the senselessness of the death penalty. But Camus soon realized, as François Guizot put it more than a century earlier, that "truth slips slowly into the spirit of power" and adopted a less subtle approach.

Camus was inspired by Arthur Koestler, the author of *Darkness at Noon* and the founder of the League Against Capital Punishment. Like Sade and Dostoyevsky, Koestler had personal reasons for his militant rejection of the death penalty: he himself had been condemned to death during the Spanish Civil War.

His seminal work on the subject, the 1955 book *Reflections on Hanging*, would be cited in parliament when England abolished the death penalty for murder in 1965 (the death penalty would remain on the books for such esoteric crimes as piracy with violence for several more decades, but the last exection in English history was held in 1964). Koestler's arguments against the death penalty were buttressed by a series of absurd hangings, notably that of young Derek Bentley in 1953. After being caught trying to break into a warehouse, Bentley, nineteen, was arrested and put in the back of a police van. Several minutes later his accomplice, sixteen-year-old Christopher Craig, shot a policeman dead. Even though Bentley was in handcuffs at the time of the shooting, both teenagers were convicted of murder; yet only Bentley was hanged, because Craig was a minor.

In 1957, two years after Koestler's book appeared, Camus published his own essay *Réflexions sur la guillotine*. He essentially argued that human systems—and humans themselves—are too unreliable to be given official power of life and death. "If murder is in the nature of man, the law is not intended to imitate or reproduce that nature," wrote Camus. "It is intended to correct it."

Distressed by society's eagerness to eliminate the rejects and psychopaths that society itself had created, Camus compared capital punishment to a father sending his son to death because he could no longer control him. He concluded that the death penalty should be replaced by hard labor. Camus was awarded the Nobel Prize Literature in 1957. Three years later, he died in a car accident along with his friend and editor, Michel Gallimard.

It was a fitting end. Camus often noted that society clung to the death penalty out of fear of murder and violent crime. The truth was, as Camus wrote in *Réflexions sur la guillotine,* for every one person murdered, twenty died in car accidents.

*

* *

IN MARSEILLE, POLITICIANS didn't quite have the time for such existentialist questions as whether society has the right to kill. Their hands were full with a more pressing concern: the heroin epidemic that was ravaging Marseille and turning the city into an international pariah.

It's true that Marseille suffers from a bad reputation. One popular book about the city evokes the phenomenon in its title: *Marseille, ou la mauvaise réputation.* Alfred W. McCoy's *Politics of Heroin in Southeast Asia* is even more damning; its chapter about the city is titled "Marseille: America's Heroin Laboratory." What's worst of all is that this reputation was richly deserved.

As made notorious by *The French Connection,* both the book (1969) and the film (1971), Marseille was the crucial link between the opium fields of Turkey and the street addicts in America. Until the 1970s, the Turkish government authorized select farmers to grow opium for pharmaceutical companies. The black market being as lucrative as it is, there was an inevitable surplus, and this raw opium paste was smuggled by boat to the port of Marseille, processed in labs scattered across the city, and then shipped to North America.

The heroin trade, like most illegal enterprises in Marseille, was run by the Corsican Mafia. But the business grew exponentially because of the legendary New York mobster Lucky Luciano. In 1936 Luciano was sentenced to thirty to fifty years in prison, but during World War II he cut a deal with naval intelligence: Luciano agreed to use his network of dockworkers to watch for Nazi infiltrators and convinced his Mafia contacts in Sicily to help Allied troops land in Italy. As Mussolini had been vigorously prosecuting organized crime, the Sicilians were more than happy to comply.

In return for this help, Luciano was released from prison on the condition he leave America. He ended up living in Italy, and during the infamous Havana Conference of 1946 that brought together organized-crime leaders from around the world, he made connections with the Marseille crime families and their heroin resources. The combination of Marseille's heroin production and Luciano's New York distribution contacts was the bonanza that created the French Connection.

The first Marseille heroin was confiscated in America in 1947 when a Corsican sailor arrived in New York City with seven pounds in his suitcase. By the 1960s, there were more than two dozen heroin labs in Marseille, and they exported on average 5,000 pounds of pure heroin to America each year. In 1965 alone, 4.8 tons—more than 10,000 pounds—were shipped. By 1969 the U.S. Bureau of Narcotics estimated that the labs in Marseille were providing between 80 and 90 percent of the heroin that hit American streets.

And aside from an Academy Award–winning film, there were other, more scandalous offshoots of the Marseille–New York heroin connection. Strong among them is the fringe theory that it was hit men from Marseille who assassinated President John F. Kennedy.

The story comes from Christian David, a member of the Marseille crime milieu in the 1960s. David told the journalist Stephen Rivele that, in the early 1960s, the crime boss and Lucky Luciano associate Antoine Guérini offered him a contract to assassinate an American politician, the "highest vegetable." According to David, he turned down the contract, but another Marseille hit man, Lucien Sarti, agreed to do the job with two associates. The story goes that the men were flown to Mexico and then drove up into Texas. Sarti was allegedly the gunman stationed on the grassy knoll.

David claims to have full proof but wants to be released from prison first. Sarti was killed by Mexican police in 1972. Antoine Guérini was shot eleven times while at a Marseille gas station in 1967. The fact that there is nobody else to confirm or deny the story only encourages its continued circulation among Marseille crime aficionados.

The bad publicity for Marseille reached its crescendo when *Time* magazine ran a cover story titled "The Global War on Heroin" that prominently featured the city. Already renowned inside France for its corruption and drug wars, Marseille now had international notoriety. It's understandable that the mayor of the besmirched city wanted to do something. But maybe he overreacted a little when, in June 1971, he lobbied the National Assembly to make drug trafficking a capital offense.

*

*   *

GASTON DEFFERRE WASN'T your typical mayor. He ruled Marseille for thirty-three consecutive years between 1953 and 1986, and the city became something of a private fiefdom. He owned three major daily newspapers, he controlled local politics, he inserted his friends and cronies into important civic positions. Even more impressively, as the French political system allows politicians to hold multiple offices, he was also a member of the National Assembly and served as everything from the head of the Socialist bloc in parliament to the minister of the interior under President François Mitterrand. He was by far the most powerful man in Marseille for almost four decades.

Fittingly for a city that loves its stories, there is no end to romantic lore surrounding Mayor Defferre. There is a mythic tale of how Defferre, an active member of the Resistance during World War II, was one of the team of commandos who freed a prominent Resistance fighter from a Nazi jail by disguising themselves as prison guards. He was also something of a political throwback and literally crossed swords with a political adversary. In 1959 Defferre had called René Ribière an *abruti* (boor) in the National Assembly. Defferre refused to apologize, so Ribière challenged him to a duel. At dawn in a garden in the Paris suburb of Neuilly, the two men fought with sabers for forty-five minutes. Ribière was pierced twice, Defferre was declared the winner, and it is considered the last official duel in French history.

This combination of gusto and belligerence that led Defferre to duel might also have fueled his response to the heroin crisis. In 1971 Defferre presented a proposal at the National Assembly for a new law to deal with the mushrooming drug problem.

"Drug traffickers who act in contempt of all human respect must be chastised," Defferre's bill read. "It does not suffice to condemn them to prison terms because too often they are the subject of reduced sentences and are given their freedom after a few short years and they recover the profits that they so carefully hid away and resume their sad activities. . . . It is necessary for all those who work in the drug business to be punished by the maximum penalty allowed by the penal code."

And, of course, in 1971 the maximum penalty allowed by law was the guillotine.

It would have marked a startling reversal of more than three hundred years of legal evolution. Since the days of Louis XIV, the number of capital crimes had steadily decreased in France. Now, while the vast majority of European countries had already abolished the death penalty, the mayor of Marseille was seeking to expand the guillotine's scope. It was a throwback to those pre-Revolutionary days when crimes such as smuggling tobacco and, yes, dueling were punishable by death.

Rival politicians in Marseille couldn't help but see a hint of cynical opportunism in the entire affair. For it was the Guérini brothers who had built up the heroin trade in Marseille and it was Defferre who helped build up the Guérini brothers.

After World War II, Marseille was a Communist stronghold, and the port was the strongest of their holds. The Communists rallied against the postwar American influence and refused to unload goods coming from the United States, so the CIA and Defferre's political party financed a band of rogues to break the Communist strikes and open up the Marseille docks. The Guérini brothers, Antoine and Barthélemy, rose to prominence through this scheme, and Defferre would rely on them repeatedly throughout his long political career. Members of the Guérini family edited one of Defferre's newspapers, worked as bodyguards for the Socialist Party, and performed innumerable other tasks.

Indeed, the general feeling was that this proposal was just Defferre, as the French say, *mettant de la poudre aux yeux* (throwing powder in the eyes) of the people to distract them from the fact that he was doing nothing to address the city's heroin problem.

Undeterred by such criticism, Defferre presented his death penalty bill to the National Assembly on June 9, 1971. It was soundly defeated.

29

IN 1974 FRENCH CRIMINAL procedure didn't provide a suspect with the right to a lawyer until after he or she had been officially charged. At the same time, a suspect was under no actual obligation to answer police questions before that moment. This made for a murky interrogation process, one that almost always favored the authorities.

As required, the police warned Hamida Djandoubi that this was a serious criminal investigation and he wasn't required to talk. "I understand you are explaining to me the legal reasons why I don't have to continue," Hamida stated, according to the rigid language of the official police report. "I think it is in my interest to tell you what happened so you can understand the reasons I could have done these things."

And so Hamida Djandoubi confessed. Along with the statements from Annie and Amaria, the mystery of the body in the cabin had been resolved. It was, of course, Elisabeth Bousquet's.*

Hamida said he had lost contact with Elisabeth after the prostitution complaint in May 1973. But, starting in June 1974, he began to hear rumors. There was a story going around that she had slept with one of his friends at the Sonacotra. Another story had Elisabeth working as a prostitute for a Corsican pimp by the name of Jean who lived in the town of La Roque d'Anthéron.

This made Hamida angry. Elisabeth knew she didn't have the right to sleep with his friends. And if she was now working the streets for somebody else, why had she filed the complaint against him in May

---

*The night of the murder is re-created from the police statements of the three participants. As I delved into the Bible and Christian philosophy for this book, while reading those three versions of the murder, each with its discrepancies but all essentially the same, I couldn't help but think of the Gospels, the same story told over and over again in slightly different manners.

1973? He told the police he wanted to find Elisabeth. He wanted to "correct" her.

He asked his friends and his brother, Ali, to let him know if they ever saw Elisabeth. On July 3, 1974, Ali arrived at the apartment on rue Villa Paradis. Elisabeth was at the Sonacotra and was asking after Hamida. She wanted to see him. She wanted to know if he would be her boyfriend again. Ali made her wait in his room while he went to get Hamida.

Hamida drove his white Simca to the Sonacotra. Back in Ali's room, Hamida gave Elisabeth a kiss on each cheek and convinced her to come back to his apartment. Ali saw them to the door. On the drive to the apartment, Elisabeth apologized for making the complaint to the police. She also asked if she could come live with him. He didn't answer.

Back at the apartment, Hamida introduced Elisabeth to Annie and Amaria. She stopped him.

"My name is Betty now," she said.

Hamida gave her a glass of Martini Blanco. Elisabeth said she was feeling drunk. Hamida brought up the prostitution complaint again. She apologized again. He slapped her anyway.

"I was overcome with anger," Hamida stated. "It must have been a nervous breakdown."

He then called Annie and Amaria from the kitchen and told them to prepare the living room. The girls rolled up the carpet, moved the lamp to the corner, and put the armchair on the bed so it would be out of the way. This gave Hamida the space he needed.

He knew his neighbor Marie-Claude and her son, Stefan, were away on vacation. In the apartment directly below, there was only an elderly Spanish woman with a hearing problem. Hamida closed the shutters on the windows. Now he had his privacy.

Annie and Amaria were made to sit on the bed. Hamida wanted them to watch.

Hamida ordered Elisabeth to undress. She hesitated. She didn't want to take off her clothes in front of the other girls. Hamida took out his wooden club. Sobbing quietly, Elisabeth took off her jeans, her light blue tank top with the anchor pattern, and her purple underwear. Once she was naked, Hamida made her lie on the floor.

It started with the belt. He hit her on the back and on the thighs. Then he started beating her with the club. Whenever Elisabeth sobbed or screamed, Hamida hit her harder.

He made her lift up her legs so he could push the club into her vagina. He made her roll onto her stomach and forced it into her anus. He made Elisabeth lick the excrement from the club.

Elisabeth started to beg for her life. She told him she would work as a prostitute for him. She said she would do anything.

"It makes me happy to see you like this," Hamida told her.

He made a false show of compassion. He took out a syringe and told her it was a painkiller. In fact, it was only tap water. He injected her in the left arm.

Elisabeth complained she was thirsty. Hamida urinated in a glass and made her drink it. She vomited it back up.

Annie and Amaria watched from the bed without a word. When Hamida went to the kitchen to fix himself a Martini and soda, Elisabeth pleaded with them. She asked them to scream from the window. She begged them to run for help. The girls said they were too scared. They did nothing.

Hamida returned and began to hit her with his wooden club again, demanding to know whom she had been sleeping with. Blood spurted from her forehead, spraying one of the walls with crimson droplets. Elisabeth could no longer form sentences. Hamida thought she was pretending, so he burned her breasts, back, and face with his cigarette. He liked the idea of fire, so he took a candle, lit it, and forced it into her vagina and anus. Then he told Annie to run out to the Simca and get the jerry can of gas.

Annie went down to the street and walked about fifty feet to where the car was parked. She retrieved the jerry can from the trunk and returned to the apartment. She didn't see anybody on the street.

Hamida took the gasoline and poured it across Elisabeth's stomach, thighs, and pubic region. Taking a box of wooden matches from the kitchen, he lit her on fire.

Now Elisabeth really started screaming. Hamida panicked. He tried to put out the fire with his hands, but it was too painful. He decided to put it out with his foot but didn't want to ruin his pants, so he rolled them up to the knee on his good leg and tried to stomp out the fire. The flames singed his leg hair, so he asked Annie to get a bucket of water from the kitchen. Finally, he doused the blaze.

Elisabeth was unconscious now, breathing unevenly and bleeding heavily. It was almost five o'clock in the afternoon. The torture had been going on for more than two hours. But Hamida wasn't finished. He went into the kitchen and got the harissa paste. He forced fingerful after fingerful into her vagina.

Elisabeth was a wreck of vomit, blood, and burned skin. Hamida began to think that maybe he'd gone too far.

And that's when he decided he was going to have to kill Elisabeth.

After Annie served him another glass of Martini, the girls began to scrub the bloodstains off the wall. With Elisabeth lying naked and bleeding on the floor, Hamida prepared dinner. At 9:30 P.M., once it began to get dark, Hamida shook Elisabeth awake and ordered Annie and Amaria to wash her with a sponge. He didn't want blood on his car seats. Then he told Elisabeth to get dressed. She was in so much pain, the girls had to help her into her clothes. Before leaving the apartment, Hamida took a length of rope, a kitchen knife, and a red scarf with fringes. The scarf had been a sixteenth-birthday present to Annie from her mother.

Elisabeth couldn't walk, so she slid down the stairs one step at a time. She was mumbling and incoherent. She said something about wanting to see her husband, Jean, in La Roque d'Anthéron.

Making sure rue Villa Paradis was empty of people, Hamida pulled the Simca to the door of the building. He pushed Elisabeth into the backseat and covered her with a green striped blanket. As the car started, Elisabeth asked where they were going. To the hospital, Hamida answered, then to see her husband.

Instead, he headed north out of the city and onto highway Nationale 113. A few months earlier, Hamida had taken Annie walking in the hills near Salon-de-Provence. He remembered there had been a deserted cabin in the middle of a field of olive trees. He thought it would be a good place to finish things.

After passing through Vitrolles, he followed the highway up the Col du Télégraphe. Halfway up, he pulled a U-turn and veered onto an old farmer's road. He stopped about sixty feet from the stone cabin.

Leaving the three women in the Simca, he took a flashlight and made sure the cabin was empty, then he ordered everyone to follow him. Elisabeth was so weak she had to crawl. Frustrated by her slow pace, Hamida looped a belt around her leg and tried to drag her. The two girls each took an arm and helped pull her along.

Inside the cabin, Hamida told Elisabeth to lie on her back. He passed the flashlight to one of the girls to hold. He gave Elisabeth a kiss on the lips. And then he strangled her with Annie's red scarf.

Hamida wanted to make sure Elisabeth was dead. She didn't move as he unwound the scarf from her neck, but nonetheless he gave her a quick kick in the face to be safe. It fractured her nose.

Driving back to Marseille, Hamida threw Elisabeth's purple high-heeled shoes and the red scarf out the window. They stopped to buy twenty francs of gas. And then they went home to the apartment.

Annie and Amaria finished cleaning the blood from the floor and the walls. They also washed the green blanket that had covered Elisabeth. In the end, the only traces of the torture were a few faded bloodstains on one wall. They slept fitfully that night. The next morning, everyone was still anxious. Hamida decided a holiday would relieve the tension, so he drove the girls to the nearby beach town of Saintes-Maries-de-la-Mer, just south of Arles.

Saintes-Maries-de-la-Mer was a strange mix of sun worshipers and religious pilgrims. According to Provençal lore, it was here that Lazarus, his sisters Mary Magdalene and Martha, and two other followers of Jesus, Mary Jacobe and Mary Salome, landed after being expelled from Israel.

When Hamida, Annie, and Amaria arrived that July, the beach cafés were full and the tourist shops were doing heady business with their religious souvenirs. They found a camping spot beside the nudist beach. Hamida liked to watch.

Throughout the vacation, Hamida never let Annie or Amaria out of his sight. The girls played in the shallow water near the shore. Neither had learned how to swim. Hamida didn't take off his pants. He was embarrassed by his prosthesis.

For the week following the murder, Hamida read *Le Provençal* and *La Marseillaise* every day. After the articles about the mysterious discovery of the body stopped appearing, he stopped buying the paper. In mid-July, they returned to the apartment on rue Villa Paradis. Life went on as it always had until the afternoon they found Houria sitting alone on the bench.

"I'm convinced I'm not normal, that's the only way I can explain this," Hamida told police after signing his confession. "Before my accident, I never touched a woman. Since then, I have felt alone and just wanted to be loved."

When the interview was concluded, there was really only one question left: would Hamida Djandoubi get the death penalty?

30

WOULD HAMIDA DJANDOUBI get the death penalty? The fact that the question was even being asked was merely a caprice of French politics.

When Charles de Gaulle resigned, in April 1969, and Georges Pompidou won the ensuing presidential election, beating Marseille mayor Gaston Defferre among others, it was supposed to usher in an era of change. Pompidou, an admirer of Hugo and Voltaire, was thought to be especially sensitive regarding the death penalty. "By temperament, I am not a bloodthirsty man," he told *Paris-Presse* while discussing the guillotine in September 1969.

This pronouncement was taken by almost everyone as a harbinger of abolition. Indeed, upon arriving at the Élysée Palace, Pompidou quickly spared two men who had killed a police officer and commuted their death sentences to life imprisonment. By October 1969, polls showed that only 33 percent of the French supported the death penalty. It was something of an embarrassing situation. France, the birthplace of the Enlightenment and of human rights, clung to the bloody heirloom that was the guillotine.

Now it seemed France would finally catch up to the rest of Europe. After the end of World War II, it had been a delicate balancing act for European governments. On one hand, they needed to forcefully redress the war crimes and so accepted the death penalty as just punishment for those found guilty at the Nuremberg Trials. Yet these same war atrocities were the motivation for governments to place a new emphasis on the sacredness of life, and the very concept of a person's "right to life" was inserted into the United Nations' *Universal Declaration of Human Rights.* By the early 1970s, the war was considered history and the European pendulum had swung almost entirely toward judicial and governmental respect for life. It was especially galling for many French that even their ancient rivals, the bloody English, had succeeded in abolishing the death penalty before they had.

Now, with Georges Pompidou ensconced in the Élysée Palace, abolition was practically a fait accompli. A special portfolio, titled "The Last Days of the Death Penalty," appeared in *Le Figaro Littéraire*, and the abolitionist lawyer Albert Naud went so far as to dedicate his book, *L'Agonie de la peine de mort*, to the president. He wrote, "To Georges Pompidou, For what he is and what he has done."

Then, in September 1971, a month before Hamida Djandoubi would lose his leg in the tractor accident, there was a hostage taking at the Clairvaux prison in the north of France. A guard and a nurse had their throats slit. And when it came to abolition, all bets were abruptly shoved off the table.

*

* *

BETWEEN THE OVERCROWDING, the crumbling facilities, and the low wages for penitentiary personnel, the 1970s were dire times in the French prisons. There were twenty-five prison revolts in 1971 and 1972 alone. Clairvaux, two hundred miles east of Paris, was especially notorious. Located on the grounds of a twelfth-century Cistercian abbey, this maximum-security prison was in such a state of decay and disarray that, seven months before the disaster, a judge from the nearby city of Troyes warned the minister of justice: "There will be, if we aren't careful or don't find a remedy soon, horrendous crimes at Clairvaux and without a doubt a hostage taking."

Sure enough, on September 22, 1971, two inmates, Claude Buffet and Roger Bontems, managed to barricade themselves inside the prison's infirmary and take a nurse and a guard hostage. Buffet was serving a life sentence for murder; Bontems was serving twenty years for robbery.

The men were armed. Buffet had a knife with an eight-inch blade that he bought from a fellow inmate for twenty packs of cigarettes while Bontems had an Opinel folding knife with a four-inch blade that was available in the prison canteen so prisoners could cut their cheese and bread. The standoff didn't last long: prison guards equipped with a fire hose stormed the infirmary. In the chaos, both hostages had their throats slit. Buffet and Bontems were charged with murder.

The public reaction was swift and angry. Newspapers assailed the lawlessness of prisons and the coddling of prisoners. A poll conducted in the days after the hostage taking revealed that the number of French in favor of the death penalty had leapt from 33 percent to 53 percent. And when Buffet and Bontems were brought to trial, a crowd of hundreds gathered outside the courthouse shouting, *"À mort! À mort!"* To death, to death.

Truth be told, if ever a case demonstrated the potential benefits of the death penalty, Claude Buffet's was it. His original crime had been atrocious. A deserter from the Foreign Legion, he stole a taxi in Paris in 1967 and then cruised the city looking for rich victims. He fell upon the beautiful Françoise Bésimensky, a fashion model and the wife of a prominent Parisian doctor. Buffet drove her down a deserted street near the Bois de Boulogne and tried to rob her at gunpoint. When Bésimensky resisted, he shot her dead. To cover his tracks, he attempted to make it look like a sex crime by stripping her corpse naked and thrusting a makeup compact into her vagina.

At that original trial, Buffet made it clear he wanted to die. He wanted to be guillotined à la Robespierre, faceup so he could see the blade rushing down toward him. In October 1970, when he was given "only" a life sentence for the murder, he was so enraged he promised to kill in prison. One year later, he masterminded the hostage taking and murdered the nurse and guard.

It was the ultimate argument for the liberal use of capital punishment: if Buffet had been guillotined for his original crime, the guard and the nurse, two innocent people, would still have been alive.

In the case of Bontems, the scenario was a little different. He had been serving time for robbery, he'd never been involved in any bloodshed, and Buffet had goaded him into joining the hostage taking. Bontems had never killed and never showed any signs of violence. He wanted to live, and not even *lex talionis*—the law of blood for blood—demanded his death.

When the hostage-taking case went to trial, Bontems's defense team included a civil lawyer from Paris named Robert Badinter. A suave and scholarly lawyer, Badinter rarely handled criminal cases but agreed to join in Bontems's defense because he was so alarmed by the bloodlust that was gripping the country. Days before the trial, the lawyer assured Bontems he would be spared. And Badinter took it as an omen that, on the same day the jury went out on the Bontems and Buffet case, June 29, 1972, the Supreme Court in America returned the verdict in the *Furman v. Georgia* case that declared the death penalty unconstitutional in the United States.

The decision involved William Henry Furman, a murderer whom psychiatrists deemed too mentally limited to understand his lawyers. The Supreme Court ruled his sentence was an example of erratic and biased use of the death penalty and declared this to be cruel and unusual punishment, in violation of the Constitution. "People live or die, dependant on the whim of one man or of twelve," wrote Justice William O. Douglas.

Badinter was elated by the news, calling it "a sign of destiny, an indication that the death penalty was but a relic from an era that was coming to an end elsewhere and might well come to an end in France as well." Yet his optimism was only partially justified. As he predicted, the jury acquitted Bontems of murder. But, amazingly, he was sentenced to die alongside Buffet for his participation in the hostage taking. When the verdict was read, shouts of "Bravo! Bravo!" rang out in the courtroom.

Buffet, in his morbid delirium, dreamed of becoming the last person guillotined in French history. "I only ask you this, Mr. President, that once the guillotine's blade chops off my head, that it permits the permanent abolition of the death penalty in France," he wrote in a letter to Pompidou. "You owe it to France."

For his part, Bontems wanted to live, and his family urged Robert Badinter to do all he could to fight for his life. At the Élysée Palace, Badinter pleaded with the president to commute his client's sentence. Once again, Badinter tried to assure Bontems: the president was on the record as being opposed to the death penalty; not a single person had been guillotined in the three years since Pompidou had been elected; and in the past twenty years only one person had been executed who hadn't actually killed somebody, Jean Bastien-Thiry, de Gaulle's attempted assassin.

"They've recognized you didn't kill anybody," Badinter told Bontems. "You will receive clemency. It is sure."

The lawyer didn't take one thing into account: the fickle nature of politics. According to the book *Tragédie à Clairvaux*, the national director of prisons warned President Pompidou that if Buffet and Bontems weren't put to death there would be a nationwide strike by prison personnel. And, for a president who was conscious of public opinion, he had to take into account a new poll released in November 1972 that showed 63 percent of the French now favored the death penalty.

Thus, the decision was made. Pompidou refused clemency for either man. On the morning of November 28, 1972, Buffet and Bontems lost their heads in the courtyard of La Santé prison in Paris. The next day, the president told journalists, "I am opposed to the suppression of the death penalty as, sadly, you have seen."

Any chances of abolition under President Georges Pompidou had been dashed. The next year, he didn't hesitate to send Ali Benyanès, the farm killer from Nice, to the guillotine.

There was a brief window of hope for abolitionists in April 1974 when François Mitterrand, an avowed opponent of the death penalty,

presented himself for the presidency in the emergency elections following Pompidou's death. Instead, Valéry Giscard d'Estaing won the
election, and he was proving to be in no great hurry to take action on
such a politically unpopular issue as abolition.

But there was a single beacon of light. One of the witnesses at the
dawn executions of Buffet and Bontems was Robert Badinter. Already
besieged by guilt at having failed his client, Badinter was utterly sick-
ened when he saw the bloody mechanics of official death. He had always been opposed to the death penalty on an intellectual level; he was
now infused with a visceral hatred for the guillotine.

"I now knew what the reality of the death penalty was," Badinter
wrote. "From that point on, I was an irreducible adversary of the death
penalty. I had passed from having an intellectual conviction to a militant passion."

Just as Martin Luther King Jr. came to embody the American civil
rights movement and Gloria Steinem took on the face of feminism, the
French abolitionist movement now had its leader. From the moment
of those twin executions, Badinter dedicated his career to the cause
and embarked on campaigns in the courts and in the media to overturn death sentences and to abolish the death penalty in France. As
Hamida Djandoubi sat in his cell at the Marseille police station, little
could he imagine that his fate might rest in the hands of a Parisian
lawyer whose name he'd never even heard mentioned.

31

August 1974

WITH TWO WITNESSES TO the murder and Hamida Djandoubi's signed confession, the police investigation was pretty much a lock. All that was left was to bring the key players—Annie, Amaria, Houria, and Hamida—before the *juge d'instruction* in Aix-en-Provence. If everyone just repeated what had been said at the Marseille police station, the charges would officially be laid and the conviction assured.

When the body was discovered, the *juge d'instruction* assigned to the case was Jean-Claude Girousse. This was a happenstance of vacation schedules. The Tribunal de Grande Instance d'Aix-en-Provence had two sitting judges who oversaw criminal investigations: Girousse and his junior, Françoise Llaurens. In the summer of 1974, Judge Llaurens took her vacation in July, meaning the body case automatically fell to Judge Girousse. But in August, it was Judge Girousse who was on vacation, so when Hamida was arrested, the file was permanently transferred to Judge Llaurens.

In the summer of 1974, Judge Llaurens was twenty-seven, only a few years older than Hamida. She was from Perpignan, near the Spanish border, and had gone to the École Supérieure in Bordeaux, the university where French judges and prosecutors were trained. (This school was a perpetual sore spot for defense lawyers, who believed the shared educational background created a subtle complicity between the two groups.) The Aix job was Llaurens's first, and she'd been in the office less than a year when Hamida came before her.

Judge Llaurens faced a delicate task: ensuring the initial confession wasn't coerced. Marseille police had a reputation for brutality and at the time of the Djandoubi case were under investigation for extracting confessions using torture. There were two high-profile incidents: in one, police were accused of sodomizing two suspects with a nightstick;

183

in the other, an accused thief was stripped naked, had a hood put over his head, was forced onto a wet table, and then given electric shocks. In the latter case, the physical evidence had been corroborated by François Vuillet, the same singing doctor who'd conducted the autopsy on Elisabeth Bousquet.

There were also retracted confessions. The most pertinent at the time involved Christian Ranucci, the young man charged with abducting and killing Marie-Dolorès Rambla. After nineteen straight hours of denials, Ranucci confessed three times: to the police, to the *juge d'instruction,* and to a court-appointed psychiatrist. Within days, Ranucci claimed he didn't remember committing any crime and said he'd only confessed because of police bullying. And the truth was, the police had misled him during questioning by insisting there were six witnesses who could prove he was the killer when in fact there wasn't a single one. By the time Hamida Djandoubi was in custody in August 1974, the furor raised by the Ranucci case had only just begun and suddenly every confession was suspect.

But Hamida didn't claim to have been tortured or bullied. Nor did he hesitate when asked to repeat the grisly details of the murder. Judge Llaurens was amazed by his attention to details. He recounted the events in a cold, technical manner, as if reciting a recipe.

"He never looked inside himself, never asked what he had done or expressed remorse," Judge Llaurens remembered. "This indifference astounded me. He spoke of the crime as if it was somebody else who had lived it. It made me think of Camus and *The Stranger.*"

Oddly, the only time Hamida showed any emotion was when confronted with the allegations that he'd prostituted Amaria. He vehemently denied this, said it was insulting that such charges could even be considered. Judge Llaurens was perplexed. How could a man so willingly admit to setting a woman aflame and raping her with a wooden club, yet become so indignant at being accused of pimping?

In the end, the judge decided to conduct further interviews before ruling on the prostitution issue. That day, initial charges were laid against Hamida Djandoubi for voluntary homicide, use of torture, and the commission of barbarous acts. A separate file was also opened for theft in connection with the stolen auto parts.

*
*   *

ONE PERSON RELIEVED by Hamida Djandoubi's arrest was Pierre Manias, as it dispersed any remaining suspicion against him. Alas, it would prove to be but a temporary reprieve from the clutches of justice.

In August 1977, three years after being questioned for the murder of Elisabeth Bousquet, Manias was charged with attempting to kill another woman. This time, he confessed.

Police had long suspected that Manias had prostitutes working out of the Auberge du Vieux Moulin. A decent clue was that one of Manias's part-time lovers, Josée di Francia, was known to turn tricks in Marseille, selling sex at fifty francs a throw on the narrow streets behind La Canebière. At the Vieux Moulin, people remembered the night Josée got drunk and did a slow striptease for a crowd of drunken truck drivers. When one among them tried to fondle her at the end, she screamed, "The show's over, you bastards!"

Manias decided Josée was out of control and had become a liability. He brought her up to one of the bedrooms, put a gun to her temple, and fired. The force of the bullet left Josée's eyes leaking from their sockets.

The case fell to the same Captain Chauley who oversaw the early stages of the Hamida Djandoubi investigation. Chauley went to visit Josée in the hospital. Miraculously, she was still alive, though blinded by the gunshot wound. She groped for his hand. She said she could feel he was a good person. And then she told him that Manias had shot her.

Nonetheless, Manias insisted Josée had merely attempted suicide, and he held this line until Chauley discovered that Manias's mother had washed the bloody sheets and blankets after the shooting. This act made her an accessory to attempted murder, so Chauley put the mother in jail and said he'd keep her there until the case got resolved. Manias, the good son, quickly confessed and spent the better part of the next decade in prison.

In the late 1980s, a few years after being released from prison, Manias was shot to death. As those in the Marseille Milieu say, it was a *règlement des comptes*. A settling of accounts.

*

*   *

THE WEEK BEFORE his arrest, Hamida made two peculiar visits. The first was to Louis and Colette Bugia. They hadn't seen their old friend "Joe" for more than a year. He appeared unannounced at their apartment one afternoon, looking haggard and tense. After some awkward small talk over glasses of pastis, Hamida told them he'd had a fight with his ex-girlfriend and it had gotten violent. He didn't say anything else and the Bugias didn't ask.

"It was as if he wanted to let something out," Colette remembers. "I think he came because he needed to confide in us, but he never said what really happened."

A few days later, Hamida telephoned Lucie Le Manchec at Jean Goudareau's office. There were still eighty francs in outstanding lawyer's fees in connection with the pension settlement. He said he wanted to pay his debt. Le Manchec told him there was no hurry; the payment wasn't due for another month. But Hamida came by the office a few hours later with the money.

"He said something about wanting to have his accounts in order because he might be going away," Le Manchec said.

That weekend, Le Manchec unfolded the morning newspaper. There, on the front page, was Hamida's picture with the bold headline pronouncing him to be the long-sought killer. The article described Hamida as a "torturer and murderer with an uncommon cruelty."

"My first thought was I couldn't believe he could do something like that," Le Manchec said. "My second thought was he was going to call Maître Goudareau."

Sure enough, as soon as she was back at the office, the phone rang. Hamida had designated Jean Goudareau as his defense lawyer.

*

* *

AS WOULD BE EXPECTED in a city with such a fascination with crime, Marseille boasted a coterie of criminal lawyers who enjoyed the status of minor celebrities. The group included Paul Lombard, Jean-Louis Pelletier, and Émile Pollak, and the majority of the big murders and major drug cases fell into their hands.

Jean Goudareau wasn't one of the chosen few. In fact, he wasn't even a criminal lawyer. He specialized in commercial and property law, and over his thirty-year career he could remember handling only a dozen or so criminal cases. And not only was Goudareau not a criminal lawyer, but law was really only a part-time occupation. He served as a city councillor from 1953 to 1977, and at the time of the Djandoubi affair, he was preoccupied with the fight to save Greek ruins that had been unearthed during the construction of a shopping mall in downtown Marseille. The ruins were twenty-six centuries old, from the very first Greek settlement in 600 B.C., but Mayor Gaston Defferre thought it ridiculous to halt progress on the shopping mall because of "four old rocks." He wanted to remove the Greek ruins and rebuild them someplace more convenient. Goudareau led the opposition and enlisted the minister of culture, André Malraux, in the fight for an open-air archaeological museum.

"We are acting with the most noble of intentions," Goudareau wrote in his campaign material, "out of the filial love we carry for our city and the pride we take from its prestigious origins."

Between his lack of criminal law experience and his political commitments, Goudareau worried he shouldn't accept the case. He was also convinced his fellow lawyers would share his concerns. "At the courthouse, of 250 lawyers, there would be 249 who would say this wasn't a client for Goudareau," he said years later.

Yet Goudareau still agreed to represent Hamida. And, shunning the French tradition of taking on a second lawyer for murder cases to fortify the defense, he chose to handle the case alone.

"Because I knew the man, because I could speak for him since I had kept up relations with him after his accident," Goudareau explained, "I could judge him with sympathy, and he was a boy who merited a lot of sympathy."

Curiously enough for a man who didn't specialize in criminal law, this wasn't Goudareau's first case involving the death penalty. After World War II, the chief of the Gestapo's special services in Marseille, Ernst Dunkel, was prosecuted for war crimes by a military tribunal. Another lawyer initially represented Dunkel, but after a falling-out midway through the trial, the German demanded another lawyer and the case went to Goudareau. The verdict was death and Dunkel was sent to the firing squad. Goudareau stood as a witness, watching as Dunkel was blindfolded and tied to the pole. He was surprised at how close the marksmen stood, only ten feet away. The scene reminded Goudareau of the Goya painting *Tres de Mayo*.

"The bullets made his body jump, and then he slid down the pole to the ground," Goudareau said. "The officer then went to the body and fired the mandatory coup de grâce into his head. . . . It's something you don't forget, you can't forget."

One capital case, one execution. Not a good sign for Hamida Djandoubi.

32

THE IDENTIFICATION OF the body as Elisabeth Bousquet allowed the police to broach another question that had hovered over the investigation: why hadn't anybody reported the dead girl missing?

Constable Pierre Vidou was charged with finding the next of kin and getting the answer. He contacted her brother Jean-Pierre Bousquet first, on August 11, two days after Hamida Djandoubi's arrest. Bousquet was working for the Marseille office of Gaz de France and living with his wife in the south end of the city, near the replica Egyptian obelisk.

Jean-Pierre simply hadn't realized his sister was missing. Elisabeth had been difficult to keep track of during the past year. She'd been hospitalized twice, she'd been in and out of women's shelters, she'd taken up with a man in La Roque d'Anthéron. Now the news of the death was a numbing blow. There had been such tremendous suffering for the Bousquet family. The motorcyle accident, the marital discord, Elisabeth's suicide attempt. As Jean-Pierre accompanied the police to identify the body, he could only wonder why life had to be so cruel.

Later in the week, Constable Vidou conducted the official interviews with Elisabeth's father, sister, and mother.

Pierre Bousquet told police he'd grown apart from his daughter because of his own problems with his health and the separation from his wife. He'd spent much of the last two years in the countryside. "From time to time, I came back to Marseille," he said. "I saw Elisabeth but I couldn't really take care of her because of the big problems I was having with my divorce."

Marie-Josée had also seen her sister sporadically over the last year.

The last time had been Saturday, June 29. "She told us she was married to a legionnaire," Marie-Josée told the police. "I didn't believe it."

Marie-Josée wasn't surprised to hear that Hamida Djandoubi was charged with Elisabeth's murder. "Ever since my sister met that Arab, she totally changed," Marie-Josée told the police.

Alphonsine Bousquet was the last person in the family to see Elisabeth alive. It was the first week of July and Elisabeth had stopped by the house her mother was now sharing with Noël Patel and his uncle in the Marseille suburbs. Alphonsine wanted her to stay and eat lunch, but Elisabeth rushed off to an "appointment."

"My daughter had a gay character. She was a little shy, and she had a really good heart," Alphonsine told the police. "I am certain that it is this fellow Hamida who led her down the wrong path."

Alphonsine was also the only person who expected the visit from Constable Vidou. The morning that the news of the arrest and the photograph of Hamida appeared in the newspaper, Noël took a copy upstairs to Alphonsine. Though it didn't identify Elisabeth, Alphonsine was overcome with dread. Call it maternal instinct.

"She started crying and sobbing," remembers Noël Patel. "I've always kept that vision of her holding that newspaper with the tears streaming down her cheeks."

*

* *

UNDER FRENCH LAW, the victim or the victim's family has the right to participate in the trial and ask for damages. This function, known as the *action civile*, allowed the Bousquets to have a lawyer of their own who had access to the court documents, could question witnesses, and could make closing arguments.

Even this simple act of choosing a lawyer reflected the fissures in the family. Pierre and the children chose Éliane Perasso, a lawyer and author who was at the forefront of the nascent feminist movement in France and who specialized in crimes against women. Alphonsine stood alone.* She selected Marc Greco, a Corsican who would go on to become head of the Marseille bar. Greco agreed to take the case on one condition: that he wouldn't request the death penalty at the trial. He was doubly opposed to capital punishment: on the moral ground that a government shouldn't have the right to kill its own citizens, and on the practical ground that he was a child of the French Resistance and had seen too many of his confrères executed.

"Historically, very few people have been condemned to death for crimes of common law," Greco said. "Many times more have been put to death for political and religious reasons."

Alphonsine agreed to the condition. Greco made her sign a contract just to be safe.

Days later, Elisabeth's story took another dreary turn. Constable Vidou drove to La Roque d'Anthéron to track down this mysterious legionnaire who was alternatively Elisabeth's boyfriend, fiancé, and husband. He discovered three items of interest.

First, the man's name was Jean-Louis Azzarello. He was the father of six children, divorced, unemployed, and he had been living in a convalescent home.

Second, he was dead. The first week of August, Azzarello had left the home to find his ex-wife. When he arrived at her house, he spent the night bingeing on alcohol and painkillers. When the ex-wife woke up the next morning, Azzarello was dead. She called the fire department and got them to take away the body. She neglected to call Azzarello's father, the convalescent home, or any of his friends. He was buried in a pauper's grave two days before Hamida Djandoubi was arrested.

---

* Alphonsine appears to have had difficulty coping with the reality of her daughter's death. According to Maryse Hugon of Langogne, several years after the murder she met Alphonsine and told her she still thought about Elisabeth. "Alphonsine looked at me and said, 'Who? Who are you talking about?'" recalled Hugon. Whether it was an attempt to block out painful memories or protect the family's privacy, Alphonsine's behavior might explain her children's reluctance to discuss the case three decades later.

And lastly, most predictably, Azzarello had lied to Elisabeth about pretty much everything. According to his father, Azzarello had never been a member of the Foreign Legion and hadn't fought in Algeria. He'd worked in a factory in Corsica and had pancreas problems. After two major stomach operations, he went on welfare. He'd been living in the convalescent home for two months when he'd met Elisabeth. And he didn't have a penny to his name.

Until the very end, Elisabeth had been blinded by her frantic need for love.

*

* *

IN MARSEILLE, THE POLICE were still dealing with Hamida Djandoubi's living victims.

For Houria, there was no doubting her physical suffering. After denouncing Hamida, she underwent her first medical examinations that same afternoon. The doctor noted how fragile she was: Houria was five feet five inches tall but straw thin, weighing barely eighty-eight pounds. The examination confirmed Houria had bruises on her shoulders, back, and legs. Her body was covered with cigarette burns. The doctor also noted that the fourth toe on her left foot had been fractured because of Djandoubi's predilection for beating the girls' feet with his club. The gynecological exam was especially troubling. The doctor verified that she had recently lost her virginity and a deposit of harissa was found near the girl's vulva.

To make matters more difficult, Houria had to cope with being rejected by her family. As her parents were still in Algeria when Houria went to the police, she was initially placed back in the youth shelter in Toulon. When her parents finally returned to Marseille and were notified of the events, their reaction was abhorrent. That fact that Houria had run away had already brought enough shame on the family; that she'd been raped was too much for them to accept. They refused to let her back into their home.

Social workers placed Houria in a Marseille shelter run by the Association Nationale d'Entraide Féminine (ANEF), a group that helped women escape violence and prostitution. The association was founded by the matron of the Michelin tire family, Marguerite-Marie Michelin. Known as "Triple M," Michelin had been deported during World War II and was appalled by how the women were treated in the camps. Afterward, she dedicated herself—and a large portion of her family's tire fortune—to the cause of French women.

The director of the ANEFs in Marseille was Jacqueline Anglade, a woman so fiercely dedicated she often spent eighteen hours a day at the shelters. She was only supposed to manage operations, but whenever there was a woman in real danger, the counselors would come to her and say, "Madame Anglade, she is for you."

So Anglade personally intervened with Houria. She was shocked by her youth, still more child than woman. And broken, so broken. "Houria lost all confidence in herself," Anglade recalled. "For her, she was nothing, she had no value in her own eyes."

Little could anyone know that for Houria there was only more agony to come.

*

* *

ANNIE AND AMARIA were in a more ambiguous predicament. Victims, most certainly. But also participants in the crime. That day at the police station, instead of being transferred to a shelter like Houria, they were taken into custody and brought to the women's wing of the Baumettes prison in Marseille.

The day after the arrest, both girls were brought up to Aix-en-Provence to be interviewed by Françoise Llaurens. Amaria was heard first. She told Judge Llaurens of meeting Hamida in the park outside her building in Lodève and falling in love and running away to Marseille. And then how her perfect boyfriend turned sadistic and lethal. Judge Llaurens was more interested in Amaria's actions on the night of the murder.

"We cleaned up the room because it was full of blood," Amaria said. And then she admitted: "The girl asked us to go get help, she asked us to call out at the window, but we were scared."

Amaria also explained how she and Annie helped carry Elisabeth to her death. "He threatened to drag her to the cabin, so Annie and I took her by the arms and helped her."

Annie was next. It was late in the afternoon, and the young woman was exhausted. She gave a few short answers and then, less than a half hour into the interview, told Judge Llaurens she couldn't continue. The judge insisted that Annie answer one key question: why hadn't they done anything to help Elisabeth on the night in question?

"Amaria and I didn't call for help because we were scared we would suffer the same fate," Annie's statement read.

Judge Llaurens understood the girls were minors and under the influence of Hamida Djandoubi. But she was also surprised by how lightly Annie and Amaria were taking the events.

"It seemed to me they didn't really feel a lot of guilt in the death of Elisabeth," Judge Llaurens remembered.

It wasn't an easy decision, but Judge Llaurens was sure it was the correct one. The girls had helped in a material fashion that night. So Annie and Amaria were charged as accomplices to murder, torture, and barbarous acts. They were to remain in prison until further notice.

33

IT WAS NAPOLEON who introduced the idea that madness might excuse crime. His criminal code of 1808 included the infamous Article 64, stating there is no offense if the offender is of unsound mind at the time of the act.

Following similar logic, in 1832 the concept of extenuating circumstances was written into French law. From that time on, rather than simply matching the crime to the list of prescribed punishments, the sentence was adapted to better fit the nature of the crime. It was a philosophy antithetical to that of Immanuel Kant. Where he saw murder as an absolute that could be punished only by death, now there were shades of gravity, and in the hands of the law, the battered wife who poisoned her abusive husband would be treated differently than the thief who murdered a family of four in their sleep.

With these developments, French justice veered into the realm of subjectivity. No longer was it a matter of proving the facts of the crime. Lawyers, prosecutors, and judges now had to peer inside the mind of the criminal and decide his or her intent. This transformation was one of the central themes of Michel Foucault's 1975 book, *Surveiller et punir* (Discipline and Punish).

"Judges have gradually, by means of a process that goes back very far indeed, taken to judging something other than crimes, namely, the 'soul' of the criminal," Foucault wrote.

Jean Goudareau realized this phenomenon was the only possible salvation for Hamida Djandoubi. There was obviously no possibility of pleading innocent. Nor was there denying the brutality of the act. The only hope was to prove there were extenuating circumstances, that Hamida's soul had been irreparably twisted by his amputation in 1971.

"This boy—young, handsome, elegant, lots of friends, success with the ladies—finds himself the next day with his leg cut off, the pain insufferable," Goudareau said. "It was a little chance, an opening. We had already cut off half of his leg so now to cut off his head. . . ."

Goudareau also believed the collection of Swedish erotica found in the apartment could prove a useful argument. In his mind, Hamida had been corrupted by pornography, and to bolster his theory, he began clipping the advertisements for porno movies that appeared in the Marseille newspapers, films such as *Adolescence perverse* and *Les Aberrations sexuelles d'un monstre.*

"There is nothing worse than pornography for developing perversity," he insisted.

Of course, Goudareau would need doctors to testify to one or both of his hypotheses. Everything rode on Hamida Djandoubi's psychiatric evaluation, which was scheduled for October 1974.

*

*   *

ANNIE'S AND AMARIA'S court-appointed lawyers were equally anxious for the psychiatric exams. Jean-Jacques Anglade and Jean-Claude Sebag were both in their twenties and members of the same left-wing movement. In the May 1974 elections in which Giscard edged out Mitterrand, Sebag actually ran for president with the fringe party Mouvement Fédéraliste Européen, and Anglade acted as his campaign manager. Sebag was eliminated in the first round of voting.

Marseille is often called a village masquerading as a city because of the unusual number of small-town coincidences that occur here. In this instance, it so happened that Jean-Jacques Anglade was the son of Jacqueline Anglade, who managed the ANEF shelters and was counseling Houria. It was his mother who politicized Anglade. In 1962 she took her teenage son to the Marseille port to welcome the *pieds-noirs* and *harkis* who had been forced from Algeria. The Anglades were among a legion of volunteers preparing sandwiches and steering refugees to the temporary lodgings set up across France.

After consulting the police files, Anglade and Sebag opted for a joint defense. For the lawyers, the girls were equal victims. Anglade still remembers the first meeting at the prison. He expected to find shattered young women; instead, the girls were happy and relieved.

"The prison was a sort of liberty after what they had endured," he recalled. "I found them smiling, aware of the dramas they had been associated with, but relaxed and almost free."

Foremost were the questions of why the girls hadn't left Hamida or done anything to help Elisabeth on the night of the murder. Annie only needed to tell the lawyers about the day she tried to escape. "The girl runs out onto the street in her underpants and bra, with burn marks and bruises on her body, and nobody helps her," Anglade said. "Then she's tied to a chair and tortured for three days. You didn't need to ask such a question twice."

The lawyers also learned of Hamida's methods of making the girls submit to him. He had them compete to avoid punishment; he would assign each a chore, say, washing the dishes for Annie and scrubbing the toilet for Amaria, and whoever completed her work first wouldn't get raped with the wooden club. He would also alternate between tortures and affection; one day he would whip Amaria with the belt and give her electric shocks; the next he would give her a gift of dried flowers and say he wanted to marry her.

"The Stockholm syndrome isn't just a theory," Anglade said. "These girls ended up attached to this man because he was their only contact."

The police in Salon-de-Provence had a similar analysis. In his report,

Commandant Yves Salendre stated: "We acquired the belief that Djandoubi, Hamida, had a strong influence over the two girls and that each one tried to be his favorite."

*

*   *

AS WITH HOURIA, there was no questioning the extreme physical abuse Annie and Amaria had suffered. The day of the arrests both were examined by a police doctor. The report on Annie noted:

• 23 circular cigarette burns, between ⅒ of an inch and ⅘ of an inch in diameter, arranged with symmetry on her stomach and breasts

• 8 scars the doctor attributed to being struck with a belt

• two razor blade cuts on each thigh, 2½ inches in length

• a burn on the inside of the right thigh, the result of a hot knife pressed into the skin

As for Amaria, the list of wounds was similar:

• multiple circular cigarette burns on her legs, stomach, rear, and breasts

• marks from a belt on her neck

• signs of recent trauma on her left thigh

• bruises on the bottom of her feet

On August 19, 1974, psychiatrists examined the girls at the Baumettes prison. As in all court-ordered evaluations, the doctors were obliged to answer six questions:

1. Does the individual suffer from any mental or physical deficiencies?

2. If so, do these deficiencies explain the infraction?

3. Does the subject present a danger?

4. Does the subject qualify for a criminal sentence?

5. Could the subject be rehabilitated?

6. At the time of the crime, was the subject demented as defined by Article 64 of the criminal code?

In their assessment of Annie, the doctors remarked on her "mediocre intellectual level." They discovered she didn't know the multiplication tables and assessed her as having the intelligence of a ten-year-old. Annie had turned eighteen two days after the murder.

"We find ourselves in the presence of a woman showing signs of light mental debilitation, who is unstable and malleable, with only a primary level of intelligence and very little imagination," the doctors wrote. "Such a subject is obviously much more apt to become submissive."

As for the six questions, they reported that Annie had a slight mental disability; the crimes she was charged with could be partially attributed to this mental disability; she presented no danger to society; she was fit to be sentenced; she could be rehabilitated; and, according to the stipulations of Article 64, her mental disability limited her responsibility.

Not a flattering assessment. But, from a legal perspective, fantastic news.

The doctors were more impressed with Amaria. Calling her "an elegant young Algerian," they complimented her "lucidity," her "precise vocabulary," and her "agreeable nature."

"The fact that she was only a mediocre student has more to do with an absence of scholastic motivation," they wrote, "than any intellectual insufficiencies."

The doctors noted she was sheltered at home and that she'd genuinely loved Hamida and believed they would marry. "These sentiments quickly turned into an immense fear, which can explain the behavior of the accused vis-à-vis the events."

As for the six questions, Amaria was found to have no mental anomaly that would have influenced her actions, she presented no danger to society, she was liable for a criminal penalty, she could be rehabilitated, and she wasn't considered demented under Article 64.

Though her report was not as exculpatory as Annie's, the doctors' evident fondness for Amaria would help her in court.

However, just as these psychiatric reports were playing in the girls' favor, Hamida was changing his story and trying to shift some of the blame for the crime onto Annie and Amaria. This emerged during a confrontation that Judge Françoise Llaurens had called to clarify the prostitution allegations.

After everyone was assembled in the judge's office in Aix-en-Provence, Hamida told Judge Llaurens that Annie was a masochist and had asked for the tortures. "It's true that I burned her with cigarettes, that I hurt her with a Gillette razor," he said. "It was because she wanted it; Annie liked to see her own blood."

Next, he blamed Amaria for Elisabeth's death. He claimed he'd wanted to drive Elisabeth to the hospital, but Amaria had intervened. "Amaria thought she would denounce us to the police, they would come and get us, and it would be over for us," Hamida said. "So she advised me to finish Elisabeth off."

Judge Llaurens reminded Hamida that this differed from his original statement. But he now claimed that the day of the arrest he had only been trying to protect Annie and Amaria from blame. "It was out of love for these two girls that I killed Elisabeth," he insisted.

The girls passionately denied these latest allegations. Amaria began crying. The confrontation was called to a halt before the prostitution questions had even been raised.

*

* *

MEANWHILE, POLICE WERE tying up loose ends on the case. They interviewed Hamida's neighbor Marie-Claude Kervella, his old friends the Comandés, his employers at the bakery and the restaurant. There was only one difficulty: his brother, Ali.

Ali was reputed to be of a dishonest bent, and he now showed why he had earned such a reputation. During his first interview, he said nothing of Elisabeth Bousquet. The police prompted him. Was Ali sure he hadn't seen any other girl with his brother during the summer? Maybe at the Sonacotra? Maybe at the end of June?

Ali stonewalled. Police let him sit in the cells overnight. The next morning, Ali relented. "I forget to tell you about one girl. . . ."

The police had a photograph of Elisabeth that Alphonsine had given them. It showed her with Noël Patel's dog, a German shepherd named Willy. She was holding a treat high above her head, and Willy was on his hind legs trying to reach it. Using this picture, Ali formally identified Elisabeth. But he still played dumb when it came to the essential question.

"You're maintaining that you don't know the circumstances in which your brother was able to bring Elisabeth to his home?" the police asked.

Ali insisted he had no idea. The police told him that Hamida had already stated that it was Ali who'd let him know that Elisabeth was at the Sonacotra.

"My brother is lying," Ali said.

"How do you explain that Amaria M. declared the same thing?"

"That girl is also lying."

The police reported the situation to Judge Llaurens. After another night in jail, Ali was informed that if he hadn't known what his brother was going to do, there would be no charges. So Ali talked and

Ali was released. The bottom line was that the police couldn't prove he'd had foreknowledge of Hamida's intentions. As things unfolded, Ali would end up being the sole beneficiary of his brother's woes.

*

* *

SEVERAL WEEKS INTO her stay at the ANEF shelter, Houria began feeling ill. Vomiting, queasiness, lack of appetite. The first assumption was a post-traumatic disorder. The truth was much, much worse.

Houria was pregnant with Hamida Djandoubi's child.

There were few options for the girl in the summer of 1974. Despite a widening campaign by women's groups, abortion remained illegal. There had even been a recent precedent when several women were charged after an illegal abortion in 1972. The *Procès de Bobigny* involved a sixteen-year-old girl, Marie-Claire, who was raped by a classmate at her high school. Her mother tried to arrange for an abortion, but the doctor demanded 4,500 francs, and she only earned 1,500 francs a month. She was forced to send Marie-Claire to an amateur. It was butchery. On the third attempt to abort the fetus, Marie-Claire hemorrhaged and had to be taken to the hospital.

The story, horrible as it was, would have ended there except that several weeks later the rapist, a boy named Daniel C., was caught stealing cars. He tried to strike a deal with police by telling them about the illegal abortion. Marie-Claire, her mother, the amateur abortionist, and two other women were charged. The case galvanized the pro-choice movement in France. The lawyer Gisèle Halimi took the case for no fee, and the likes of Simone de Beauvoir began a national awareness campaign on behalf of the women.

At the trial in October 1972, Marie-Claire's mother told the court, "*Mais, monsieur le juge, je ne suis pas coupable! C'est votre loi qui est coupable.*" I'm not guilty, your law is guilty.

She had summed up the sentiments of the majority of the nation. But to no avail. The mother was fined five hundred francs, and the amateur abortionist sentenced to one year in prison. Georges Pompidou, already embroiled in the question of the death penalty, announced he was "repulsed" by the abortion issue and refused to address it.

The fallout was electric. There were mass protests and petitions among women's groups, and when Valéry Giscard d'Estaing won the 1974 elections, there was a promise of progress. The credit would belong to Simone Veil, a lawyer and activist renowned for her perseverance. When she was seventeen, her entire family was arrested and put in the Auschwitz-Birkenau camp. Veil survived, returned to France, completed her education, and entered politics. After gradually ascending the ranks, she was appointed minister of health in May 1974.

In September 1974, Veil launched her program to transform women's health care. First, it was contraception. At the time, birth control was sold only by doctor's prescription, so Veil introduced a law making birth control more accessible.

The abortion law would be a tougher battle, as it was opposed by religious groups and a bloc of politicians on the right. The issue became further complicated when it was linked to the capital punishment debate. Pro-life groups attacked politicians like Veil who supported both the abolition of the death penalty and the legalization of abortion. Did they respect life or not?

In Paris, Robert Badinter was furious at what he saw as a sophist ruse. In his eyes, there was no conflict between the two beliefs. "The death penalty is a torture imposed by society onto a condemned individual, while the choice of abortion is left to each woman's personal decision," he wrote. "Women are given the liberty to choose; it is not at all the same with the death penalty."

Although several deputies labeled her bill the "law of genocide," Veil won over the National Assembly. The law passed by a vote of 284 to 189, and on January 17, 1975, abortion was legalized in France.

But that would be too late for Houria.

Jean-Jacques Anglade solved the dilemma. Having learned of Houria's predicament from his mother, he found a doctor willing to perform an illegal abortion. Initially, the doctor was reluctant to operate on a fourteen-year-old girl without her parents' consent. Anglade illicitly photocopied parts of the police dossier to present to the doctor. The abortion was performed.

"I knew I was breaking the law, but it was the only option," Jean-Jacques Anglade said.

For Jacqueline Anglade, her role in the abortion was apostasy. A practicing Catholic, she abhorred abortion and was vehemently opposed to Veil's reforms. But for the only time in her life, she made an exception.

"I was against abortion and I am still absolutely against abortion," she said decades later. "But in that type of situation . . ."

Hamida never knew he could have been a father.

34

SUMMER FADED INTO FALL and the pace of Marseille life became as brisk as it ever does in a Mediterranean city. The beach crowds thinned and long-sleeved shirts appeared, high schools and universities were back in session, and, for those with jobs, the August vacations were now distant memories.

Hamida Djandoubi's initial psychiatric assessment was held October 7, almost three years to the day after his leg was amputated. It would be a challenge to convince doctors to show any sympathy. Several years earlier, a man named Thomas Ferrandini had broken into a Marseille hotel and killed its owner. Ferrandini had been released from a mental hospital just six weeks earlier, and the widow complained that the psychiatrists had been too lenient in allowing his discharge and bore responsibility for her husband's death. Reviews of hospital measures were under way, and doctors were being doubly cautious. The consensus was to err on the side of incarceration.

Hamida's assessment was conducted by Dr. Suttel and Dr. Merlin. Again, the six questions were to be answered, and again the key issue would be his mental state at the time of the murder.

When the examination began, it didn't take long for his darkness to emerge. Hamida quickly paraded out his hideous new story: the torture of the girls was sadomasochistic sex play. "I would cut Annie with a Gillette blade, I would suck her blood and then spit it back in her mouth. It gave her an orgasm," he told the doctors.

Still, he insisted that he didn't take any sexual pleasure in torturing Elisabeth. It was just a matter of punishment. "I was mad because she was prostituting herself," he said. "And she slept with anybody."

The doctors' conclusions were damning. Hamida was "an authentic executioner who took pleasure from the suffering of others" and represented "a colossal social danger." They detected no mental abnormalities to explain the crime and declared that Hamida wasn't suitable for rehabilitation. In other words, he was a prime candidate for the guillotine.

*

* *

HAMIDA DIDN'T DO himself any favors during the reconstruction of the crime either.

On the morning of November 8, 1974, he, Annie, and Amaria were brought from Baumettes prison to the apartment on rue Villa Paradis. Already present were the three defense lawyers, Judge Llaurens and her assistants, the police doctor, and the landlord, Victor Barrielle. A police secretary, Nadine Pache, had been asked to play the role of Elisabeth Bousquet.

Starting at 9:30 A.M., the murder was re-created in thirty-two scenes. Hamida pretended to slap "Elisabeth" in the first scene, followed by a picture of Annie and Amaria moving the rug to prepare the room for the torture. So it went, until Annie acted out the scene where she fetched the gas can from the Simca 1000. Here, Hamida again showed his haunting attention to detail. When Judge Llaurens asked him to pose for a picture holding the gas can over Elisabeth, he protested.

"He told me, 'No, no, I poured gas from the jerry can into a glass and poured the glass of gas onto Elisabeth,'" Llaurens remembered. "He was very insistent."

It was also at this moment that Hamida's story once more diverged from his earlier confessions. He had said he attempted to stomp on Elisabeth's stomach to put out the fire; now he claimed he wouldn't have used his foot because his prosthesis didn't allow him enough balance. As a compromise, Hamida agreed to reenact both versions for the camera.

When it came to the other tortures, Hamida was less cooperative.

He now denied sodomizing Elisabeth with a lit candle and making her drink his urine, and refused to pose for these pictures. He did, however, allow himself to be photographed fetching a tin of harissa from the kitchen shelf.

By one o'clock, the events of the apartment had been covered. As the crowd filed down the stairs, Hamida found himself next to Amaria. Despite the presence of the police and court officials, he gave her a hefty kick, sending the girl sprawling against the wall.

He said it had been an involuntary action. The police noticed his prosthesis hadn't hindered his balance in this particular circumstance.

The afternoon session at the cabin was shorter, consisting of only ten photographs. Once again, there were conflicting versions of events. Annie and Amaria claimed Hamida had tied a belt to Elisabeth's leg and dragged her from the car; Hamida now denied this. Again, both versions were photographed.

There was no disagreement about the last two pictures. Number 31 showed Hamida kicking Elisabeth in the face to make sure she was dead. Number 32 showed him removing the scarf from her neck.

One person pleased by the day's events was the landlord, Victor Barrielle. With the reconstruction now complete, he would get the keys to the apartment back. Barrielle submitted a demand for 812 francs and 50 centimes to compensate for the rent lost while his apartment had been under police stewardship.

*

* *

ONCE THE RECONSTRUCTION was finished, Anglade and Sebag requested the release of Annie and Amaria from prison. They'd made an earlier motion, but Judge Llaurens had rejected it, wanting to ensure all the accused were present for the reconstruction. Now, with the girls having fully cooperated and their parents willing to sign guarantees, the lawyers felt they had a better chance.

"My client, to the contrary, can be considered another victim of the principal accused," wrote Anglade. "A victim of having been lured from her home and her parents, where she led a serious life, a victim of the physical and moral domination exercised by this individual over her."

Jean Goudareau wasn't convinced by his colleague's argument. He saw the girls more as accomplices. "It's absolutely incredible that the two girls would watch this torture and not cry for help," he said. "The two girls contributed."

It was a murky issue, but with the parents to act as guarantors, there was no justification for keeping the girls in prison for the months and years it would take for the case to go to trial. Judge Llaurens signed the release, and on November 14, Annie and Amaria left Baumettes and went their separate ways: Annie to her family's apartment in Marseille, Amaria to Lodève.

The only girl not back with her parents was Houria. She still lived in the shelter and things weren't hopeful.

"She had no self-esteem," Jacqueline Anglade said. "She would go out every day to meet men, to sleep with men. We tried to talk to her but she wouldn't listen."

*

*   *

WHEN THE APARTMENT on rue Villa Paradis was emptied, Hamida's belongings went to his brother. On November 25, Ali received a bounty: three suitcases of clothes, a Europhon record player with two speakers, twenty-one audio tapes, a Radialva television, a transistor radio, a tape recorder, a gas oven, and various dishes and cutlery.

The real prize was the cherished Simca 1000, with a manageable 76,238 kilometers on the odometer. From prison, Hamida asked Goudareau to withdraw money from his bank account. He wanted to make the final four car payments for his brother.

It should be noted that Hamida wasn't entirely satisfied with the inventory of items recovered from his apartment. On December 13,

1974, Goudareau wrote a letter to Judge Llaurens on his behalf. He claimed that certain personal papers and pay stubs were missing.

"Also, since the apartment has been liberated, we haven't found the twenty pornographic books that my client brought from Sweden," Goudareau wrote.

The pornography was never located.

*

*   *

IN THE SPRING OF 1975, three more doctors assessed Hamida to determine the mental implications of his amputation. The accident was key to his defense, and it had surely been a traumatic incident; but as police investigators like Jacques Chauley were quick to note, not every amputee becomes a depraved rapist and murderer.

The doctors decided the amputation, "a symbolic castration of his social ambitions," prompted his downward spiral. "As a result," they wrote, "he turned in on himself and returned to the ethnic attitudes of his origins (polygamy) and a strong aggression that he channeled and let out only with his sadistic tendencies during the sexual acts."

They also concluded that the amputation hadn't spawned any mental illness that might mitigate his acts. The only improvement in this second assessment was that these doctors believed there was a slim chance he could be rehabilitated.

"It wasn't what I was expecting," Goudareau admitted. "I was very disappointed with the doctors. They spent hardly any time at all with him."

In fact, nothing was going Goudareau's way. The medical and psychiatric reports gave him no legal ammunition. His client was constantly changing his story and had physically attacked Amaria in the presence of the judge and police officers. And the two girls, who he felt shared some responsibility for the crime, had been released from his prison. His frustration mounting, he lashed out at the worst possible target: Judge Françoise Llaurens.

It was a money issue. At the time of his arrest, Hamida had 11,700 francs in his bank account. It was in August 1974 that Goudareau first requested that 6,000 francs be released so Hamida could settle his debts and pay his lawyer's fees. Goudareau repeated the request on November 12, 1974; on December 15, 1974; on January 17, 1975; and on February 25, 1975. Each time, Judge Llaurens informed Goudareau that the police still weren't ready to release the bank account. Finally, on March 21, 1975, Goudareau was given authorization to withdraw the money, but when he arrived at Baumettes, the paperwork needed to obtain Hamida's signature hadn't been prepared.

Goudareau was furious with the "casualness" of Judge Llaurens and rashly dictated a letter.

"If lawyers owe magistrates their deference, then magistrates owe lawyers their respect, and, I add, especially when there is a difference of age as large as that which separates us," wrote Goudareau. "I will not allow myself to be treated the way you are treating me."

Goudareau sent copies to the president of the court in Aix-en-Provence, the head of the Marseille bar, and a local representative of the Ministry of Justice. The money was eventually released. But Goudareau, like his client, wasn't making any friends.

*

*   *

ALMOST A YEAR INTO Giscard's presidency, the French government still showed no signs of moving on the death penalty. In February 1975, the minister of the interior declared that the death penalty had to be maintained for murders involving children, police officers, and hostages. The following month, Prime Minister Jacques Chirac announced he too was in favor of the death penalty in cases of hostage takings that ended in death.

The government's resolve would be tested in 1975 after General Franco had five men executed in Spain after highly dubious trials on terrorism charges. Around Europe, the decision and the death penalty were roundly condemned. In Paris, where a large community of Spanish political refugees lived, the executions sparked the biggest street demonstrations since May '68. A cadre of French celebrities, including the actor Yves Montand, even flew to Madrid to protest in person.

Yet the French government refused to censure the executions or question the death penalty. And the Spanish government was quick to point out the reason behind the French silence. In an official statement, the Spanish government noted there had been ten executions in France since 1964; meanwhile, Spain had only held eight executions since 1960. The pot had wisely avoided exchanging insults with the kettle.

At roughly the same time, a French teenager was brought to trial for murdering an elderly woman. Bruno T. was only seventeen at the time of the crime, and his lawyer argued that the boy's volatile childhood explained the violence. Bruno had been abandoned by his parents at the age of three, juggled between foster homes, and eventually consigned to a juvenile detention center for problem children. The jury wasn't convinced. The verdict was death.

Bruno T. couldn't be guillotined, as France had signed a 1966 United Nations treaty that banned the execution of minors. But that didn't stop the public from crying for the teenager's head. After the verdict, a poll revealed that 58 percent of the population felt a minor should be executed for "especially odious" crimes. The minister of justice said the decision showed people were more concerned about the violence of the crime than the age of the offender. And *Le Figaro* editorialized, "We are entering the age of executioners because we have entered the age of murderers."

*

*   *

IN JANUARY 1976, four years after hosting the trial of Claude Buffet and Roger Bontems, the city of Troyes was the scene of another drama that would be pivotal to the death penalty debate.

After leaving school one afternoon, an eight-year-old boy by the name of Philippe Bertrand disappeared. That evening, the family received an anonymous phone call demanding one million francs in ransom. It was a ludicrous proposition. The Bertrands were a working family with little money. Who would target them for a kidnapping?

The case became a national obsession. Philippe's photograph was distributed to the media, and his mother and father appeared on television to beg for his return. The family managed to borrow money for the ransom and were sent on the most pitiless of treasure hunts. A letter with one of their son's gloves was left at a church, which directed them to a billboard with another letter pinned to one of his boots. Finally, they were led to parking lot where their child's jacket hung on a fence post. They were instructed to leave the ransom in its place.

The money was never taken. But a young man named Patrick Henry had twice come into a neighboring café during the night. Henry was in debt, giving him motive; and Henry's family knew the Bertrands, giving him access to Philippe. Police questioned Henry for forty-eight hours, but he revealed nothing and was released.

When Henry left the police station, he told journalists: "I am for the death penalty in this sort of case. They don't have the right to attack the life of a child."

Three weeks after the boy went missing, the police discovered Henry had been secretly renting a second apartment. Under the bed, they found the corpse of Philippe Bertrand.

There was a maelstrom of anger. The mayor of Troyes demanded the courts make an example of Patrick Henry. The minister of the interior said if he were a member of the jury, he would send Henry to the guillotine. On the evening news, Patrick Henry's photograph was brandished and the anchor announced: "Bastard. There, the word has been said." And newspapers trumpeted the news that "even his own mother is asking for the ultimate punishment."

The case was so vile that the lawyers contacted by Patrick Henry refused the case. In Marseille, Émile Pollak stepped forward. Pollak was a Provençal legend, a character from one the *polars,* the crime novels that were a Marseille specialty. He was sixty years old, smoked three packs of Craven A cigarettes a day, gambled incessantly on the horse races, and had fourteen cats living with him at his house on avenue du Prado.

Pollak wrote in his memoir that a lawyer's duty was "to defend with all our courage, with all our soul." It was no surprise then that he announced that he would accept the Patrick Henry case if asked. And it was fair measure of the emotion surrounding the affair that he immediately lost several clients, and death threats were made against his grandson.

But in the end, Patrick Henry didn't contact Pollak. He'd heard of a lawyer in Paris who was on a personal crusade against the death penalty. And so he called Robert Badinter. The consensus was it would be an impossible case to win. The consensus also was that if Badinter could win it, it would be the end of the death penalty in France.

35

HAMIDA DJANDOUBI'S MORE celebrated cellmate at the Baumettes prison would be the first to have his day in court.

The Christian Ranucci case was as befuddling as ever. At first glance, the evidence was overwhelming. Ranucci had confessed to abducting Marie-Dolorès Rambla, stabbing her to death, then hiding the body under a bush at a mushroom farm. The manager at the mushroom farm identified Ranucci as the young man who had gotten his car stuck on their road the day of the abduction. And, based on Ranucci's instructions, the police were able to find the murder weapon buried in the soft earth of the farm.

Yet his lawyers, led by Paul Lombard, believed him innocent. Ranucci insisted his confession was made under duress. The two witnesses to the actual abduction, one of whom was a mechanic, testified that Marie-Dolorès was forced into a Simca, while Ranucci drove a Peugeot. Even with a metal detector, the murder weapon took almost an hour to find, despite Ranucci's apparently detailed description of its location. And, most peculiarly, in the weeks prior to the abduction, there were complaints of a man in a red sweater trying to lure children into his car, and police had found a red sweater at the mushroom farm. It didn't belong to Ranucci.

It is impossible to know what happened. In the bestselling book *Le Pull-over rouge*, the French writer Gilles Perrault advanced the theory that Ranucci had the bad luck of pulling into the mushroom farm to take a nap at the same time the murderer in the red sweater buried the girl nearby. Whatever the truth, Ranucci's lawyers thought there was enough doubt to avoid the death penalty. Ranucci was young, only twenty-two years old at the time of the trial; he had no prior police record and was considered a hard worker and loving son; and there was the greatest abolitionist argument of all, the prospect that an innocent man might be put to death.

What the lawyers didn't anticipate was the Patrick Henry effect.

Ranucci went to trial just two weeks after Henry's arrest for the murder of young Philippe Bertrand, and the French people were traumatized by the idea that child killers were running amok in their country. One television poll showed support for the death penalty edging close to 80 percent. As Roger Gicquel, the host of a major evening news program on French television, declared, "*La France a peur.*" France is scared.

The night before Ranucci's trial, the eighteenth-century courthouse in Aix-en-Provence was graffitied with *A mort Ranucci* (Death to Ranucci). The next morning, heaving crowds surrounded the courthouse, crying out for the guillotine. Ranucci's mother was repeatedly spit upon as she entered the building.

In the witness box, Ranucci couldn't have performed more poorly. Newspapers described him as arrogant, combative, and having the "eyes of a dead fish." Lombard denounced the "collective hysteria" following the Henry arrest and argued that his client was both innocent and mentally unstable. Why else would he confess to a crime he didn't commit and behave so erratically in court?

"If you give death to Ranucci, you will reopen the doors to barbarity," Lombard told the jury. "You will fatten the bloody tome of judicial errors, you will become executioners, you will have ceded to the anger, the fear, the panic. But I know you will not do that."

Lombard was wrong. After two and a half hours of deliberation, the jury sentenced Ranucci to death. Four and a half months later, on July 28, 1976, Ranucci was guillotined at the Baumettes prison. Witnesses say his head bounced twice after the assistant executioner tossed it into the basket.*

---

*Because of the publicity surrounding the Ranucci case (the film about his case is still regularly shown on French television), many people in France believe him to be the last man guillotined. When conducting research for this book, I was forced to carry newspaper clippings and other references with me to convince people that other men were indeed guillotined after Ranucci.

It was the first execution of Valéry Giscard d'Estaing's presidency. Like Pompidou before him, Giscard had told people he was "personally not in favor of the death penalty." Like Pompidou before him, politics had gotten in the way of his personal beliefs. With repeated polls announcing the vast majority of the French people now wanted to keep the death penalty, the sitting government wasn't going to instigate a debate on an issue as controversial as abolition.

In Paris, Robert Badinter, who was in the midst of preparing for Patrick Henry's trial, called the verdict a "shock." Both he and Jean Goudareau knew what it meant: if Ranucci wasn't granted clemency, nobody would be granted clemency. The only way to spare their clients' lives was to convince a jury they didn't deserve to die.

*

* *

IT WASN'T ONLY Giscard who was embracing the death penalty. Days before Ranucci was guillotined, the United States welcomed capital punishment back into its criminal codes.

After *Furman v. Georgia* declared the death penalty unconstitutional, several states revamped their laws and applied to reinstate capital punishment. The lead case, *Gregg v. Georgia,* involved Troy Gregg, a hitchhiker who'd murdered two men who'd picked him up. In hopes of executing Gregg, Georgia had changed its trial procedure, separating the verdict from the sentencing. Before, a guilty verdict in a capital case automatically meant the death penalty; now there would be a sentencing hearing during which mitigating factors could be presented.

This safeguard was enough for the Supreme Court. "Certain crimes are themselves so grievous an affront to humanity that the only adequate response may be the penalty of death" read the majority opinion in the 7–2 Supreme Court decision that allowed the restoration of capital punishment.

This concept of an "affront to humanity" was at the heart of society's attachment to the death penalty. In the book *Eichmann in Jerusalem,* which traced the agonizing trial and execution of Nazi leader Adolf Eichmann in Israel in 1962, Hannah Arendt called that case the "supreme justification" for the death penalty. She wrote of crimes that so offend nature "the very earth cries out for vengeance." There were echoes of Plato, who argued in the *Gorgias* that, for the vilest of criminals, death was the only "way in which they can be delivered from their evil."

Left to decide was which crimes constituted such an affront to nature, such an embodiment of evil. Over the centuries, there had been an intriguing inverse trend in Western countries: the horror of execution methods radically diminished while the horror of the crimes that qualified for execution increased exponentially. Gone were the days when a thief was broken on the wheel and rolled around town for all to see; now only the cruelest and most sadistic of murders merited death, and the executions were meted out in the most sanitized and humane ways possible. Perhaps this was the "civilizing process" Sir Henry Maine wrote about in *Ancient Law*.

Whatever the case, the brief parenthesis of American abolition had ended, and this only served to escalate the debate in France. Europe had profoundly rejected the death penalty; America was once again embracing it. Which way would France fall?

That summer, the unions for the French lawyers, judges, and police officers all announced they were in favor of abolition. But the government wasn't moved.

"There are crimes that raise the anger, the disgust, to the point that the State must take charge and make their authors disappear," Jean Lecanuet, the former minister of justice, explained. "If not, the anger will turn against the State, against justice, and it will install a climate of vengeance and settling of accounts."

There was the inevitable rush of books weighing in on the subject. Some of the most insightful work was published by Jacques Léauté at the Institute of Criminology in Paris. He compiled statistics from the

Western European countries where the death penalty had been eliminated to show there had been no rise in either murders or violent crimes after abolition.

It was compelling material, but over the decades there had been endless academic studies released that either supported or discredited the deterrence value of the death penalty, depending on how their authors had juggled the numbers. In the end, perhaps the best evidence was simply anecdotal: in nineteenth-century England, when theft was a capital offense, the police noted a huge number of thefts reported during the public hangings; pickpockets were working the distracted crowds, reaping small fortunes as people watched their fellow thieves' necks get snapped.

Even pop stars entered the fray. Michel Sardou was one of the bestselling French musicians of the 1970s and was a source of constant controversy. He'd been accused of misogyny for lyrics such as "I want to rape women and force them to admire me" and of glorifying French colonial days with lines like "I had lots of black servants / And four girls in my bed."

Then there was "*Je suis pour*" (I Am For). In this angry song that manages to combine both disco and anthem rock, Sardou adopts the voice of a father whose son has been murdered. After denouncing the imbeciles and philosophers who oppose the death penalty, Sardou claims even Jesus wouldn't stand beside a child killer. His chorus screams:

> *You killed a child of love.*
> *I will have your death.*
> *I am for.*

At the same time, Julien Clerc advocated for abolition. Clerc made his name by creating the French version of the musical *Hair* in 1969, and he went on to release more than twenty albums. In 1976, he recorded "*L'Assassin assassiné*" (The Murderer Murdered), the reflections of a musician on the afternoon a man is guillotined. He sings:

> *The blood of a condemned man*
> *Is still the blood of a man.*
> *When the blade falls,*
> *The crime changes sides.*

So it was that, from bookstores to radio stations to editorial columns, the death penalty debate consumed France. But at least one person wouldn't be swayed by these polemics. Jean Goudareau already knew exactly how he felt about the guillotine. He was all for it.

"I was in favor of the death penalty for certain cases," Goudareau explained. "Drug dealers, the killers of children, the killers of police officers."

And not only was Hamida Djandoubi's lawyer in favor of capital punishment, he actually felt it should be carried out more often. In dismissing the work of Jacques Léauté, Goudareau argued: "They always say the death penalty isn't dissuasive. Why not? Because it is only applied every two years."

An unusual philosophy for a defense lawyer handling one of the most important death penalty cases of the decade.

36

AFTER SO MANY MONTHS of torture and hell, Annie and Amaria were slowly reassembling their lives.

Upon being released from prison, Annie got a job minding children for a family in her neighborhood. Her employer was happy enough, reporting that she was "conscientious, gentle, and honest around the house." At home, her parents said Annie was quiet and respectful, mostly watching television or spending time with her brothers and sisters.

Throughout that first year, Annie showed signs of lethargy and depression. In August 1975, just before the anniversary of the arrests, her doctor recommended she take a vacation in hopes that the change in scenery would do her good. Judge Llaurens gave her permission to leave Marseille, and on that trip, she met a young man. Annie was grateful for a chance to start again, and things developed quickly. In April 1976, the couple was married. Judge Llaurens amended Annie's release conditions to allow her to live with her new husband in the west of France.*

As for Amaria, if she thought her parents had been strict prior to her meeting Hamida Djandoubi, it was nothing compared to life after her release from prison. She could see only a select group of friends, she was never allowed beyond the confines of the apartment complex without explicit permission, and there was once more talk of an arranged marriage in Algeria. Slowly, after proving herself to her parents and local social workers, Amaria began to earn more freedom

---

* I have kept the details of both Annie's and Amaria's new lives to a minimum in an effort to reduce any chance that the women might be identified. The use of their names and last initials was considered appropriate by both court officials and women's counselors.

and responsibility. By 1976, she was working in a fabric factory and was described as a "wise and attentive" worker.

But neither woman could stop thinking about the impending trial. There was no sign that the charges against them were going to be dropped, and their lawyers were preparing them for the possibility that they might have to return to prison. Amaria couldn't bear the thought.

"I beg you to help me," she wrote her lawyer. "I want to forget everything. I am so ashamed."

*

*   *

HAMIDA'S LIFE WAS gray and routine. He was kept in the QHS—the Quartier Haute Sécurité—at the Baumettes prison and was allowed little contact with other prisoners. Yet despite his relative isolation, he continued to aggravate people. The QHS was also the location of *le cachot* (the cell for solitary confinement) for prisoners who'd broken prison rules by mouthing off to guards, fighting, being caught with hashish, or any number of offenses. Everybody in the wing resented Hamida because he would sleep all day and then pace his cell all night. The noise kept the other prisoners awake.

"It was *thump-click, thump-click, thump-click,* the sound of his fake leg, all night long," remembers Patrick Dallari, one of those prisoners.* "We asked him to stop. He didn't care. He was a real *casse-couilles.*" A ball-breaker.

Hamida didn't avail himself of the prison library or the array of remedial courses on offer inside the prison. That made for a minimum of distractions. In January 1976, he pled guilty to the theft charges stemming from the stolen auto parts. He was sentenced to six months in jail and fined 175 francs and 25 centimes. A few months later, his amputated leg, which would be so pivotal at his trial, began

---

* The director of the prison's cultural program arranged for me to visit the QHS on the condition that I repay the favor by giving seminars in the multimedia center. By chance, Dallari attended one of my seminars and shared his memories of Hamida Djandoubi.

swelling. After numerous complaints, he was fitted for another prosthesis in May 1976. He was escorted by three police officers the day he received his new plastic leg.

By this point, Hamida had dropped all contact with his old friends, refusing to answer their letters. His brother had disappeared with the Simca, and Hamida didn't let Goudareau notify his family in Tunisia. At first, the prison imam tried to convince him to return to Islam, but Hamida wouldn't accept the man's visits. Nor did he respond to entreaties from a Catholic priest by the name of Paul Edmonds, who assured him that from heaven Elisabeth Bousquet had already forgiven him.

The only person Hamida really spoke with was Goudareau. They met several times a month in the lawyer's room at the prison. It was a sparse setting, furnished with nothing but two wooden chairs and a table. Goudareau always brought American cigarettes because Hamida preferred blond tobacco to the dark French cigarettes available at the prison canteen.

"We talked a lot about the time before his accident, how much he loved Marseille," Goudareau remembered. "I tried to get him to talk about his family, his childhood, but he never wanted to, so I abandoned the subject."

There was also the case to discuss. Goudareau had made progress on one important front. After attending a conference in Nice on the aftereffects of amputation, he became convinced that the psychiatric evaluations Hamida had undergone had been prejudicial. He suspected that one of the court doctors, René Suttel, was biased and slanted his reports to favor the prosecution. Goudareau's instinct would ultimately be proven corect. In an interview with *Le Nouvel Observateur*, Dr. Suttel explained that he'd become a court psychiatrist in the 1940s because he wanted to help the countless men and women who were wrongfully ensnared in prison when they should be in psychiatric hospitals. After decades in the system, however, he'd succumbed to cynicism and become a proponent of the death penalty.

"When it comes to punishments, I tell you this is the only one that completely excludes any chance of recidivism," Dr. Suttel told the magazine. "I tell you, there are types who will kill and kill again otherwise."

Goudareau was able to convince Judge Llaurens that a more balanced opinion was needed, and one final evaluation was ordered. It was to be Hamida's last chance to curry medical favor, and Goudareau urged him to try to be more sympathetic. Alas, the results were barely more positive.

"Underneath an appearance of calm, levelheadedness, and equilibrium, Djandoubi in fact lacks emotional control and stability," the doctors wrote. Their conclusion was that Hamida's aggression stemmed "to a large part" from the amputation, but this same physical handicap would limit any efforts at rehabilitation.

It wasn't what Goudareau wanted. He would have preferred the conclusion that Dostoyevsky reached in *The House of the Dead*: "The criminal, at the moment he accomplishes his crime, is always sick."

For Goudareau, it was the latest blow to his defense. He had no doctors to support his theories, and there were few people willing to come forward to testify on Hamida's behalf. And since under French law there is no such thing as a plea bargain, Goudareau couldn't even throw in the towel and have Hamida plead guilty in hopes of getting a life sentence instead of the guillotine.

It was the most difficult of defenses. There was no question of innocence; the crime was utterly barbaric; and the criminal himself had no redeeming qualities. The only reason to reject the death penalty for Hamida Djandoubi was if one morally and philosophically rejected the very principle of the death penalty. And this is what truly undermined Goudareau's efforts.

In Paris, Robert Badinter was weaving the moral and religious arguments against capital punishment into his defense of Patrick Henry. Goudareau couldn't avail himself of this same tactic; how could he appeal to the jurors' consciences when he himself wasn't troubled by the guillotine?

"It is a just penalty," Goudareau would say. "I was one of the few defense lawyers who would say so. Nine out of ten lawyers didn't have the courage to support the death penalty publicly, but I did."

But this "courage" was exposing Goudareau to criticism. In Marseille and in Aix-en-Provence, the courthouses were already buzzing over the fact that Goudareau would be handling the biggest death penalty case of the coming year.

"We can have all the opinions we want on the condition that we do our job properly," said Jean-Daniel Bruschi, the lawyer representing Houria and her family in their *action civile*. "If you don't like Arabs, and your client is an Arab, and if he faces the death penalty and you are for the death penalty, well, at that point, you have to make a little effort."

By November 1976, Judge Llaurens declared the investigation complete. In the end, she filed prostitution charges against Hamida. Although the police hadn't obtained any additional physical evidence or outside corroboration, she decided the testimony of the girls was enough to warrant the charges.

As per French law, the file was sent to another court, the *chambre d'accusation*, for a form of pretrial to ensure there was enough evidence to proceed and to make the charges official. The lawyers and defendants were convoked at the end of November 1976. To no one's surprise, on December 1 the decision was announced: Hamida, Annie, and Amaria would go to trial in February 1977.

*

*   *

THE NEW YEAR broke with the return of capital punishment in the United States. Gary Gilmore was executed by firing squad in Utah on January 17, 1977. The ACLU and various abolitionist groups had wanted to use the case as a challenge to the *Gregg v. Georgia* ruling, but Gilmore, convicted of murdering a motel owner, would have none of it. He wanted to die and had twice attempted to take his own life while in prison.

The Gilmore case added another hue to the abolition discussion. The death penalty could now be seen as state-assisted suicide. It was a modern variation on Kant's eighteenth-century philosophy: at times, the death penalty was an act of mercy because for certain men death was a lesser punishment than having to endure a lifetime of shame in a prison cell.

And the Gilmore execution conveniently marked another major step in Robert Badinter's fight against the death penalty in France. In 1972 the U.S. Supreme Court had abolished capital punishment the same day his client Roger Bontems was sentenced to die. Now, the day before the most important trial of his life, events in America once again provided a chilling juxtaposition to Badinter's work.

*

*   *

ONE OF THE VICTIMS of the bedlam surrounding the Patrick Henry affair was Robert Badinter himself. He received so much hate mail that he filled a garbage bag, which his children affectionately called "Madame Poubelle," Madame Trashcan. One evening, he and his wife came home from a dinner to find fire trucks and police officers in front of their apartment building beside the Jardin du Luxembourg. A homemade bomb had gone off outside their door. The lawyer was under siege for his beliefs.

On January 18, 1977, a little more than a month before Hamida's trial was scheduled to begin, Henry's got under way in Troyes. As with Hamida, there was no question of guilt or innocence. Henry had confessed to murdering the little boy. All that remained to be answered was whether the punishment would be life imprisonment or the guillotine.

Badinter's strategy was to attack the death penalty itself. He called upon Father Clavier, the priest who escorted prisoners to the guillotine, to describe the cold ritual of official death. "Society should not respond to horror with horror," the priest told the jury. Then the criminologist Jacques Léauté testified that the death penalty had no effect on crime rates, calling the dissuasive value of the guillotine a "myth." Badinter also read a letter from Christian Ranucci's mother. "The partisans of the death penalty are proving their ferocity in this case," she wrote. "They can never imagine that their son or their brother might find themselves in such a place."

And finally, there was Badinter himself. Taking the same spot where he argued so fruitlessly for Bontems, Badinter now told the jury they would be killing Henry themselves if they voted for the death penalty. There were no grounds of appeal. And as President Giscard had shown with Ranucci, there was no clemency for child killers.

"We are going to abolish the death penalty, which means you will be left alone with your verdict, forever," he told the jurors. "Your children will know that one day you condemned a young man to death. And you will see how they look at you."

After an hour and a half of deliberation, the jury came back with its decision. Patrick Henry was sentenced to life in prison. There would be no guillotining.*

It was also almost certainly the end of the death penalty. If the reviled Patrick Henry couldn't be put to death, who could? The national

---

*Patrick Henry further tarnished his name and undermined the efforts made on his behalf by fumbling his second chance at life. After being granted parole in 2001, he was first caught shoplifting in June 2002 and then arrested and found guilty of smuggling more than twenty pounds of hashish into France.

news magazines came to this very conclusion. *Le Nouvel Observateur* decided, "It wasn't Patrick Henry that the jurors absolved, it was the death penalty that they condemned." *Le Point* ran its story under the headline: "THE DEATH OF THE DEATH PENALTY."

In Marseille, it was the best news Hamida Djandoubi had heard since his arrest.

37

UNLIKE THE PATRICK HENRY affair, there wasn't a glimmer of national media coverage leading up to Hamida Djandoubi's trial. As a rule, the big newspapers were more concerned with French politics and international events. That week, there was the usual round of French strikes; a raft of gossip surrounding Jacques Chirac's run for the Paris mayor's office; in Israel, Yitzhak Rabin had beaten Shimon Peres to become leader of the Labour Party; Jimmy Carter announced there would be a sixty-eight-billion-dollar budget deficit in the U.S.; and Quebec had elected a separatist leader named René Lévesque, reigniting talk that Canada would break into two countries.

It wasn't that national newspapers didn't follow crime. Even if there wasn't a case of the magnitude of Patrick Henry's or Christian Ranucci's, *Le Monde, Le Figaro,* and *Libération* nonetheless devoted a page or half page a day to police matters. It just so happened that the week of Hamida's trial, that slot was filled by another murderous amputee in the south of France.

Jean-Baptiste Dorkel, or "the Madman of the 504," as the newspapers called him, had been cruising around in his Peugeot 504 and running cars off the highway at random. This little game came to a tragic head in August 1975. A family of four was driving home in their small Citroën when Dorkel raced up from behind and forced their car off a cliff. Miraculously, the father and the two daughters suffered only minor injuries, but the mother was killed.

Farther up the same highway, Dorkel tried to run a Fiat off the road. This time, the driver escaped and jotted down the license plate. Police arrested Dorkel and discovered that the nineteen-year-old man was both functionally and emotionally illiterate. He was so perplexed by life he couldn't even explain when or how his right arm had been amputated. Psychiatrists described him as having "*Clockwork Orange*–type sadism."

Dorkel's trial was held the same week as Hamida's. For a full day, he steadfastly denied all charges. Then the prosecutor brought up his father.

"Imagine if your father, who you loved so much, was here and said, 'Calotte'—because that is what he called you when you were a little boy—'Calotte, if you don't tell me the truth, I'm going to lose my temper like you've never seen before.' What would you say?"

"I would tell him," answered Dorkel.

"Tell him what?"

"Yes, it was me."

Dorkel was found guilty and sentenced to eighteen years in prison.

*

*　*

THE COMPASSION SHOWN to one amputee with a troubled past might have been encouraging for Hamida Djandoubi. Except Dorkel hadn't brutally tortured his victims for three hours before driving them off the road. And his skin was white.

Race was always a consideration when justice was dispensed in the south of France. In his memoir, Émile Pollak wrote, "A ghost prowls the high courts, a ghost that is odious and still active: racism."

Pollak knew from experience. He'd defended an Algerian man in an assault case that should have been an obvious acquittal. Two drunken legionnaires had chased the Algerian through the streets of Marseille, threatening to kill him. When the Algerian was finally cornered, he took out a knife and stabbed one of the legionnaires. Astonishingly, the judge rejected the argument of self-defense despite the injured legionnaire's admission that he had provoked the attack. Under sentencing guidelines, the Algerian should have received between one and five years in prison. The guilty verdict itself was so outrageous, Pollak assumed the sentence would be on the low end of the scale. Instead, his client got twenty years in prison. *Le Figaro* drily observed that, when it comes to French justice, "It's better to be named Marius than Mohamed."

This same racism infiltrated the Hamida Djandoubi case. Some of the prejudice was laughable: several psychiatrists and police officers accused him of having a cultural inclination toward polygamy. Some of it was plainly distasteful: "A certain number of people said, 'Well, Elisabeth got what she deserved for sleeping with an Arab, or Annie got what she deserved for dating an Arab,'" remembered Jean-Jacques Anglade.

Not that the French president was setting any positive examples. In Paris, Valéry Giscard d'Estaing had organized a forum between religious communities and the French government. Catholics, Protestants, Lutherans, Baptists, Jews—all received invitations to the Élysée Palace. But not a single imam.

*

* *

IF ONE WERE LOOKING for portentous events in the days before Hamida's trial opened, there was no shortage.

In Paris, Albert Naud, the lawyer who had been such a vigilant opponent of the death penalty, died of edema of the lungs. In his obituary, *Le Monde* observed: "He will not, then, see the success of the fight which he led for more than 30 years against the death penalty."

Naud, in the belief that everyone deserved a defense, had represented some of the more nauseating characters in twentieth-century France. It was Naud, for example, who defended Louis-Ferdinand Céline on obscenity charges. Céline, whose *Voyage to the End of the Night* remains a classic of French literature, had asserted that the Vichy government hadn't gone far enough by shipping Jews to the camps; he thought all Africans and children of mixed parents should have been gassed. Naud also defended Pierre Laval, the

Vichy politician who attempted to avoid execution by committing suicide.

"The death penalty," wrote Naud of the experience. "From the moment it is pronounced, it becomes a cross for the lawyer to bear."

Yet if Naud's death was a bad omen, there were some concretely positive signs as well. At the same Aix-en-Provence courthouse where Hamida would be tried, a prosecutor denounced the Patrick Henry verdict and requested the death penalty. He was rebuffed by the jury, leading *Libération* to declare, *"Le test Patrick Henry a fonctionné."* The Patrick Henry test worked.

Still, not everybody was quite so convinced. In Troyes, the members of the jury who spared Patrick Henry were receiving death threats at their homes. A television poll determined 83 percent of the French supported the death penalty. And Giscard announced there was still both "pressure and need" to maintain the guillotine.

Jean Goudareau certainly didn't put any faith in the Patrick Henry "test," for he too believed the jurors had made a mistake. "Personally," Goudareau said, "I would have cut his . . . I would have condemned him to death three times, not once."

*

*   *

TROUBLED BY HIS CLIENT'S poor performance before the psychiatrists, Goudareau thought Hamida should work on his court demeanor.

"He had trouble speaking in public," Goudareau said. "He was always very sociable with me, but if there were large groups he would become quiet and have trouble expressing himself."

Goudareau thought the best solution was to have Hamida prepare a statement apologizing for his crime, something that would give him a base to work from in court. In the final days before his trial, Hamida wrote about his life. He said he wasn't very bright as a child, he talked about his fights with his uncle and his desire to move to France. He concluded:

I used to be very nice to everybody. I gave presents to everybody who helped me. I had confidence in anybody. I never hung out with thugs.

During these two years I have been living in prison, I have reflected a lot. What I did was terrible. I did it in a moment of madness and I regret it from the bottom of my heart.

*

*   *

IF HAMIDA DJANDOUBI was making a halfhearted attempt to apologize, some members of the Bousquet family were making a genuine effort to forgive—not Hamida, but Annie and Amaria.

After reviewing the court documents, Éliane Perasso, the lawyer representing Pierre, Jean-Pierre, and Marie-Josée Bousquet, concluded the girls were victims, not criminals.

The conclusion wasn't surprising: Perasso had been working on women's issues in France for more than a decade and was a leading authority on feminism in Marseille. Her 1973 book, *Ne pleure pas, hurle!* (Don't Cry, Yell!), attacked the blatant machismo of French politics. Her arguments were persuasive: in the early 1970s, 53 percent of voters were women but only 2 percent of elected politicians were women.

"This world is unjust, and, as a result, murderous. I refuse to submit to it because it has been constructed against the Woman and the Child," Perasso wrote. "I will not ignore that women have only barely left the darkness, that the liberation movements have left them behind."

Nothing proved Perasso's point better than the French rape laws in the 1970s. At the time, rape was still considered a minor offense and tried in the correctional courts, along with shoplifting and traffic infractions. Worse, the choice of whether or not the case would be tried in a closed courtroom wasn't up to the victim: it was the man charged with rape who got to decide whether the hearing would be public or private.

In Marseille, these laws were thrust into the spotlight by the Calanques rape case. The Calanques are the staggeringly beautiful cliffs that run along the coast between Marseille and Cassis and are the home of the famous Grotte Cosquet and the thirty-five-thousand-year-old handprints. In August 1974, two young Belgian women were camping overnight when several drunken men stumbled upon their tent and raped them. When the women tried to resist, they were beaten with a hammer.

The two women hiked back into Marseille that night to report the rape. But the authorities refused to take the case seriously. The men claimed the sex was consensual, and the police were more concerned with what two women were doing camping alone in the Calanques. It was only after the women enlisted Gisèle Halimi, the lawyer who'd handled the Bobigny abortion case, that the police gave the case the attention it begged for.

Perasso saw Annie and Amaria as victims of the same strain of violence and discrimination that was plaguing France. She raised her concerns with the Bousquet family and found a receptive audience. The Bousquets, despite their profound suffering, remained deeply compassionate. After having the facts of the ordeal suffered by Annie and Amaria laid out before them, they agreed to drop their civil prosecution of the girls.

"Hamida Djandoubi killed one woman and destroyed the lives of three others," Perasso said. "It seemed absurd that we would make life harder for those two young women."

Perasso wasn't the only one alarmed by the misogyny of Hamida Djandoubi's crimes. A nonprofit association that worked on behalf of women who were the victims of violence successfully petitioned to be heard at the trial. Part of its complaint read: "Djandoubi used prostitution's sadistic repertoire of sadism, perversion, cruelty, and, without the least bit of humanity, ground down the souls of those whom he captured."

The case was rightfully placed in the context of the larger problem of violence against French women. Yet, unthinkably, once the trial began Goudareau would further stoke the anger the women's groups felt toward his client.

*

* *

THE PROSECUTOR WHO had the Hamida Djandoubi case was Yves Chauvy. He was a man who was relentless in the pursuit of his goals. After taking an interest in mountaineering a few years earlier, he'd completely devoted himself to climbing. He'd already reached the summit of both Mont Blanc, at 15,750 feet the highest mountain in Western Europe, and Mont Rose, the second-highest peak in the Alps at 15,100 feet.

Chauvy moved just as determinedly through the prosecutorial ranks. When choosing his law career, he decided he had an accusatory personality—"*Je suis plutôt répressif,*" he would say—so he became a state attorney. His first position was in Montélimar, the famous nougat town an hour north of Marseille, where he married his wife in 1957. He would hold another fourteen posts in eleven different cites in his career. What earned him notice at the ministry of justice was organizing a mass prosecution single-handedly in 1969. A group of small-business owners held a protest against high taxes, and things turned riotous, with rocks thrown and injuries inflicted. Chauvy managed to charge thirty-three men and win seventeen convictions.

In 1975 Chauvy arrived in Aix-en-Provence and quickly established a law-and-order reputation. When the Djandoubi file landed on his desk in November 1976, the vital question was what sentence he would request. The Bousquet family had made it clear they were opposed to the death penalty. "We believe that an evolved society cannot dispense death, not even to murderers, not even to Monsieur Djandoubi," they said through a spokesperson.

But the decision was up to Chauvy and Chauvy alone. He felt there were "extremely grave facts." He approved of the Christian Ranucci execution: "I have confidence in the jury and my colleagues." And he felt the Patrick Henry decision was "deplorable."

It was a healthy indication of what punishment he would ask the jury to deliver.

*
* *

IF THE NATIONAL MEDIA were oblivious to the Hamida Djandoubi affair, the Marseille newspapers certainly weren't going to overlook such tantalizing material.

The crime was too sensational to abide by any notion of maintaining a fair trial. On Tuesday, February 23, 1977, two days before the trial was to begin, *Le Provençal* ran a smiling picture of Hamida with the headline "*TORTURÉE À MORT PAR UN PROXÉNÈTE.*" Tortured to Death by a Pimp. The crime was described in explicit detail, right down to the very cigarette burns.

La Marseillaise decided to lead with the abolition issue. The day of the trial, under the headline "A HORRIBLE CRIME," the article began: "The death penalty and above all horror will hover over the debates today at the courthouse in Aix-en-Provence."

The right-wing newspaper *Le Méridional* wasn't known to mince words. Its preview article began, "A 27-year-old Tunisian, Hamida Djandoubi, a perverse, cruel, and sadistic pimp who is guilty of having committed a crime more horrible than the most perverted soul could even imagine, will appear today before the Cour d'Assises in Aix-en-Provence."

As dramatic as the lead was, the article's conclusion was ultimately more pertinent.

"Will the death penalty be requested? Will it be obtained?"

38

THE COURTHOUSE IS IN the heart of Aix-en-Provence, just a few dozen paces off the tree-lined cours Mirabeau. Like most everything in this city, it sits atop ruins: Aix was the first Roman city in France, founded as "Aquae Sextiae" in 122 B.C., a time when Massalia to the south was still firmly in the hands of the Greeks.

Construction on the courthouse began in 1787, and the building was inaugurated in 1847. Busts of Siméon and Portalis, two of the more famous Aixois lawyers, stand on either side of the broad main entrance, and the courtrooms are arranged around a large square atrium. The most distinguishing feature is the lack of a roof over this atrium, a rather unsubtle message from the architect: the light of truth will shine here.

In France, justice is incredibly succinct. Instead of trials that drag on for weeks or months, even the most complicated cases are heard in three or four days. With Hamida Djandoubi, as the question of innocence or guilt wasn't to be decided, the courtroom was reserved for only two days.

The trial was to begin at 8:30 A.M. on Thursday, February 24, 1977. There weren't the same frothing crowds as when Ranucci was tried in the same courtroom the year before. But the evil of the crime—and the lurid articles in the newspapers—drew no small number of onlookers. By one estimate, more than a hundred people huddled outside the courthouse in the chilly dawn air, hoping to get a seat at the show.

That morning, Hamida wore a beige suit with a patterned shirt underneath. Two guards escorted him into the courtroom, but he was neither handcuffed nor chained at the feet. He paused to shake Jean Goudareau's hand before being steered to the prisoner's dock. When he turned to survey the crowd, there was a murmur of awe from the assembled journalists. Although much had been made of Hamida's looks, this was the first time the reporters had seen him in person.

"It is true, he is a handsome man with his matte complexion, his black hair, his dark, alert eyes," wrote Micheline Deville in *Le Soir*. "I have asked myself who he made me think of. The answer came: Harry Belafonte, that sweet American singer, that supple dancer. So it is, we don't always have the face of our soul."

*

*   *

THE PRESIDING JUDGE on the case was Henri Vuillet, a thirty-year veteran of the court. He was known for his rigid control over trials. He called the court to session precisely on time.

The first task was jury selection. Twenty-three potential jurors—nineteen men and four women—had been selected at random from the voters' lists and summoned to the courthouse. Their names were written on index cards and pulled one at a time from an urn until they had a jury of nine. The prosecutor, Yves Chauvy, had the right to exclude four jurors, and Jean Goudareau, five. Neither was allowed to ask questions; they could only consult the voters' list that gave the name, age, place of birth, and profession of each potential juror.

Goudareau ended up excluding four potential jurors. All four of the women's names were pulled from the urn, and Goudareau rejected each one. "Considering the circumstances of the offense, I thought it best to avoid the women," Goudareau later said.

At the front of the courtroom was a long desk on a raised platform. Judge Vuillet was seated at the center, and the jury fanned out on either side. At the ends were two more judges, court-appointed magistrates who sat with the jury, answered questions on the technicalities of law, and voted on the verdict.

The list of witnesses was called to make sure all were in attendance. Summonses had gone out to more than two dozen people, but there were still key absences: several psychiatrists had prior engagements; Elisabeth's mother, Alphonsine, claimed she was too ill to attend the trial; Houria's mother hadn't made the trip from Lodève; and Ali Djandoubi was conveniently missing. Of greatest consequence would be the fact that Marie-Claude Kervella, Hamida's neighbor at 17, rue Villa Paradis, wasn't there. The police hadn't been able to deliver her summons because she'd moved.

*

*   *

UNLIKE AMERICAN AND English courts, where the judge serves as an impartial observer and intervenes only on points of law, in France the judge propels all aspects of the trial. He chooses the order in which witnesses are heard and leads the questioning of those witnesses. In the Hamida Djandoubi case, Judge Vuillet began by summarizing the dossier. He read out each excruciating detail of the torture, every observation from the autopsy, each nuance of Hamida's confession. The travesties cataloged, Judge Vuillet turned to the accused. Why?

"I wanted to know why she made the complaint against me," Hamida answered. "I started to hit her and then I don't know what happened."

"You hit her with a club, you hit her with a belt. You made her get undressed. You forced the club into her vagina. Isn't that true?"

"I don't remember," he claimed. "I was drunk. I had taken LSD."

Judge Vuillet reminded him that none of the medical tests revealed any drug other than alcohol in his system at the time of his arrest. Now was not the time to start a fresh round of lies.

"Since my amputation, I am not the same man," Hamida tried to continue. "I don't know what happened."

"Come on, take responsibility for your acts," snapped the judge. "You're not an amnesiac."

This much was true. Hamida would have no trouble recalling certain details.

"You poured gas onto her stomach and lit her on fire, isn't that true?" asked Judge Vuillet.

"It was only a couple of drops," Hamida protested.

Word by word, Hamida was digging his grave. Even his lawyer seemed surprised by the aloof answers. Observers in the courtroom covered their faces in despair. A journalist described the scene: "We have penetrated the hell described by Pasolini in *Salò, or the 120 Days of Sodom.*"

Others were more melodramatic. "The public's trembling faces reflected all the pity in the world for this martyr, but also all the horror her perverse executioner inspired. We speak of the Christian martyrs, those who suffered under Hitler, and, now, this woman."

*

* *

HAMIDA LEFT THE STAND having done nothing to win sympathy from the jurors. Now Judge Vuillet called the psychiatrists. They would only heap more misery upon the accused.

"There is no therapy whatsoever that can help a pervert," Dr. Merlin told the court. "There is only one criminal sentence that will be efficient."

Yves Chauvy pressed for more. Could Hamida's behavior be attributed to his amputation?

"What I wanted to say was that this perversity has always been in him," Merlin obligingly added.

Dr. Boukson appeared as the key expert for the defense, and under guidance from Goudareau, he spoke of the tractor accident. "The amputated leg isn't a negligible trauma," Boukson told the court. "This social check, without a doubt, triggered a regression that, without a doubt, ended with this explosion of sadism."

Before breaking for lunch, Dr. Boukson added one more thing: "It was an escalation of violence and perversity. It was like he was a gambler who turns himself over to his vice and is willing to play until his own suicide." The news of the original prostitution complaint against Hamida sent a wave of murmurs through the courtroom. "I couldn't help but think," wrote the journalist Riou Rouvet, "that if the complaint made by the unhappy Elisabeth in 1973 had been properly handled . . . maybe this young woman would be alive today."

That afternoon the police witnesses gave the details of the investigation and the arrest.

Once the police were finished, it was the girls' turn. Annie went first, and under gentle questioning from Judge Vuillet, recounted the details of the event. She spoke in a calm voice, looked the judge in the eye, and barely glanced at where Hamida was sitting.

First Annie and then Amaria explained how Hamida had caught them in his violent trap and took control of their lives. The jurors began nodding in compassion. But it was Houria who truly absolved the girls when she took the stand.

"It was a nightmare for all of us," she told the court. "I don't blame Annie and Amaria. There was nothing we could do."

Throughout, Goudareau chose not to challenge the facts or aggressively question the witnesses. In his mind, his best chance—his only chance—was the final plea. There was only one moment when Goudareau made a true objection. Near the end of the day, as the final witnesses were being called, he pounced on the fact that the police hadn't been able to deliver the summons to Marie-Claude Kervella. He quickly jotted a letter to the judge and placed it on Judge Vuillet's desk.

"It is indispensable to the manifestation of the truth that the witness Kervella, who was requested by the Public Minister by the normal regulations, be searched for in all possible locations," Goudareau wrote.

He asked to have the trial postponed at least twenty-four hours, and preferably for several weeks, until the next court session. Judge Vuillet reviewed the petition but rejected it as "baseless."

The actual value of Kervella as a witness was minimal; the best she could do was speak to Hamida's human side. But her absence could prove pivotal. The failure to deliver the summons was grounds for appeal.

*

*   *

THE DAY CLOSED with those who knew Hamida Djandoubi from before the accident. Goudareau asked them each to describe their friendship with Hamida and any changes they'd noticed. "He was just a different person," Louis Bugia told the court. "I can't explain how he could have changed like this."

Bugia was the final witness. As he walked to the door of the courtroom, he glanced back and saw Hamida staring after him. "I thought I saw a tear on his cheek," Bugia remembered.

At 7:30 P.M., the session closed for the day. Court would reconvene the next morning with the closing arguments from the prosecution and the defense.

The newspaper reporters hurried to meet their deadlines. They were unanimous in their revulsion. "THE TORTURING PIMP" announced one headline. "HIS DEMONIC SOUL" was another. Or simply "THE PIMP'S HORRIBLE CRIME."

The journalists were also in agreement when it came to Goudareau's task the next day.

"Hopeless," wrote Alex Panzani in *La Marseillaise*.

*

*   *

ON FRIDAY, THE proceedings got off to a calamitous beginning for the defense. The jury was seated, Hamida Djandoubi was in the prisoner's dock, and the prosecution was ready to proceed. But Jean Goudareau was missing.

Judge Vuillet, who wanted his judicial ship run tightly, was obviously annoyed. After a brief wait, he saw Jean-Jacques Anglade sitting in the audience. Vuillet ordered him, the only lawyer in the room not directly involved in the Djandoubi trial, to stand in for Goudareau.

Anglade was flabbergasted. That afternoon, he had to defend Annie and Amaria in youth court. He was only in the courtroom to observe Hamida's trial on the chance he could glean something helpful for his clients. Ethically, he didn't think he could actually represent Hamida Djandoubi.

Anglade told the judge he was opposed to the request and called the head of the Aix bar to consult on the matter. The two lawyers agreed that Anglade had no business stepping in for Goudareau. He reentered the court and officially refused the request.

According to Anglade, the judge smiled and called a recess. As the courtroom emptied, Vuillet took Anglade aside and said, "You have put the jury's backs up; I will have his head."

"He wasn't upset at all," Anglade remembered. "He just wanted to force me to decline in front of the jury, to show that defense lawyers had attitudes, that they respect nothing. It was a manner of devaluing the defense."

Goudareau arrived a short time later. He'd been stuck in traffic.

*

*   *

FRIDAY MORNING HELD another curiosity for those in the courtroom. On Thursday, Pierre Bousquet had watched the trial alongside his lawyer, Éliane Perasso. As he heard the appalling details of his daughter's death, his face crumpled in anguish and despair. Still, nobody expected the change in him. When he arrived the next day, his hair had turned nearly completely white.*

"It looked as if he'd aged twenty years," Perasso remembered. "I couldn't believe it was the same man."

---

* There is at least one happy ending in the Bousquet story: the trauma of their daughter's murder eventually brought Pierre and Alphonsine back together and they were able to repair their marriage.

This sad transformation of the murdered girl's father only added more weight to what Yves Chauvy was planning to say.

Whenever Chauvy wrote his final submissions, he always had the same intention: to place the jury in the shoes of the victim and the victim's family so they would see the need for extreme justice. As he stood in the courtroom that morning, with the traumatized Bousquet family behind him, this is exactly what he did.

"Enter into Djandoubi's hell. We see a sordid and cruel scene, a collection of the most shameful perversions, a man lazy to his very being, unstable in his work even before his accident, a demonic soul dedicated to evil. Evil is his gourmet pleasure. It is for this type of hell, this torture, this murder, this barbarity, that the law has created a fundamental penalty: the death penalty.

"Beware of the school quarrels and parlor discussions. I do not need to debate this penalty because it exists today. When someone rapes, someone tortures, and someone kills, we must think of the victims. You are a jury of men who have the honor of protecting women. Remember, a large majority of French people favor a firm and efficient justice.

"You are not here today to judge the law. You are not here to judge the penalty. You are here to judge an individual case and your role is to apply the law in the name of this nation.

"The penalty that I claim for society is the death penalty."

*

* *

GOUDAREAU BEGAN HIS defense of Hamida's life with friendship. His clientele, he told the jury, didn't consist of hoods and criminals. He was a business lawyer. But, as he knew Hamida and liked him, he was standing by him in court.

"After his crime, he extended his hand toward me, and I didn't believe it possible to refuse him mine," he told the jury. "This job weighs heavily on my shoulders."

Surprisingly, Goudareau used much of his final plea to denounce those accusations that most bothered Hamida: that he had acted as a pimp. Goudareau told the jury that the girls were lying, that his client didn't need the money, that he had never wanted his girlfriends to prostitute for him.

"My client made mistakes, but in his heart he loved those girls and wanted no harm to come to them," Goudareau said. "He would not have put them on the street and he did not put them on the street."

Then Goudareau raised the issue of the amputated leg. He chose a metaphor that mystified many in the courtroom. At the time, there was a popular French quiz show, *La Tête et les jambes*. The gimmick of the show was that two contestants worked together: one noted for his or her cultural acumen, the "head," and the other an athletic type, the "legs." As the show unfolded, the "head" was asked a series of questions; if he or she couldn't answer them correctly, the "legs" would have to perform ridiculous physical challenges such as crossing muddy ponds blindfolded. The "head" could thus save the "legs" from painful exertions.

"In this case, it is the reverse," Goudareau told the jury. "My client's leg will save his head."

Unaware of the general puzzlement in the courtroom, Goudareau explained again how Hamida had lost his leg and described the downward spiral of his life since that fateful accident.

"It is not a matter of forgiving this man, but understanding him," Goudareau said. "He suffered a horrible trauma and it resulted in his transformation. He suffered so he began to drink, and as he began to drink he became violent."

Goudareau concluded by fighting the accusation that the crime had been planned. Without premeditation, there could be no death penalty.

"Yes, the death was atrocious and lasted all afternoon and into the evening," Goudareau explained. "The accused was overcome by his rage and anger and didn't know how to stop the madness. I ask you to understand this man's sickness and to act accordingly. This man deserves to spend the rest of his life in prison for what he did. But his death will solve nothing."

Goudareau retook his seat at the defense bench. Judge Vuillet offered Hamida the last word. Rising from the prisoner's dock, he began to speak.

"What I did was horrible and I know I regret it. Since my amputation, I haven't been the same. I have been edgy, very different. Nobody wanted me for work and I became crazy. I ask Elisabeth's parents to forgive me. I ask everybody to forgive me, and I ask the jurors to understand me."

Everyone in the courtroom thought it sounded like Hamida was reciting from a text.

The jury retired to the deliberation room. In the meantime, Hamida was escorted back to his cell. By all accounts, he was stunned by what had transpired. A guard reported back to the judge that he kept protesting, "The death penalty? I don't understand. Why didn't anybody tell me this was so serious?"

Less than an hour later, the bell sounded. The jury had come to a decision.

*

* *

THERE WERE MULTIPLE questions for the jury to answer in connection with the murder. The first several were uneventful in light of the confession; the last, asking if there were extenuating circumstances that would preclude the death penalty, was essential. The questions began:

Did Djandoubi voluntarily kill Elisabeth Bousquet between July 3 and 4, 1974?
Yes, answered the jury, with a majority of at least eight votes.

Did Djandoubi act with premeditation?
Yes, with a majority of at least eight votes.

Did Djandoubi commit torture and barbarous acts in the process of the murder?
Yes, with a majority of at least eight votes.

And then thick silence fell on the courtroom. Goudareau clasped his hands before him. Chauvy watched the jurors. Hamida stared at the floor.

Do any extenuating circumstances exist in favor of Hamida Djandoubi?
No, with a majority of at least eight votes.

It would be death.
Applause rippled through the courtroom.

39

June 1977

LAWYERS WHO HAVE HEARD the death penalty pronounced say a pall envelops those who played a role in the judgment. There are no celebrations. Eyes are averted. Conversations are reduced to muttered banalities. Leave is taken of one another as quickly as possible.

"There are no victors when the death sentence is won," said the admittedly partisan Robert Badinter, "simply an odor of shame."

After Hamida Djandoubi's death sentence fell, Jean Goudareau went to his client and assured him there was hope. The trial could be thrown out for technical failings. Or the president could grant him clemency. Hamida listened to these comforts just as he had listened to the verdict: impassively.

"I wouldn't say he accepted it," Goudareau recalled. "It was more that he wouldn't or couldn't even process this event. It was unreal to him."

Shortly after noon, Hamida was transferred back to Baumettes. Goudareau, meanwhile, returned to Marseille. It was clearly not his day: he'd arrived late, he'd lost the case, and now he found a parking ticket tucked onto his windshield.

Back inside the courthouse, there was little time to digest the verdict. Two hours later, the trial of Annie and Amaria began with much of the same cast. Henri Vuillet would serve as the judge, Yves Chauvy as the prosecutor. This time, a special adviser for cases involving minors, the *juge des enfants,* would oversee the proceedings.

Another jury of nine was drawn, this time without a single exclusion. The girls faced between two and five years in prison, and it was an unbearable prospect for them. Amaria had already broken down because, as per court procedure, she'd been forced to spend the eve of her trial in a cell at Baumettes.

At least the lawyers were now more optimistic that the previous night in prison would be the extent of their clients' incarceration. There was much working in the girls' favor. The Bousquets and Houria had publicly forgiven Annie and Amaria and were no longer taking part in the prosecution. At his own trial, Hamida had appeared hostile and unsympathetic, lending authority to the defense that he had completely manipulated the girls. Then there was the matter of timing.

"The fact that Djandoubi was condemned to death played into our case," said Jean-Jacques Anglade. "There is a subconscious movement to balance things; when a heavy penalty is pronounced, the next might be lighter."

At the girls' trial, the most important testimony came from Houria. Having been forced to submit to Hamida, she knew how paralyzing the fear could be. "We were all victims," she told the court. "We all suffered together."

Still, Yves Chauvy pushed, if not for a heavy sentence, at least for a conviction and a slap on the girls' wrists. He told the jury how Annie fetched the jerry can of gasoline, how the two girls had watched as Elisabeth was tortured, how they helped drag her to the cabin.

"Yes, this was a horrible situation for them, but they should have acted," Chauvy said. "A human life was in the balance, and not only did they do nothing, these girls actually carried Elisabeth to her death."

Anglade was enraged by the prosecutor's submission. In his final plea, he compared Annie and Amaria to none other than the saint who helped Jesus carry his crucifix. "These girls were compassionate when they helped Elisabeth to the cabin, they made her last moments bearable," Anglade told the jury. "In the Passion of Christ, Simon of Cyrene helped Christ carry his cross. Did we charge Simon of Cyrene as an accomplice to the Romans in the murder of Christ?"

The trial lasted less than five hours, and the final arguments were heard just before seven o'clock at night. The jury took less than fifteen minutes to come to its decision: not guilty of all charges.

Annie and Amaria wept.

*

    *   *

A DEATH SENTENCE was front-page news, and in their coverage the Marseille newspapers followed their editorial lines. *Le Méridional* proclaimed that Hamida had received the sentence he "merited." The abolitionist paper, *La Marseillaise,* was disappointed by Goudareau's defense, especially the fact that he didn't cite the Patrick Henry verdict or argue against capital punishment itself. "The lawyer chose not to address the moral issue of the death penalty," the article noted.

And it wasn't just *La Marseillaise* that was surprised by Goudareau's omissions. The other lawyers involved in the case were all abolitionists, and they were all shocked by Goudareau's approach. "The defense presented by Jean Goudareau represented a complete scandal," Anglade said. "If we don't plead the case against the death penalty, we sacrifice 50 percent of the client's chances."

Perhaps the most anguished of the lawyers was Jean-Daniel Bruschi, who had represented Houria and her family at Hamida's trial. He'd planned to lash out against the death penalty in his final submissions but was unable to because Goudareau hadn't even raised the issue.

"The debate could only have been philosophical because Djandoubi had admitted to the facts," Bruschi said. "In a case like Ranucci, where there was a question that he was innocent, you could plead the case and hope to get the benefit of the doubt. With Djandoubi, you had to argue the grand principles of the death penalty."

Others also came in for criticism. In the preceding decade, top lawyers had made a point of attaching themselves to death penalty cases in order to argue these very grand principles. Yet there wasn't a flicker of interest in the Djandoubi case.

"The big tenors didn't jump into the case. Robert Badinter didn't volunteer for the case, Émile Pollak didn't volunteer for the case," says Bruschi. "This affair didn't interest anybody."

There would be other repercussions to Goudareau's trial tactics.

The same afternoon Hamida was condemned to death, three of the four women excluded from the jury filed an official complaint with the ministry of justice and held an impromptu press conference at the Aix courthouse. Just as with the Bobigny abortion trial and the Calanques rape case, French women were no longer willing to have their issues decided by men.

"We believe that in trials involving violence against women or against female children, women must not be excluded from the juries," their statement read.

Still, it wasn't all criticism for Goudareau. Among the police officers in the courtroom, the lawyer had won nigh universal respect.

"He was an extraordinary man who made an extraordinary argument," Captain Jacques Chauley recalled. "Normally, criminal lawyers use their techniques. This was a business lawyer, so he made a plea as a human, from the heart. It was so extremely moving I ask myself if he didn't make me cry. I never saw such a beautiful plea. He brought out all the Christian sentiments, all the human emotions."

And for others, far away from the Aix-en-Provence courthourse, the verdict illuminated the reality of the death penalty. The boy who found Elisabeth's body that sweltering July day was now a law student in Bordeaux. Though Frederick Bartoli hadn't thought about the implications of his discovery when he was fifteen, he was now fully involved in those "school quarrels" and "parlor debates" that Yves Chauvy had derided at the trial.

"With that trial, I realized how challenging it was to be opposed to the guillotine," Bartoli said. "The woman had been beaten, tortured, everything. It was simply inhumane. But just because the act was inhumane, it didn't mean the state shouldn't be human."

*

* *

IT was the seventh death sentence delivered since the beginning of Giscard's presidency. Of the previous six, four men had been granted clemency, one man was still waiting for his clemency hearing, and Christian Ranucci had gone to the guillotine.

Strictly speaking, there was at least a two-in-three chance of receiving clemency. Reassuring odds, but Goudareau hoped the case wouldn't reach the president.

In France in the 1970s, it wasn't possible to appeal the verdict simply because a lawyer felt there had been an error in the jury's judgment. The only way to overturn a trial was to prove there had been quantifiable errors in the judicial process. This was Goudareau's task in the weeks following the death sentence, to examine the mechanics of the trial in hopes of finding procedural mistakes. In the end, he came up with several grounds for appeal:

• the court clerk had failed to note in the official trial record when potential jurors were excluded during the selection process

• the official record didn't make note of a lunch break taken between one o'clock and three o'clock on the first day of the trial

• the judge erred by not postponing the trial until Marie-Claude Kervella could be found

On the surface, niggling details. But the aim was to give the appeals court justification for annulling the verdict. Within the legal community, the feeling was that this court, the *cour de cassation,* was opposed to the guillotine and would use any excuse to overturn a death penalty. In the past year, the court had annulled three death verdicts for reasons that were mostly benign: in two cases, the names of jurors hadn't been properly pulled from the urn, and in the final case there hadn't been an Algerian interpreter in the room for a five-minute period during a two-day trial.

But although the *cour de cassation* had embraced the most minor judicial error as cause for retrial, it had also ignored the most blatant. During the trial of Bontems and Buffet, the entire court proceedings were accidentally broadcast over the courthouse loudspeakers, thus tainting witnesses waiting outside the courtroom to testify. With the pressure for expedited justice, the appeals court decided this wasn't a problem.

By March 1977, Goudareau had the appeal ready. As the *cour de cassation* was a unique jurisdiction, only a handful of Paris firms were qualified to appear before the court. Goudareau contacted one such lawyer, Guillaume Devolvé, who agreed to handle the appeal. Normally, it took two to three months for a decision to be reached.

*

*   *

MEANWHILE, THE DRUMBEAT of the abolition movement quickened. One week after Goudareau sent in the appeal, an international conference against the death penalty was organized in Paris. Later that same month, it was a group of artists and militants who organized street festivals and concerts to rally support for abolition. "It was like breathing the air of May '68 again," Robert Badinter said.

One of the major weaknesses of the abolition movement was that the majority of French didn't believe there was an adequate replacement. As it stood, "perpetual" imprisonment in France often meant the offender was eligible for parole after fifteen years, and the average "life" sentence was over after a little more than nineteen and a half years. To address these concerns, in June 1977, Paul Lombard, the lawyer who had acted for Christian Ranucci, proposed a guaranteed fixed-term sentence to replace the guillotine. Under this proposition, the offender wouldn't receive a parole hearing until twenty years had passed, and that hearing would only be to determine if he or she was ready to begin the parole process.

There was also increased spiritual pressure for abolition. As part of his earlier *Humanae vitae* (On Human Life), Pope Paul VI had reversed centuries of church thought by condemning the death penalty and eliminating it from the criminal code that governed Vatican City. Now the official newspaper of the Vatican, *L'Osservatore romano,* was asking Catholics around the world to embrace its position. In France, the message was eagerly received by a coalition of bishops who quickly issued a joint statement urging abolition.

Yet, as Badinter himself was fond of noting, the choice of whether or not to support the death penalty is a moral one; but the decision to implement such a choice is ultimately political. This is why French abolitionists were most encouraged by a government report that came out in June 1977.

In an attempt to sidestep the furor surrounding the death penalty, President Giscard had created a committee to study crime in France. In its report, the committee, which included the minister of justice and the former national director of police, recommended the death penalty be replaced with a guaranteed long-term sentence. For abolitionists, it was cause for rejoicing. The smart money now said the government would introduce legislation to abolish the death penalty when the fall session of the National Assembly opened in September.

In Marseille, Goudareau was especially relieved. The same week the committee's report was released, the decision from the *cour de cassation* came back. The appeal had been rejected. The Kervella issue came close to convincing the court, but in the end the verdict stood.

"It is so painful to see a condemnation to death," wrote Devolvé. "When it comes to the request for clemency, I assure you that I will provide all my support."

Goudareau could only hope that the request for clemency wouldn't be necessary. With a consensus forming between the French religious, legal, and political communities to move ahead on abolition, there was a chance he wouldn't even have to make the trip to the Élysée to see the president.

40

JEAN GOUDAREAU WASN'T oblivious to the muttered criticisms. He'd never felt part of the Marseille legal clique, and his right-wing politics isolated him from many of the court's more left-leaning lawyers. Now it seemed everyone had an idea about what he *should* have done on the case, and all the ideas started in the same place: why hadn't he sought out Émile Pollak?

"If it had been Pollak defending him, the verdict would have been different," as Marc Greco, the civil lawyer representing Alphonsine Bousquet, bluntly put it.

It wasn't just his fellow lawyers who were asking the questions.

"I understand that Monsieur Goudareau wanted to stand by him as a friend, but he should have taken on another lawyer as well to handle the criminal aspect of the case," Louis Bugia said years afterward.

And, with the trial over, Ali Djandoubi had conveniently resurfaced. Friends were telling him that if he wanted to save his brother's life, he needed to get Émile Pollak on the case.

"Ali came to me and told me, Maître, sadly we have come to our last chance," Goudareau remembered. "He wanted me to take Pollak as an assistant."

So the day after the appeal was rejected, Goudareau went to see his more celebrated colleague. Pollak hadn't appeared at the Marseille courthouse in months, and there were rumors of a sickness. Sure enough, when Gouadreau arrived at the house with the fourteen cats, it took Pollak ages to descend from his bedroom, and he received his visitor in a bathrobe. But Pollak lit a Craven A and listened. As soon as he realized it was a death penalty case, he agreed to help.

Pollak was a man completely in love with the law. He was fond of repeating a recipe for life success: "If you want to be happy one day, get drunk; if you want to be happy two days, get married; if you want to be happy your entire life, become a lawyer." And as a lawyer, nothing motivated him like the death penalty. Pollak understood how a person could kill, whether out of sickness or madness or anger. But he couldn't fathom how a court could kill after cold and sober reflection. There was also the matter of his religion. He was one of those who took the commandment "Thou Shalt Not Kill" literally.

"He was a strong, strong believer," recalled his daughter, Nicole Pollak. "He didn't see how Christ's teachings allowed the death penalty."

Even with the possibility of abolition looming, the two lawyers needed at least to file their request for clemency. So that afternoon, interrupted by Pollak's regular bouts of coughing, they took out their notepads and began to work.

That same week, Goudareau also contacted Georgie Viennet, president of the Association for the Abolition of the Death Penalty, and asked her to help organize a letter-writing campaign to President Giscard on behalf of Hamida. At last, Goudareau was reaching out to the abolitionists and activists whose cause he'd long rejected.

*

* *

THESE EFFORTS BY Goudareau would soon become more urgent. For, even in the face of his own governmental committee's recommendation to end the death penalty, President Giscard didn't hesitate to send a second man to the guillotine.

Jérôme Carrein was a thirty-five-year-old alcoholic from northeast France who'd abducted the eight-year-old daughter of a waitress he knew. After trying to rape the little girl, he drowned her in a swamp. The girl's last words were "No, no, I'm going to tell my parents."

Carrein had been sentenced to death twice. The original verdict had been overturned by the *cour de cassation*, but a second jury came to the same conclusion as the first: the murder of the little girl was so vile that the guillotine was the only appropriate punishment. In May 1977, Carrein's lawyer, Pierre Lefranc, went to the Élysée to ask President Giscard d'Estaing for clemency. He pointed to his client's alcoholism and traumatic childhood as mitigating factors. But on June 22, 1977, just one week after the committee report was made public, the president gave his answer: Carrein was to die.

The next morning, on June 23, 1977, Lefranc entered his client's cell with the official entourage of guards and court officials. Carrein knew what it meant. All he asked was that Lefranc pass a message to his mother.

"Tell her, Maître, that I regret all the bad things I have done. Ask her to forgive me. Tell her, Maître, that I am thinking of her up to the last minute."

As was tradition, Carrein was offered a last drink. He took one look at the bottle of cognac and shook his head. "If it wasn't for alcohol, I wouldn't have hurt a fly."

Then Carrein lost his head to the guillotine.

Nothing made any sense anymore in that long summer of 1977. Every indication pointed toward imminent abolition, yet the president of France didn't hesitate to use the guillotine. Clearly, Goudareau and Pollak would have to make that trip to the Élysée after all.

*

* *

THE RIGHT TO GRANT clemency is a remnant of Roman law, the consecration of the notion that rulers had the power of life or death over their subjects. Under the French monarchies, the king was the closest link to God, and his right to grant clemency was considered the most divine of his powers. In the seventeenth century, the Parlement de Paris went so far as to decree such mercy "the most beautiful flower in the crown."

As France moved from monarchy to democracy, the right to grant clemency was transferred to the president. But this "beautiful flower" of kings was soon called "a lottery of blood" when used by politicians.

"It depends on the lawyer, the mood of the president, the mood of the people," Robert Badinter said. "It excuses a jury because they are not actually condemning a man to death; they are merely offering the 'King' the choice of whether that man lives or dies."

Even the most cursory review of the dispensation of clemency in twentieth-century France is alarming for its inconsistencies. In 1965, for instance, Charles de Gaulle was about to refuse to grant clemency to an Italian man who had committed an especially debased murder on French territory. Then he realized the famous Mont Blanc tunnel between France and Italy would be opening soon. De Gaulle thought it improper to sever an Italian's head with such an auspicious Franco-Italian project on the verge of being inaugurated. The death penalty was commuted to life imprisonment.

Nor was Giscard d'Estaing immune to such pressures. In April 1976, he outlined the types of cases he thought deserving of the guillotine: premeditated abductions of children that resulted in their death and the murder of the elderly in order to steal their savings. The latter perfectly described the crime of Moussa Benzahra. He killed an eighty-three-year-old woman and robbed her of her last few hundred francs. But Giscard granted him clemency anyway.

It was political, of course. Benzahra was a *harki,* and in the 1970s there were hundreds of thousands of *harkis* in France. They formed a well-organized lobby, and there were massive petitions for the president to show mercy. With such a major bloc of voters engaged in the campaign, Giscard spared Benzahra.

Hamida Djandoubi had no powerful lobby group behind him. But he did have Goudareau and Pollak. Their written appeal for clemency proved to be an eloquent voice for life.

Above all, they questioned the finding of premeditation. "If killing

Elisabeth was a premeditated decision, can we believe that he would have brought her to his own apartment, separated from his neighbor by only a thin wall, and then subjected her to these tortures in front of two girls who lived with him, and finally, strangled her in front of them so he would be at the mercy of two witnesses?"

Gouadreau and Pollak also claimed that the psychiatrists had shown a "rare incompetence," and Annie and Amaria had "partially distorted the facts in order to assure their own acquittals."

"Is it necessary to execute a crippled man?" they concluded. "Does it correspond with your ideal of justice that a crime where destiny played such a part, a destiny that transformed a young, handsome and morally irreproachable man, should end in death?"

The document was couriered to the Élysée Palace. On July 11, they received confirmation that President Giscard d'Estaing had received the document and was considering their request.

*

*   *

AS JULY CAME TO A CLOSE, Goudareau allowed himself to relax. August was the national month of vacation, and there was no chance that the president would call the lawyers to Paris. What the government could do, however, was use this window of summer tranquillity to deliver some highly controversial news.

Ever since the committee had recommended eliminating the death penalty, abolitionists optimistically awaited the government's response. The minister of justice, Alain Peyrefitte, gave his answer in mid-August, when most of official France was on vacation and away from their newspapers and televisions. In an essay that appeared in *Le Monde*, Peyrefitte began in a sympathetic fashion:

"It is hard to believe that the death penalty is still admissible in countries that pretend to found their institutions on logic," he wrote. "If a judge condemns a criminal to death or a criminal perpetrates this crime, it is equally a crime."

But there was a catch. Peyrefitte said the French people weren't ready for abolition. Polls showed that at least 60 percent were still in favor of the guillotine, and "responsible men cannot accept to act when the current conditions are so unfavorable." Most grotesquely, Peyrefitte justified the decision by quoting Albert Camus's play *Caligula*: "You did well to calm us. It is too soon to act: the people, today, are against us. Do you want to watch with us for the moment to conclude?"

It was an audacious gesture, using the words of perhaps the most famous abolitionist of twentieth-century France to justify maintaining the guillotine. If corpses turn in their graves, Camus was spinning.

The irony of Peyrefitte's declaration was that the French people's attachment to the guillotine was actually beginning to impede justice. As part of a 1975 treaty, several countries, including Holland, refused to extradite suspects to countries using the death penalty. This meant that one of the prime suspects in the sensational case of "*Les Tueurs d'Ardèche*" (The Killers of Ardèche) was left in judicial limbo.

Three men had robbed a bank in the town of Ardèche. They were so lackadaisical, they stopped on the way out of the bank to eat tomatoes they found in a grocery bag in the lobby. Predictably, police were waiting for them, and in the ensuing shoot-out, one officer and two bystanders were killed. One of the three robbers that day was Stéphane Viaux-Peccate, a boxer who was the reigning French lightweight champion. He managed to escape amid the chaos and fled to a small village in Holland. Aware of the French enthusiasm for the guillotine, the Dutch refused to deliver Viaux-Peccate unless there were assurances he would not be put to death. But by law, the French government couldn't interfere with the courts.

After seven months of mounting embarrassment, a covert agreement was reached: President Giscard d'Estaing promised that if Viaux-Peccate were to be condemned to death, he would grant him clemency. Viaux-Peccate was delivered to French police, found guilty of murder, and sentenced to eighteen years in prison.

*

* *

THE SUMMONS ARRIVED in early September. Jean Goudareau and Émile Pollak were invited to appear before the president at 3:30 P.M. on September 6, 1977.

They awoke early that day, flew to Paris, and made their way to the presidential palace near the Champs-Élysées. The entire meeting took less than half an hour. Giscard was well versed in the case. He had read the defense appeal, and, in accordance with the clemency process, had received reports from the trial judge, the prosecutor, and the head of prosecution in Aix. The dossier was also reviewed by several high-ranking justice officials, including the director of penitentiaries and the minister of justice.

There was a peculiar coincidence to the case. Elisabeth's family came from Estaing, the town where Giscard d'Estaing had his family castle. Did the president know the murderer's victim was one of his townspeople?

It didn't come up in the meeting with Goudareau and Pollak. The president only wanted small details filled in, most prominently asking about the public reaction to the crime. Here, Goudareau sensed an opportunity. He was convinced that justice had been hijacked by media sensationalism and popular hysteria. He said the people of Marseille had been "inflamed" by the case, and it had prevented Hamida Djandoubi from receiving a fair trial.

Near the end of their conversation, the president confided that the time was coming to abolish the death penalty in France. According to Goudareau, Giscard even hinted that the issue would be addressed when the National Assembly reconvened at the end of the month. Then the president thanked them for their efforts and promised to have a decision shortly.

On the flight back to Marseille, the two lawyers were of different minds. Goudareau was optimistic. "He is sure to receive clemency," he told Pollak. "It would be absurd to execute somebody just one month before the parliament abolishes the death penalty."

But Pollak wasn't so sure. While Goudareau was reacting to the president's warm reception and the promise of impending abolition, Pollak couldn't get past the facts of the case. They were too ugly to allow for the sentence to be easily commuted.

And Goudareau would succumb to doubts of his own. He thought that maybe he'd erred by mentioning the anger swirling around the case. Initially, he'd hoped the president would correct an act of mob injustice. He'd forgotten that Giscard d'Estaing was obsessed with polls and hesistated to do anything that jeopardized his public standing.

"I feared I had made a mistake," Goudareau recalled. "I suddenly realized this could be the end."

In one sense, it was the end. There was nothing left for the lawyers to do. There was nothing left for anybody to do. But wait.

41

IT WAS TIME FOR MARCEL Chevalier to inspect the machine. With a clemency request pending, there was a chance it would be needed in the coming weeks. Considering how highly charged each execution had become, a broken bolt or clogged bearing would never do if that lethal dawn came.

Chevalier was fifty-six years old in 1977. When he was a child, his life seemed destined for a more conventional path. He was born in Montrouge, a suburb south of Paris, where his father ran a candy shop and his mother made the candy. His parents hoped he would join the family business, but, in what seemed an act of rebellion at the time, Chevalier refused. Instead, he learned typesetting and at the age of thirteen got his first job in a print shop.

After serving in World War II, he returned to Montrouge. His life changed in 1947 when he met a young lady named Marcelle Louise Obrecht at a picnic. She was twenty-two, four years younger than Chevalier, had flashing eyes, and worked as a seamstress in his neighborhood. He began the courtship that day at the picnic, and less than a year later they were married.

Even on his wedding day, Chevalier didn't know his wife's secret.

It came out a few years later, at a family dinner with her father and uncles. Sitting at the table, a fair quantity of red wine already drunk, Chevalier learned his father-in-law, Georges Obrecht, was an assistant executioner. His uncle, André Obrecht, was the chief executioner of France. And, as Chevalier would soon discover, these types of jobs always stayed in the family.

*
*   *

UNTIL THE SEVENTEENTH century, there was no real pattern to who did or didn't get the job of state killer. Those who had a taste for death seemed drawn to the profession, a phenomenon epitomized by a fellow named Capeluche, who served as an executioner under Charles VI. This Capeluche had a deft touch with the decapitating sword and no small bloodlust. Not sated by his official duties, he committed a string of murders on the side. When he was arrested, the inevitable question arose: when the executioner is to be executed, who does the executing?

The answer turned out to be his valet. With Capeluche giving step-by-step instructions, he kneeled, held firm, and was beheaded on August 22, 1418.

Capeluche was applauded for his professionalism that morning, but that should come as no surprise. French executioners have always enjoyed a good reputation. One need only remember that Henry VIII imported a Frenchman to behead his beloved Anne Boleyn in 1536. Having heard great things about an executioner named Jean Rombaud, the king sent his aides across the Channel to investigate. Eager to win the lucrative assignment, Rombaud performed a special double execution for the visiting dignitaries: he sat the two men down in chairs, stood between them, and with one fluid stroke of his two-handed sword, lopped off both their heads at once. Rombaud got the royal job.

Anne thought it amusing. "I heard say that the executioner was very expert," she said minutes before her death, "and I have a little neck!"

A century and a half later, the first grand lineage of executioners was founded. In 1675 a lusty young man named Charles Sanson de Longval tempted a young woman into a shadowy corner of her family apartment. The father burst in, catching the young couple in a compromising position. Sanson was dragged into the father's study and saw walls lined with swords, axes, and other instruments of death. He'd just seduced the executioner's daughter. He now had a new wife and a new profession.

Though the tale has been lovingly embroidered over the years, it did mark the beginning of the Sanson family dynasty. In 1688 Charles Sanson was named official executioner of Paris, and for the next two hundred years his descendants worked the trade in all corners of France. Charles Sanson's son, Charles Sanson Jr., was an executioner; his grandson, Charles Jean-Baptiste Sanson, was an executioner; and his great-grandson, Charles-Henri Sanson, was the most famous of them all, executing Louis XVI, Marie-Antoinette, and the motley crew of French Revolutionaries.

In all, there were nineteen Sanson executioners. The legacy ended only in 1847 with the scandalous Henri-Clément Sanson. Henri-Clément hated the job and broke out in red blotches and suffered bouts of trembling whenever he received his orders. Understandably, he began to drink, gamble, frequent prostitutes, and, it being Paris, collect expensive antique furniture. His expensive habits proved his downfall in March 1847, when Henri-Clément did the unthinkable: he pawned the official Paris guillotine. A week later, on March 17, 1847, he received an execution order and didn't have enough money to reclaim his instrument. The ministry of justice paid to free the guillotine. Henri-Clément performed this one final beheading and then was promptly fired. A Sanson never killed for France again.

The nepotism, however, continued. By 1870, with the introduction of the railroads and the decrease in the number of executions, the system changed. As opposed to 1 executioner for each jurisdiction (at the peak of the Reign of Terror there were actually 160 licensed executioners in France), there was now but 1 chief executioner who traveled the entire country. The first chief executioner was Nicolas Roch, whose forefathers included executioners in Auxerre, Lyon, Montpellier, and Rennes. And in 1879, when Roch retired, Louis Deibler, whose father, grandfather, and great-grandfather had been executioners, was named to the post. And on January 2, 1899, his son Anatole succeeded him.

"Ah, my son, what a beautiful New Year's gift," Louis Deibler said at the time.

Anatole Deibler continued the family tradition, hiring his nephews, Jules-Henri Desfourneaux and André Obrecht, as his assistants. It should be mentioned that Obrecht continued to work with his uncle even though he was the latest in a long line of executioners whose romantic lives suffered because of the profession. Shortly after taking on the job, he proposed to the young woman he was dating. Her father, an abolitionist, opposed the marriage. Obrecht wrote a letter of complaint:

"You are opposed to capital punishment and make this clear by refusing her hand to an executioner. . . . But if you were to come home one night and find your wife murdered, your daughter strangled, and the murderer still in the house and about to escape—what would you do? You have a revolver in your pocket: will you fire or not?"

Deaf ears met the argument. Obrecht was forced to find another bride.

When Antoine Deibler died in 1939, the title of chief executioner first passed to Jules-Henri Desfourneaux, who would conduct the Weidmann execution, the final public guillotining in French history. Upon Desfourneaux's death in 1951, André Obrecht was named the chief executioner of France. The appointment came just as Obrecht was taking a liking to his niece's husband, Marcel Chevalier.

*

*   *

IT DIDN'T TAKE MUCH convincing for Marcel Chevalier to join the profession. The money was too good to refuse: the monthly salary of an average government worker for a job that had to be performed at most a handful of times every year.

In October 1958, Chevalier received the title "executioner's assistant, second class." The first time it took some getting used to. He made small mistakes—he forgot to put the bucket for the head next to the guillotine, for example—and was generally flustered by the blood.

"It's something you never forget," he would say afterward.

Especially disagreeable for the assistants was the position of "photographer," which involved crouching down in front of the guillotine and tugging on the condemned man's ears to ensure he didn't pull his head back when the blade fell. Not only did your clothes get soaked and the head come off in your hands, but throughout the centuries more than one photographer had lost a finger as a result of a little too much casualness in his approach.

Still, there was no turning back, especially with his uncle and father-in-law on the execution team. Chevalier kept his job in the print shop, working out the travel schedule with his employer. Few people knew what he did. It wasn't that he cared what they thought; he just found most people were jealous of the extra money he earned for so little work.

It was an agreeable life. Chevalier and his wife raised their two children in suburban Paris and spent holidays in the French countryside, where Chevalier kept a little garden and fished for trout. By the 1970s, with André Obrecht developing Parkinson's disease, it was decided Chevalier should replace him after the Ranucci execution.

Chevalier was named the new chief executioner of France on July 30, 1976. When the articles noting the appointment appeared in the newspapers, they were filled with the usual fabulous tales. That four hundred people had applied for the job. That the executioner's money was free from taxation. That he received a six-thousand-franc bonus called the *prime de panier* for every head he cut off. All lies. But, as it was government policy not to comment on the executioner, editors allowed the elaborations.

Maybe this is why Chevalier didn't like the press. Or perhaps it was the way it hounded him. Paparazzi tried to take a picture of him waiting at a bus stop. Two more photographers bribed a bank employee to tell them when he was leaving the building so they could get his picture. Whatever the case, during his more than two decades as an executioner's assistant and then chief executioner, he granted only one interview.*

"I am a man like any other. I have a wife, two children, a mother-in-law in the country. I don't hide. I have nothing to hide," he told a journalist from *Paris-Match*.

As for abolition, Chevalier was curt: "I don't allow myself an opinion. I'll wait to see what happens." Still, Chevalier said the most despicable criminals had to be eliminated. Why waste public money feeding them? But if the death penalty were to be abolished, Chevalier thought the reestablishment of the prison colony in Cayenne would be the best possible replacement.

Chevalier was first called into service as chief executioner in June 1977, when Jérôme Carrein was guillotined. By all accounts, the decapitation went smoothly and Chevalier was commended for his work that morning.

Now, in that first week of September 1977, Chevalier went over the guillotine to make sure all was in working order. He oiled the blade release, he checked the bolts, he made sure the wooden braces were solid and true. For if the clemency was refused, Hamida Djandoubi would become Marcel Chevalier's second "client," and he wanted this guillotining to go smoothly as well.

---

* Not all executioners are so reticent. Fernand Meyssonnier, who was an executioner in French Algeria, often entertains journalists' questions and even ran a guillotine museum from his home for a short while. It is through Meyssonnier that I learned the exact mechanics of the guillotine.

42

September 1977

THE OFFICIALS FROM THE Ministry of Justice began looking for Jean Goudareau late on the afternoon of Friday, September 9, 1977. They learned from his secretary, Lucie Le Manchec, that he was in Paris on business and would be back early in the evening.

They waited for his plane to land at the Marseille airport. They somehow missed him amid the rush of disembarkation. An agent was dispatched to his apartment building to wait outside. It was almost eight o'clock when Goudareau finally arrived home. The agent handed him a letter. It was remorselessly precise:

MAÎTRE GOUDAREAU
AVOCAT AU BARREAU DE MARSEILLE

I have the honor to let you know that following a decision by Monsieur le Président de la Répubique, the request for clemency of the individual named Hamida DJANDOUBI has been rejected.

As a consequence, the order of the Cour d'Assises des Bouches-du-Rhône that condemned Hamida DJANDOUBI to the death penalty will be carried out Saturday 10 September 1977 at 04h15.

I am sending you this notification to permit you to assist your client.

Please accept my assurances, my Cher Maître, that you have my highest regards.

LE PROCUREUR DE LA RÉPUBLIQUE

As a rule, these letters of death were delivered to the defense lawyers after visiting hours had ended at the prison where the condemned man was being held. This policy prevented suicide attempts or last-night belligerence, but it also created unending panic. For men awaiting clemency, any morning at dawn their cell door could open and they could be led to the guillotine. In *The Stranger,* Camus described the agony of Meursault's nights.

"The worst part of the night was the vague hour when I knew they usually come; once it was after midnight I waited, listening intently. Never before had my ears perceived so many noises, such tiny sounds. . . . Mother used to say that however miserable one is, there's always something to be thankful for. And each morning, when the sky brightened and light began to flood my cell, I agreed with her."

Hamida Djandoubi had been living this uncertainty for days. Prison guards told laughing stories that he'd even started sleeping beneath his bunk in hopes he wouldn't be found if the dawn reckoning came.

Having read the letter, Goudareau telephoned Pollak, whose sickness had worsened. Pollak's daughter, Nicole, begged him not to attend the execution. She even offered to bear witness in his place. Pollak refused, but he did accept two small favors. Nicole's husband would wait for him outside the prison gates; and Nicole herself would be responsible for waking him up.

Nicole was so nervous she set two alarms and ordered a wake-up call from France Télécom. "It left me feeling ill," Nicole remembers. "When that telephone rang it meant a man was going to die. It was so final, it was terrifying."

Goudareau laid out a dark suit, but not the one he wore to funerals. That, he thought, would be inappropriate. He chose not to sleep at his apartment that night. His grandchildren were staying with him, and he didn't want them asking any questions. They were too young to understand.

He went to his office. As a city councillor, he had a chauffeur-driven car at his disposal, so he arranged to be picked up at 2:30 A.M. Just before midnight, he finally lay down on the couch and closed his eyes. Sleep never came.

*

*   *

YVES CHAUVY LEARNED that clemency had been refused earlier that day. He was the one charged with organizing the execution, and there were countless details to see to: preparing for the arrival of Marcel Chevalier and the guillotine, ordering the police to cordon off the prison, arranging for the presence of the required witnesses.

It made for a frantic pace, one that allowed little time for reflection. But even if it had, Chauvy wouldn't have thought twice. He felt a lot of prosecutors requested the death penalty with the hidden hope that the president would spare the condemned man and they wouldn't have blood on their hands. Not Chauvy.

"I never had a doubt, not a regret," he said years later. "If the dossier was to arrive on my desk again today, I would ask for death again."

Chauvy was proud of his role in the justice system. He saw himself as the avenger of crimes and a protector of the vulnerable. His sentiments echoed those of Hammurabi some 3,700 years earlier, when he wrote his famous code to protect the "widows and orphans."

"I would like all the abolitionists to be able to see how horrifying these crimes are," Chauvy said. "I would like them to put themselves in the situation of the victim and the victim's family."

And even though Chauvy was a devout Catholic, he saw no conflict between his actions and the church's new stance against the death penalty. He also respectfully disagreed with Émile Pollak's interpretation of the teachings of Jesus.

"The church, through history, has always held a very ambiguous position toward the death penalty. I didn't take it into consideration."

So he made his phone calls, he prepared the official death, and never once did he feel a twinge of ambivalence.

*

*   *

MARCEL CHEVALIER AND his two assistants retrieved the guillotine from the basement storage room at the Fresnes prison outside Paris early on the morning of September 9.

For most of the twentieth century, there had been two operational guillotines in France: one based in Paris, and one that traveled the country and was left wherever it had last been used. But in 1964, when André Obrecht was chief executioner, the guillotine was sent to Martinique to execute a man who had raped and killed a little girl. It was left in Fort-de-France for future "territorial" executions, meaning that the Paris guillotine now served all of continental France.

As per tradition, Chevalier took the train to the site of the execution while his assistants were responsible for delivering the guillotine. They took to the road hours earlier than necessary. The official executioner's van was more than twenty years old and notoriously unreliable. On the way to the Ranucci execution, it had even broken down on the highway. Police were alerted and the guillotine was transferred into a spare truck, then escorted to Marseille at high speed. It arrived at the Baumettes prison less than half an hour before the execution was to be held. The truck had been repaired and had posed no troubles on the Carrein execution. But Chevalier was a cautious sort and ordered his assistants to leave early. Why take unnecessary risks?

The actual guillotine being transported from Fresnes to Marseille had evolved from the machine used to end the life of Nicolas-Jacques Pelletier in April 1792. The grooves on the insides of the uprights had been lined with metal, small wheels had been placed on the sides of the blade to speed its descent, and the *lunette,* which clasped the condemned man's neck into place, was made adjustable so there was less wriggle room.

But, despite these changes, the guillotine that would kill Hamida Djandoubi was essentially the same machine. According to French government statistics:

- the entire guillotine weighed 1,278 pounds

- the blade, with the *mouton,* weighed 88 pounds

- the guillotine blade dropped 8 feet and 4 inches

- it took ⁷/₁₀ of second for the blade to fall

And, most crucially for Hamida Djandoubi:

- the actual beheading took 2/100 of a second

The official witnesses began to arrive shortly before four in the morning. The prison was located in the south end of Marseille, its back against the cliffs that led into the Calanques. Those who visited Baumettes always noticed the sculptures that adorned the outside of the prison wall. Lust, Gluttony, Greed, Sloth, Anger, Envy, and Pride— the Seven Deadly Sins, each represented by an acutely unattractive persona. A none too subtle message on what to avoid if you didn't want to end up on the wrong side of those sublimely decorated walls.

There were twelve official witnesses that morning: the trial judge, Henri Vuillet; the prosecutor, Yves Chauvy; an envoy from the Ministry of Justice, Pierre Berge Lefranc; three representatives from the prison, Messieurs Rousseau, Cubaynes, and Maurel; the *juge d'instruction* from Marseille, Madame Mabelly; Dr. Tosti; Jean Goudareau and Émile Pollak; Imam Hocine Saidi; and the court clerk, Alphonse Rihet.

Counting the executioner, his aides, and the prison guards, the crowd would exceed twenty.

Once inside Baumettes, the witnesses were led to a ground-floor office. The long corridor that led to the Quartier Haute Sécurité where Hamida was kept had been lined with blankets to muffle the approaching footsteps. Once everyone was gathered, the long walk began. Pollak, coughing and gasping for breath, had trouble keeping up with the procession as it marched the three hundred feet along the corridor. Goudareau remained with his colleague until they arrived at the death row cells, then hurried to the front of the group. He wanted Hamida to see his face first.

Hamida was gently shaken awake. He looked surprised to see the crowd in the cell but didn't say anything. As he slept without his prosthesis, extra time was taken to strap it into place. After getting dressed, he splashed cold water over his face, then the procession made its way back down the corridor. The footsteps were once again muffled. But in the heavy silence, all could hear the click-click-click of Hamida's plastic leg.

As they walked, the imam approached, offering a final chance at spiritual redemption. Hamida waved him away.

At the end of the corridor was a small office where Chevalier and his two assistants waited. There was a little table covered in wax paper. On top was the traditional bottle of cognac, a glass of water, a pack of cigarettes, and a pen and paper in case Hamida wanted to write any last words.

Hamida accepted a glass of cognac despite the iman's wince of disapproval. He downed it one long swallow and asked for another, which he drank just as quickly.

He took a cigarette and smoked it down to the filter. He asked for a second and smoked that one to the filter as well. Then he complained. He'd wanted blond tobacco, not dark. Several men offered him a third cigarette, but Chevalier was impatient.

"*Ah non*," Chevalier said. "That's enough. We've already lost enough time."

It was time for the prisoner's *toilette*. As he sat, the executioner's assistants used scissors to trim his hair and cut away the collar and back of his prison shirt. They wanted the guillotine to have unimpeded access to the neck.

With a thin cord, Hamida's hands were then bound behind his back. Chevalier's assistants each took an arm and lifted him to his feet. As they moved him toward the second door in the room, Hamida tried to turn back. "I want to see my lawyer."

Goudareau moved closer. Hamida asked that Goudareau tell his brother he'd been executed. He had nothing else to say.

The executioner's assistants kept him moving. The door was opened onto a small courtyard. There stood the guillotine.

Goudareau had two reactions: shock and disgust. Shock at how small the guillotine was in real life; he felt that if he reached up he could touch the blade. And disgust that this was the sanctioned means of French death. "It wasn't sacred," Goudareau said. "Good, they took it out of the streets and it was no longer a public spectacle, but then, to put us in a terrible basement room with cracked walls and a dirty table . . ."

The courtyard wasn't large enough for the witnesses, so they stayed inside, fanning out on the other side of the doorway. Goudareau and Pollak made sure they were near the front, where Hamida could see them.

Hamida was strapped onto the *bascule*. The *bascule* was lowered into place. The *lunette* was dropped around his head. He made one last effort to call out for his lawyer. And then the blade fell.

Goudareau turned his head away. But thirty years later, he remembered the sound as clearly as if it were yesterday. The gush of blood. It was as if somebody had thrown a bucket of water against the wall.

Having requested the death sentence, Chauvy felt it was his responsibility to watch. The French poet La Rochefoucauld once said that neither the sun nor death could be looked upon with a steady gaze. Chauvy was determined to prove him wrong. He purposely stood close to the machine. He purposely watched every detail. The head that fell and bounced in the basket. The crimson fountain that spurted from the arteries. And the puddle of blood that slowly crept out from under the machine. Chauvy stood his ground. The blood stained the tip of his right shoe.

43

FOR JEAN GOUDAREAU, his work that Saturday morning was not yet done. From the prison, he went to the Sonacotra at Pointe-Rouge where the two brothers had once lived together. Goudareau roused the director, and together they went to Ali's room.

Ali sat on the edge of the bed in his pajamas and listened. He hunched over and put his head in his hands. He didn't cry.

*

*   *

ALI WAS THE SOURCE of other concerns that morning. There were courthouse rumors that he had sworn to avenge himself on Houria if his brother was guillotined. Jean-Jacques Anglade was on his way to catch a train in Avignon when news of the execution came across the radio. He called his mother at the ANEF shelter with the warning, and Houria was given special protection over the next days.

No harm came to Houria. Police could never confirm the legitimacy of the threat.

*

*   *

WHEN GOUDAREAU FINALLY arrived home, the streets were filling with morning traffic. His wife had a cup of coffee waiting for him. He didn't drink it. "I just told my wife it was finished, then I went to the bedroom," he said.

Émile Pollak was already back in his bathrobe, his health more fragile than ever. "He was compacted, gray, silent," remembers his daughter, Nicole. "Facing the death penalty was an emotional burden that nearly crushed him every time. This time it was too much."

Four months later, in January 1978, Émile Pollak died of lung cancer. In Marseille, a street beside the courthouse would be named after him; in Paris, Badinter dedicated his battle for abolition to his fallen comrade.

*

*　　*

AFTER THE GUILLOTINING, Hamida Djandoubi's corpse was placed in the wooden disposal box. As was tradition, his head was placed between his legs.

His remains were transferred to the city morgue, and then to the Saint Pierre cemetery. For centuries, a back corner of the cemetery had been reserved for the men and women who had been executed in Marseille. Hamida's body lies there to this day in an unmarked grave.

*

*　　*

THAT SATURDAY MORNING, after signing all the paperwork, sending the official report to the ministry, and tacking the public notice of the execution to the prison door, Chauvy drove from Baumettes to his home in Aix-en-Provence. As he approached the city, he realized it had been months since he'd last donated blood, so he decided to stop at the Red Cross clinic.

Chauvy was immensely proud of his status as a blood donor. To this day, he keeps his battered Red Cross card in his wallet and is quick to point out that over the years he has given blood precisely 123 times.

"*Par humanité*," Chauvy said.

It was after 10 A.M. and the clinic was always open on Saturday mornings to cater to working donors. Chauvy was surprised when the door wouldn't open. He jiggled the handle to make sure. He looked to see if a note had been posted, an explanation. Nothing. The clinic was inexplicably closed.

Chauvy got back in his car and drove home to his wife.

*

*　　*

IN THE *Provençal-Dimanche,* the story took up almost the entirety of the front page, with a picture of Hamida in handcuffs and the bold, capitalized, underlined title "GUILLOTINÉ." It occupied similar space in *La Marseillaise* and *Le Méridional.*

What differed were the newspapers' reactions: The *Provençal* ran an editorial on the middle pages denouncing the death penalty. "A man is dead. A monstrous man, I will repeat it, a perverted, uncorrectable, and indefensible man, but a man all the same. There is nothing that will beautify this. His execution doesn't fix anything."

La Marseillaise ran an even stronger editorial on the front page titled "USELESS CRUELTY." It read: "This is a remnant from the age of barbarity and there is no justification for it."

Le Méridional didn't run an editorial. Its articles were subjective enough. The headlines read "DJANDOUBI HAS PAID" and "JUSTICE HAS BEEN DONE."

The guillotining hit the middle pages of the national newspapers, always accompanied by analysis of its political ramifications. *Le Monde* quickly moved the debate forward, publishing a three-part essay on the death penalty by Robert Badinter.

The Marseille papers also pushed ahead. There were new crimes to report. The day after Hamida's guillotining, a twenty-four-year-old woman was stripped half-naked, had her skull crushed in with a glass bottle, and then was strangled to death. The papers were calling it "the Mysterious Crime of Berre," after the town outside Marseille where the murder occurred.

*

*   *

SINCE SAVING PATRICK Henry's life, Robert Badinter had become known as a miracle worker among the condemned men in French prisons. The reputation was deserved. In the months and years following the Hamida Djandoubi execution, he took on the cases of five men who were facing the death penalty.

In Nantes, in November 1977, he and Nicole Pollak represented Michel Bodin, who had killed a man in a wheelchair in order to steal a few thousand francs. The murder was aggravated by the fact that the man's eyes had been pierced neatly in the center of the irises by a needle. Along with his traditional anti–death penalty arguments, Badinter said his client had been too drunk for such an exact torture, meaning it had to have been done by his accomplices. It won the day and Bodin was sentenced to life in prison.

In December 1978, Badinter defended Mohamed Yahiaoui, a Tunisian baker who killed his employers after a dispute over unpaid overtime. Using a medical report that suggested Yahiaoui had undiagnosed epilepsy, Badinter convinced the jury to choose life imprisonment.

In January 1979, it was Michel Rousseau, an alcoholic who had beaten his neighbor's daughter to death. Again, using the defense of alcoholism, Badinter saved his client's head.

In Dijon in March 1979, Jean Portais faced death for killing a young woman and a police officer during a robbery. Portais was in his sixties. He would die in jail, so why opt for the guillotine? Again, the jury chose life imprisonment.

Finally, in Toulouse in March 1980, there was Norbert Garceau. This was the most challenging of the cases. In the 1950s, Garceau had strangled a woman to death and been spared the guillotine. After serving more than two decades in prison, he was released and, in almost exactly the same scenario, strangled another woman. As with Claude Buffet, it was the most penetrating argument for the death penalty: if Garceau had been guillotined in 1952, a young woman would still have been alive in 1979. Badinter argued that Garceau, who'd served with the French military, had been made psychotic by his experiences with the death squads in Indochina. The jury sentenced him to life in prison.

"I hope they massacre your wives," a man in the courtroom screamed at Badinter and his team of lawyers after the Garceau verdict was read.

Five death penalty cases, five exhausting victories. Only more files would come.

*

*　　*

IN 1978, GILLES PERRAULT's *Le Pull-over rouge* was released, and the Ranucci case was once more pushed to the forefront of the death penalty debate. Just as Voltaire had done with the Calas case in 1765, Perrault exposed the biases and frailties of the justice system. Michel Foucault, reviewing the book in *Le Nouvel Observateur,* wrote: "Was Ranucci, guillotined the 28th of July, 1976, innocent of the murder of a little girl two years earlier? We still don't know. Maybe we will never know. But we do know, in an irrefutable manner, that justice was guilty."

The abolitionist movement was steadily gaining momentum. In Spain, Franco was dead, and, in 1978, one of the early moves of the democratic government was to jettison capital punishment for common crimes. This was the generally accepted first step toward total abolition: first eliminate the death penalty from the criminal code, then ban it even in times of war.

The only Western European country other than France still to have the death penalty in its laws was Belgium, and this was a judicial ruse. To delineate the very worst crimes, Belgian courts liked to sentence criminals to death, but they were then universally shown clemency. There hadn't been an execution in Belgium since 1950; it was de facto abolition. This meant France was the last to send its prisoners to death. The Swedish justice minister, Karl Libdom, said, "We, the representatives of numerous European countries who are profoundly attached to France and would like to see France at the front lines of the fight for human rights, we are stupefied and distressed to see France dishonored by this sad record."

A backdoor abolition effort was made. Abolitionists introduced a bill in parliament that would have eliminated the 185,000 francs in budget funds that went to Marcel Chevalier, his aides, and the maintenance of the guillotine. Pierre Bas, one of the bill's most vociferous supporters, asked the National Assembly: "Do you find it normal that we are the last country in Europe to keep an executioner?"

The National Assembly decided it was normal. The bill failed.

It was hard to blame the politicians. The polls showed the people wanted the death penalty, usually by a majority of between 55 and 65 percent. And in the fall of 1980, four more men were sentenced to death in the space of six weeks. In one case, the prosecutor hadn't even requested the death penalty, but the jury chose to deliver it nonetheless. In November 1980, the minister of justice was quoted as saying, "At a moment when police officers are shot every day as if they are rabbits cornered in the woods, a government conscious of its responsibilities cannot propose the suppression of the death penalty."

The message was unmistakable: the Giscard government was never going to renounce the guillotine. Abolition would come only if the government were to be deposed.

*

* *

IN THE 1981 presidential elections, the hope of the Left—and the abolitionists—was once again François Mitterrand. Mitterrand had already lost two bids for the presidency: to Charles de Gaulle in 1965 and to Valéry Giscard d'Estaing in 1974. His losses had become something of a bad joke, and he was compared to Raymond Poulidor, the famous French cyclist who always came close to winning, but never won, the Tour de France.

As the election approached, the polls had Giscard d'Estaing and Mitterrand even. The most incendiary issue before the candidates was the death penalty. In January, *France-Soir* published a poll that had 63 percent of the French in favor of capital punishment, 31 percent opposed, and 6 percent undecided. The guillotine alone could turn the election.

Giscard was unambiguous in his statements: "At this moment, the government must not propose to abolish the death penalty. It would go against the profound beliefs of the French people, and I believe that we don't have the right to go against the profound beliefs of the people we represent and govern."

Politically, pragmatically, it was obvious what Mitterrand should have done: woo the voters and avoid the subject of the death penalty at all costs. Instead, he announced on national television: "In my conscience, in my faith, I am against the death penalty," he said. "I don't need to read the polls."

The first round of the election was held on April 24, 1981. Voters were presented with more than a dozen candidates from the extreme Right (Jean-Marie Le Pen of the Front National) to the extreme Left (Arlette Laguiller of the Lutte Ouvrière). The top two vote winners would move to the second round. Giscard and Mitterrand were the obvious choices, but there was a dark horse, the sitting prime minister, Jacques Chirac. When the votes were counted after the first round:

Giscard d'Estaing: 28 percent
Mitterrand: 26 percent
Chirac: 18 percent

Pundits now predicted Giscard d'Estaing would win because his disciple, Jacques Chirac, would surely swing his votes to him. But a week before the second round, Chirac made an odd pronouncement. He would vote for Giscard d'Estaing but wouldn't tell his supporters what to do. This might have made the difference. On May 10, 1981, Mitterrand won the election, 52 percent to 48 percent.

Mitterrand didn't falter. His first month in office, he granted clemency to a man convicted of killing a police officer. Then he appointed Robert Badinter as minister of justice.

During the summer of 1981, Badinter began to write the legislation that would abolish the death penalty. Now inside the system, he began to feel the tug of political compromises. Certain members of the National Assembly wanted a clause that would allow for the death penalty in times of war; others wanted a simultaneous provision to extend prison sentences, thus silencing critics who thought abolition was soft on crime.

Badinter refused both requests. He quoted Victor Hugo: "Abolition must be pure, simple, and definitive."

The bill reached the National Assembly in September 1981. The day the debates were to be held, *Le Figaro* announced the latest poll results: 63 percent of the people were for the death penalty. Undaunted, in a speech that was nationally televised, Badinter told the National Assembly why it must abolish the guillotine.

"In countries where liberty reigns, abolition is almost universally the law; in countries ruled by a dictator, the death penalty is everywhere. This division is not the result of a simple coincidence; there is a correlation. The true political significance of the death penalty is that it comes from the belief that the State has the right to dispose of its citizens as it sees fit, up until the point they can be put to death. This is why the death penalty is so popular in totalitarian regimes.

"We must fight with all our forces so that crime and violence are reduced in our society, but this belief and this fight does not mean it is necessary to kill the guilty. That the parents or the loved ones of a victim wish for this death, I understand because it is the natural reaction of a person who is hurt. But it is a human reaction based on nature. And all of the historical progress in the realm of justice has been to overcome this idea of private vengeance. And how do we overcome it if we don't first abolish *lex talionis*?

"For those of us who believe in God, God alone has the power to choose the hour of our death. For we abolitionists, we understand that it is impossible for the justice of men to have the power of death because we understand human justice to be flawed.

"Tomorrow, thanks to you, French justice will no longer be a justice that kills. . . . Tomorrow, the bloody pages of our justice will have turned."

The vote wasn't close: 363 for abolition; 117 against.

The Senate confirmed the vote, 160 to 126 in favor of abolition.

On October 9, 1981, the death penalty was abolished and the guillotine was relegated to the museum. A moral and political struggle that had impassioned the nation for almost two centuries had ended.

At least for the time being.

Later

IN 1996 GEORGIA STATE legislator Doug Teper (Democrat-Atlanta) put forward a curious proposal: that the state of Georgia adopt the guillotine for certain executions.

House Bill 1274 proposed:

BE IT ENACTED BY THE GENERAL ASSEMBLY OF GEORGIA:

The General Assembly finds that while prisoners condemned to death may wish to donate one or more of their organs for transplant, any such desire is thwarted by the fact that electrocution makes all such organs unsuitable for transplant. The intent of the General Assembly in enacting this legislation is to provide for a method of execution which is compatible with the donation of organs by a condemned prisoner.

The bill failed on second reading.

Later Still

IN 2007 RETIRING PRESIDENT Jacques Chirac oversaw a constitutional amendment that, in theory, permanently banned the death penalty in France. The Front National wasn't dissuaded and continues to fight for the restoration of capital punishment. The following proposal is part of the party's envisioned overhaul of the French justice system.

ARTICLE 14: *Reestablish the death penalty for the most serious crimes*

In the context of the new European politic, France withdraws from the portions of the treaties that make this reestablishment impossible.

The death penalty would then be reestablished and applied for the following crimes:

- *international crime and trafficking rings (drugs, mafia, espionage)*

- *terrorism and hostage taking*

- *the murder of children, elderly people, members of police forces, the national guard, and prison personnel*

- *assassinations and murder with rape*

- *acts of torture and barbarity*

The leader of the Front National, Jean-Marie Le Pen, has said executions would be conducted by guillotine or firing squad. In the 2002 national elections, Le Pen made it to the second round and received 18 percent of the vote in the race for president. That same year, for the third straight election, he was the leading vote-getter among presidential candidates in Marseille.

In the 2007 national elections, which were won by Nicolas Sarkozy, Le Pen received a little more than 10 percent of the national vote and was eliminated in the first round. Sarkozy also carried Marseille.

Now

RETENTIONIST COUNTRIES: 62

AS OF NOVEMBER 2007, sixty-two countries continue to execute their prisoners. This group includes Afghanistan, Barbados, China, Cuba, India, Iran, Japan, Pakistan, Syria, Thailand, and the United States of America.

ABOLITIONIST COUNTRIES: 135

MEANWHILE, 135 COUNTRIES can be considered to have abolished the death penalty. Ninety-two countries have banned capital punishment outright; 10 countries keep the death penalty in their laws only for exceptional circumstances, such as war crimes; and 33 countries are considered de facto abolitionist, as the death penalty is against current government policy and there have been no executions for ten years or more. Among the 135 countries are:

COUNTRY	LAST EXECUTION
Australia	1967
Belgium	1950
Canada	1962
Colombia	1909
Finland	1944
Greece	1972
Honduras	1940
Iceland	1830
Ireland	1954
Italy	1947
Mexico	1937
Nicaragua	1930

Rwanda	1998
Switzerland	1944
Turkey	1984
United Kingdom	1964

Source: Amnesty International

To see exclusive photographs
and documents from the
Hamida Djandoubi case, visit
WWW.JEREMYMERCER.NET

Acknowledgments

AS EXHILARATING AS SUCCESS would be for me personally, a greater reason to hope the literary gods smile upon this book is to justify the astounding faith of my family and friends.

One does not travel this rutted road long before learning a writer's journey abounds with emotional and financial disruption. One simply cannot manage alone. For the better part of a decade, my parents, Ross and Patricia, have been the most stalwart of supporters. I couldn't imagine a better birthright for an author than a father who is a devoted grammarian and a mother who is an assiduous financial manager. As always, I love and thank them both.

I am equally amazed by the good souls who continue to provide me with warm meals, comfortable couches, and unconditional kindness. Meredith and John Olson, Buster Burk, Quinn Comendant, Julie Delaney, Dave Ebner, Colin Freeze, Sparkle Hayter, William Murray, Viken Berberian, and J. E. Friar, I am spoiled to know you.

Many are those who have offered suggestions on this manuscript, but I would be remiss not to draw attention to one person in particular. Adrian Hornsby continues to be the most demanding, insightful, and inspiring of readers. I await the honor of returning his editorial favors.

In terms of logistics, this book couldn't have been written without the help of several individuals and institutions. During my sojourn in the village of Oia, Atlantis Books provided vital resources, while the benefits of Wikipedia and Project Gutenberg are abundantly obvious when working on a remote Greek island. In Marseille, Soraya Amrane and Lucille Lagier of the Atelier de Visu provided a most creative working environment, while in upstate New York Jonny Diamond and Amanda Park Taylor provided a quiet farm retreat. The thesis work of Robert Grimm introduced me to the contradictions of Belsunce;

Nadia Drici went hunting for abandoned roadside cabins with me; and at the *cour d'appel* in Aix-en-Provence, Jean-Yves Lourgouilloux and Roland Mahy were generous with their assistance. Without the help of Marie Moses Delgado, my French correspondence would have been brutish. And to Robert Badinter, a special thank-you.

Of course, all of this would merely translate into a stack of coffee-stained manuscript pages were it not for the confidence of publishing professionals. I thank my agent, Kristin Lindstrom, and my editor, Michael Flamini.

Finally, this project encompassed three years and two loves. The first research on this book came in my waning days with Julie de Robillard; two and a half years later, the final edits were made at the dawn of my time with Géraldine Van Pée. Without love, work is hollow. I am a lucky man.

Interviews

Anglade, Jacqueline—June 2006, Marseille

Anglade, Jean-Jacques—June 2006, Vitrolles

Badinter, Robert—March 2005, Paris

Bartoli, Frederick—January 2006, Bordeaux

Bruschi, Jean-Daniel—June 2006, Marseille

Bugia, Louis and Colette—June 2006, Marseille

Ceccaldi, François—July 2006, Marseille

Ceccaldi, Paulette—June 2006, Marseille

Chauley, Jacques—August 2006, Cannes

Chauvy, Yves—April 2007, Nîmes

Comandé, Bruno—September 2004, Marseille

Dallari, Patrick—April 2007, Marseille

Goudareau, Jean—August 2004, September 2004, and
December 2006, Marseille

Greco, Marc—June 2006, Marseille

Guiard, Marie-Solange—April 2007, Marseille

Hugon, Maryse—September 2005, Langogne

Kervella, Marie-Claude—August 2004, Marseille

Lafout, Sister Odette—November 2006, Langogne

Le Manchec, Lucie—September 2004, Marseille

Llaurens, Françoise—July 2006, Aix-en-Provence

Meyssonnier, Fernand—July 2007, Fontaine de Vaucluse

Patel, Noël—August 2007, Roquevaire

Perasso, Éliane—March 2007, Marseille

Pollak, Nicole—August 2004, Marseille

Sciverel, Marianne—July 2005, Marseille

Thain, Jean—August 2006, Sisteron

Bibliography

Agostini, Julie, and Yannick Forno, eds. *Les Écrivains et Marseille.* Marseille: Éditions Jeanne Laffitte, 1997.

Andrews, William. *Bygone Punishments.* London: William Andrews, 1899.

Arendt, Hannah. *Eichmann in Jerusalem: A Report on the Banality of Evil.* New York: Viking Press, 1963; New York: Penguin, 2006.

Badinter, Robert. *L'Abolition.* Paris: Fayard, 2000.

———. *L'Exécution.* Paris: Éditions Grasset Fasquelle, 1973.

Barnes, Harry Elmer. *The Story of Punishment: A Record of Man's Inhumanity to Man.* 2nd ed. Montclair, N.J.: Patterson Smith, 1972.

Bedau, Hugo Adam, and Paul G. Cassell, eds. *Debating the Death Penalty.* Oxford: Oxford University Press, 2004.

Berns, Walter. *For Capital Punishment: Crime and the Morality of the Death Penalty.* New York: Basic Books, 1979.

Berry, James. *My Experiences as an Executioner.* Devon, England: David & Charles Reprints, 1972.

Bishop, George V. *Executions: The Legal Ways of Death.* Los Angeles: Sherbourne Press, 1965.

Bouscaren, Lincoln T., and Adam C. Ellis. *Canon Law: A Text and Commentary.* Milwaukee, Wis.: Bruce Publishing Company, 1946.

Brouqui, Serge. *Marseille bombardée.* Gap, France: Imprimerie des Alpes, 1998.

Brugger, E. Christian. *Capital Punishment and Roman Catholic Moral Tradition.* Notre Dame, Ind.: University of Notre Dame Press, 2003.

Busquet, Raoul. *Histoire de Marseille.* Marseille: Éditions Jeanne Laffitte, 1999.

Camus, Albert. *Resistance, Rebellion and Death.* Translated by Justin O'Brien. London: Hamish Hamilton, 1961.

———. *The Outsider.* Translated by Joseph Laredo. London: Penguin Classics, 2000.

Casanova. *Histoire de ma vie.* Paris: Laffont, 1993.

Clavel-Leveque, Monique. *Marseille grecque*. Marseille: Éditions Jeanne Laffitte, 1985.

Cobb, Richard. *Death in Paris*. Oxford: Oxford University Press, 1978.

Costa, Sandrine, ed. *La Peine de mort: De Voltaire à Badinter*. Paris: Flammarion, 2001.

Darnton, Robert. *The Great Cat Massacre and Other Episodes in French Cultural History*. New York: Vintage, 1985.

Delarue, Jacques. *Le Métier de bourreau: Du moyen âge à aujourd'hui*. Paris: Fayard, 1979.

Driver, G. R., and John C. Miles, eds. *The Babylonian Laws*. Oxford: Clarendon Press, 1955.

Duff, Charles. *A Handbook on Hanging*. London: Putnam, 1961; New York: New York Review of Books, 2001.

Dumas, Alexandre (père). *The Count of Monte Cristo*. Reprint, Hertfordshire, England: Wordsworth Editions, 1997.

Foucault, Michel. *Discipline and Punish, The Birth of the Prison*. Translated by Alan Sheridan. London: Penguin Books, 1991.

Froment, Pascale. *René Bousquet*. Paris: Fayard, 2001.

Gerould, Daniel. *Guillotine: Its Legend and Lore*. New York: Blast Books, 1992.

Giscard d'Estaing, Valéry. *Le Pouvoir et la vie*. Paris: Éditions Compagnie 12, 1988.

Gonod, Michel. *La Deuxième Porte: Les dernières jours de la guillotine*. Paris: Éditions Jean Picollec, 1981.

Gorecki, Jan. *Capital Punishment: Criminal Law and Social Evolution*. New York: Columbia University Press, 1983.

Gouiran, Maurice. *Marseille, la ville où est mort Kennedy*. Paris: Éditions Jigal, 2007.

Grossman, Mark. *Encyclopedia of Capital Punishment*. Santa Barbara, Calif.: ABC-Clio, 1998.

Guizot, François. *Des conspirations et de la justice politique* and *De la peine de mort en matière politique*. Paris: Fayard, 1974.

Hanks, Gardner C. *Against the Death Penalty: Christian and Secular*

Arguments Against Capital Punishment. Scottsdale, Pa.: Herald Press, 1997.

Hearn, Daniel. *Legal Executions in New England: A Comprehensive Reference, 1623–1960.* Jefferson, N.C.: McFarland & Company, 1999.

Hermary, Antonie, Antoinette Hesnard, and Henri Treziny, eds. *Marseille grecque: 600–49 av. J.-C., La cité phocéenne.* Paris: Éditions Errance, 1999.

Hugo, Victor. *The Last Days of a Condemned Man.* Translated by Geoff Woollen. Oxford: Oxford University Press, 1992; London: Hesperus Classics, 2004.

Hustak, Alan. *They Were Hanged.* Toronto: James Lorimer & Company, 1987.

Innes, Brian. *The History of Torture.* New York: St. Martin's Press, 1998.

Janes, Regina. *Losing Our Heads: Beheadings in Culture and Literature.* New York: New York University Press, 2005.

Jolowicz, H. F. *Historical Introduction to the Study of Roman Law.* Cambridge, England: Cambridge University Press, 1965.

Joutard, Philippe, ed. *Histoire de Marseille en treize événements.* Marseille: Éditions Jeanne Laffitte, 1998.

Kant, Immanuel. *Metaphysical Elements of Justice.* Translated by John Ladd. New York: Macmillan, 1965.

Kershaw, Alister. *A History of the Guillotine.* London: John Calder; London: Tandem Books, 1965.

Koestler, Arthur. *Darkness at Noon.* New York: Macmillan, 1941; New York: Time, 1962.

Larguier, Jean. *Que sais-je: La procédure pénale.* 12th ed. Paris: Presses Universitaires de France, 2005.

Laurence, John. *A History of Capital Punishment.* New York: Citadel Press, 1960.

Le Dantec, Bruno. *La Ville-Sans-Nom: Marseille dans la bouche de ceux qui l'assassinent.* Marseille: Éditions Le Chien Rouge, 2007.

Lupoi, Maurizio. *The Origins of the European Legal Order.* Translated by Adrian Belton. Cambridge, England: Cambridge University Press, 1994.

Mackey, Philip English, ed. *Voices Against Death: American Opposition to Capital Punishment, 1787–1975*. New York: Burt Franklin, 1976.

Maine, Sir Henry Sumner. *Ancient Law*. London: John Murray, 1883.

Marion, Georges. *Gaston Defferre*. Paris: Albin Michel, 1989.

McCoy, Alfred W. *The Politics of Heroin in Southeast Asia*. New York: Harper & Row, 1972.

Meyssonnier, Fernand, with Jean-Michel Bessette. *Paroles de bourreau: Témoignage unique d'un exécuteur des arrêts criminals*. Paris: Éditions Imago, 2002.

Michelot, Jean-Claude. *La Guillotine sèche*. Paris: Fayard, 1981.

Montagu, Basil, ed. *The Opinions of Different Authors upon the Punishment of Death*, vol. 1. London: Longman, Hurst, Rees, and Paternoster Row, 1809; Buffalo, N.Y.: William S. Hein Company, 1984.

———. *The Opinions of Different Authors upon the Punishment of Death*, vol. 2. London: Longman, Hurst, Rees, and Paternoster Row, 1812; Buffalo, N.Y.: William S. Hein Company, 1984.

Morris, Norval, and David J. Rothman, eds. *Oxford History of the Prison*. Oxford: Oxford University Press, 1995.

Mousourakis, George. *The Historical and Institutional Context of Roman Law*. Hampshire, England: Ashgate, 2003.

Naish, Camille. *Death Comes to the Maiden: Sex and Execution 1431–1933*. London: Routledge, 1991.

Nathanson, Stephen. *An Eye for an Eye: The Immorality of Punishing by Death*. 2nd ed. Lanham, Md.: Rowan & Littlefield Publishers, 2001.

Opie, Robert Frederick. *Guillotine: The Timbers of Justice*. Thrupp, England: Sutton Publishing, 2003.

Perasso, Éliane. *Ne pleure pas, hurle!* Paris: Éditions Stock, 1973.

———. "Le Passage à l'acte criminel, une signature?" In *La Psychanalyse, encore*, edited by Claude Boukobza. Ramonville, France: Éditions Érès, 2006.

Perdu, Charles, and Patrick Rebell, eds. *La Résistible Ascension de l'extrême droite à Marseille*. Lyon: Atelier de Création Libertine, 1989.

Perrault, Gilles. *Le Pull-over rouge*. Paris: Fayard, 1994.

Plato. *The Dialogues*. Translated by Benjamin Jowett. Oxford: Clarendon Press, 1875.

———. *Protagoras, Philebus, and Gorgias*. Translated by Benjamin Jowett. Amherst, N.Y.: Prometheus Books, 1996.

———. *The Republic*. Translated by Benjamin Jowett. Oxford: Clarendon Press, 1881.

Plutarch. *The Lives of Noble Grecians and Romans*. Translated by John Dryden and Arthur Hugh Clough. Chicago: Encyclopedia Britannica, 1952.

Pollak, Émile. *La Parole est à la défense*. Paris: Robert Laffont, 1975.

Prejean, Helen. *Dead Man Walking*. New York: Random House, 1993; London: Fount Paperbacks, 1996.

Owens, Erik C., John D. Carlson, and Eric P. Elshtain, eds. *Religion and the Death Penalty*. Grand Rapids, Mich.: William B. Eerdmans Publishing Company, 2004.

Robb, Graham. *Victor Hugo*. London: Picador, 1997.

Sarat, Austin. *When the State Kills: Capital Punishment and the American Condition*. Princeton, N.J.: Princeton University Press, 2001.

Savey-Casard, Paul. *La Peine de mort: Esquisse historique et juridique*. Geneva: Librairie Droz, 1968.

Schabbas, William A. *The Abolition of the Death Penalty in International Law*. 3rd ed. Cambridge, England: Cambridge University Press, 2002.

Schultz, Fritz. *Principles of Roman Law*. Translated by Marguerite Wolff. London: Oxford at the Clarendon Press, 1936.

Scott, George Ryley. *The History of Capital Punishment*. London: Torchstream Press, 1950.

Simon, Rita J., and Dagny A. Blaskovich. *A Comparative Analysis of Capital Punishment*. Lanham, Md.: Lexington Books, 2002.

Slim, Iceberg. *Pimp: The Story of My Life*. New York: Holloway, 1965; London: Canongate Books, 1996.

Society's Final Solution: A History and Discussion of the Death Penalty. Lanham, Md.: University Press of America, 1997.

Sorell, Tom. *Moral Theory and Capital Punishment*. Oxford: Basil Blackwell (Open University), 1987.

Stassen, Glen H., ed. *Capital Punishment, A Reader*. Cleveland, Ohio: Pilgrim Press, 1988.

Tellegen-Couperus, Olga. *A Short History of Roman Law*. London: Routledge, 1993.

The Terrible and Deserved Death of Francis Ravilliack. Edinburgh: Robert Charteris, 1610.

Thucydides. *History of the Peloponnesian War*. Translated by Rex Warner. London: Penguin Books, 1972.

Toulat, Jean. *La Peine de mort en question*. Paris: Éditions Pygmalion, 1977.

Twain, Mark [Samuel Clemens]. *The Innocents Abroad*. London: J. C. Hotten, 1869.

Walker, Peter N. *Punishment: An Illustrated History*. Newton Abbot, England: David & Charles, 1972.

Wekesser, Carol, ed. *The Death Penalty: Opposing Viewpoints*. Farmington Hills, Mich.: Greenhaven Press, 1986.

Wright, Gordon. *Between the Guillotine and Liberty: Two Centuries of the Crime Problem in France*. Oxford: Oxford University Press, 1983.

Index

Les Aberrations sexuelles d'un monstre (film),
  196
*Abolition of the Death Penalty in International
  Law* (Schabas), 13n
abortion, 50, 91, 156, 202–4, 250
Académie Chirurgicale, 112
Académie de Médecine, 155
Ackermann, Françoise, 144, 145, 149–50
Les Actes des Apôtres (newspaper), 99
action civile (French legal function), 190–91,
  224
Adolescence perverse (film), 196
L'Agonie de la peine de mort (Naud), 178
Aix-en-Provence, France, 236
Akiba, 54
Algeria, 7
  Amaria M. and, 78–79, 81, 82
  Azzarello, Jean-Louis, 92
  de Gaulle, Charles, 157
  France, 35–37, 38, 46, 49, 165
  harkis, 36, 78, 146, 197, 257
  Houria S. and, 192
  pieds-noirs, 36, 145, 146, 197
  racism, 229–30
  torture, 147
Altamira caves, Spain, 12–13
Amaria M.
  abuse of, 197–98
  crime reconstruction, 206–7
  defense of, 197–98, 233
  Djandoubi, Ali and, 201
  Djandoubi, Hamida and, 78–79, 81–83, 89,
    101–3, 104–7, 159, 160–62, 164,
    200–201
  psychiatric evaluation, 196, 198–200
  recovery of, 220–21
  release from prison, 207–8
  testimony of, 240, 258
  trial of, 247–48
  witness role, 171–76, 183, 193–94, 224
Ambrose, Saint (bishop of Milan), 64
American Civil Liberties Union (ACLU),
  225
American Revolution, 98, 114
Ancient Law (Maine), 22, 217
Anglade, Jacqueline, 193, 196–97, 203–4,
  207–8, 275

Anglade, Jean-Jacques, 196–97, 241–42, 248,
  249, 275
animals, 74–75, 75n, 123
Anne de Gaulle Foundation for Down
  syndrome, 50
Annie V.
  abuse of, 197–98
  crime reconstruction, 206–7
  defense of, 197–98, 233
  Djandoubi, Hamida and, 77–78, 89,
    101–3, 104–7, 159, 160–62,
    200–201
  psychiatric evaluation, 196, 198–200
  recovery of, 220
  release from prison, 207–8
  trial of, 247–48
  witness role, 171–76, 183, 193–94, 224, 240,
    258
Anti-Sacrilege Act, 137
anti-Semitism, 140
Antony, Mark, 43
appeals court process, 251–52, 253
Aquinas, Saint Thomas, 65–66, 73, 157
archaeology, France, 12–13
Ardèche, France, 259
Ardourel, Henri, 81
Arendt, Hannah, 216–17
Aristotle, 26
art, Stone Age culture, 12–13
Artaud, Antonin, 109
"L'Assassin assassiné" (song), 218
assassination, 157
Association for the Abolition of the Death
  Penalty, 255
Association Nationale d'Entraide Féminine
  (ANEF), 193, 196–97, 202, 275
Athens (antiquity), death penalty, 30–32
Augustine of Hippo, Saint, 64–65
Auschwitz-Birkenau concentration camp,
  203
Australia, 140
Austria, 157
autopsy, 131–32
Avis motivé sur le mode de décollation (Louis),
  112–13
Azzarello, Jean-Louis, and Elisabeth Bousquet,
  92–94, 107, 191–92

Babylon, 21–23
Badinter, Robert, 180, 181, 182, 203, 213, 224,
    225, 226, 247, 249, 252, 253, 257, 276,
    277–79, 281–82
Banjo (McKay), 47
Barrès, Maurice, 143
Barrielle, Victor, 79–81, 206, 207
Bartoli, Antoine, 116, 118–19, 121, 130
Bartoli, Frederick, 116–17, 118, 121, 130, 250
Bartoli, Yvette, 116, 118–19, 121, 130
Bas, Pierre, 279–80
Basque territories, 74
Bastien-Thiry, Jean, 157
Bastille, storming of, 97
Beaurieux, Jacques, 155
Beauvoir, Simone de, 202
Beccaria, Cesare, 96–97, 110, 122
Belafonte, Harry, 7, 237
Belgium, 279
Bentley, Derek, 165–66
Benyanès, Ali, 133, 181
Benzahra, Moussa, 257
Bertrand, Philippe, 212, 215
Bésimensky, Françoise, 179
Béziers, France, massacre at, 74
Bible, crime, 52–54, 63–66
Bicêtre (prison, hospital, old-age home, near
    Paris), 113, 139
Blackstone, William, 85
blasphemy, 52
Bodin, Michel, 278
Boleyn, Anne, 85, 263
Bontems, Roger, 48, 178–82, 211, 225, 226,
    252
botched executions, guillotine, 2–3, 262
Boudouresques (doctor), 72
Boukson (doctor), 239–40
Bousquet, Alphonsine, 201, 254
    divorce of, 189
    Elisabeth and, 48, 51, 52, 71, 94, 190, 191n
    marriage, 28–29, 60–61, 62, 242n
    Marseille, 14–15, 17, 28
    Patel, Noël and, 60–61, 61n
    trial, 190–91
Bousquet, Elisabeth
    Azzarello, Jean-Louis, and, 92–94, 107, 192
    childhood of, 14, 17–18
    Djandoubi, Ali and, 201–2
    Djandoubi, Hamida and, 25, 27, 28, 29, 45,
        46–48, 50–51, 60, 61–62, 67–68,
        106–7, 162, 222
    family life, 29, 60–61, 62

family notification, 189–90
Foyer Ariane (women's shelter), 67, 68–69
Marseille, 18–19
media, 70
mental health of, 72, 89–90
murder investigation, 119–21, 134–35,
    171–76, 185, 206–7
personality of, 50
prostitution, 62, 67–68, 71–72, 90
suicide attempt, 90, 189
Bousquet, Jean-Pierre, 14–15, 17, 18n, 45,
    50–51, 89–90, 189, 232
Bousquet, Marie-Josée, 14, 17, 18, 20, 28, 48,
    94, 189–90, 232
Bousquet, Pierre, 90–91, 189
    Djandoubi trial, 242–43
    Elisabeth and, 48, 51, 94
    finances of, 28
    injury of, 18–19, 24, 48, 61
    marriage of, 61
    Marseille, 14–15, 17, 18
    personality of, 28–29
    trial, 190–91, 232
Bousquet, René, 16–17
Bousquet, Roland, 14, 17, 18, 18n
Bouverie, Tuant de la, 111
Breton, André, 15
Briand, Aristide, 141–42
Bruschi, Jean-Daniel, 224, 249
Buffet, Claude, 48, 178–82, 211, 252, 278
Bugia, Colette, 57, 106, 186
Bugia, Louis, 25, 34, 57–58, 106, 186, 241, 254
Bugia, Salvatore, 34, 106

Caesar, Julius, 43
Il Caffè (journal), 96
Caius, Marcus, 42
Calais, Count, 108
Calanques rape case, 233–34
Calas, Jean, 87, 88, 112
Calas, Marc-Antoine, 87
Caligula (Camus), 259
Caligula (emperor of Rome), 42–43
Camus, Albert, 36, 152–53, 165, 166, 184, 259,
    269
Candide (Voltaire), 87
Canute (king of England), 84
Capeluche, 263
capital punishment, term of, 43. *See also* death
    penalty; executions; guillotine
Carbone, Paul, 118
Carrein, Jérôme, 255–56, 267, 271

Carter, Jimmy, 228
Carthage, Tunisia, 7, 55–56, 63
Casanova, Giacomo, 27, 87
Cascio, Carmelo, 93
Cassius, 44
Catalina, Lucius, 43
Cathars (gnostic group), 73–74, 75
Catherine, Saint, 95
Catherine of Aragon, 85
Catherine wheel, 95
Catholic Church. *See* Christianity
cave paintings, Stone Age culture, 12–13
Cayenne (French Guiana penal colony), 140, 142, 267
Ceccaldi, François, 18–19, 45, 51, 90
Ceccaldi, Paulette, 19, 29, 51
Céline, Louis-Ferdinand, 230
Cenci, Beatrice, 109
Central Intelligence Agency (CIA), 170
Chaillan, Alain, 148, 149
chambre d'accusation, 224
Champcenetz, Chevalier de, 100, 100n
Charlemagne (Holy Roman Emperor), 65
Charles VII (king of France), 147
Charles X (king of France), 137
Château d'If (prison), 139
Chauley, Jacques, 119, 120–21, 132–34, 144, 185–86, 250
Chauvy, Yves, 234, 237, 239, 243, 246, 247, 248, 250, 270, 272, 274, 276
Chevalier, Marcel, 2, 3–4, 262, 265–67, 270, 271, 279
Les Chevaliers du Fiel (group), 59–60
China, 153
Chirac, Jacques, 210, 228, 281, 285
Christianity, 54, 63–66
    crime, 84–88
    death penalty, 84, 252–53, 270
    Marseille, France, 80
    Middle Ages, 73–76, 84
    social forces, 97
Chronicles of England, Scotland and Irelande (Holinshed), 108–9
Chronique de Paris (newspaper), 115
Cicero, 43–44
Cingle de la Mola Remigia cave, Spain, 13
Cîteaux, abbot of, 74
Clairvaux prison hostage taking, 48, 178–82
Clarke, Arthur C., 12
Clavier, Father, 226
clemency requests, 256–58, 262, 268–70, 279, 281

Cleon (Athenian general), 32
Clerc, Julien, 218–19
clock tower in Schaumburg, 109
Clovis (king of the Franks), 65
Code civil des français (Napoleonic Code), 136
Code d'instruction criminelle (Napoleonic criminal law), 136
Code pénal, 152
Colbert, Jean-Baptiste, 85–86
Columban, Roger, 83
Columbus, Christopher, 114
Comandé, Bruno, 25, 56, 58, 106, 201
Comandé, Katherine, 9, 34–35, 46, 106, 201
Comandé, Vincent, 9, 34–35, 46, 106, 201
Commentaries on the Laws of England (Blackstone), 85
Commentary on the Sermon on the Mount (Augustine), 65
Committee of Public Safety, 123–24, 126
Communist Party, 129, 170
Concordance of Discordant Canons (legal system), 73
confession, torture and, 86
Constantine (emperor of Rome), 64
contraception, 50, 91, 203
"Contre la peine de mort (Au peuple du 19 octobre 1830) (Lamartine), 138
Corday, Charlotte, 153–54, 157
Corpus Iuris Civilis (Roman legal code), 41, 73, 120, 136
Corsica, 116, 121
Corsican Mafia, 167
Cosquer, Henri, 12–13
Côte d'Azur, archaeology, 12
The Count of Monte Cristo (Dumas), 8, 159
cour de cassation, 251–52, 253, 255
Craig, Christopher, 166
crime
    Beccaria, Cesare, 96–97, 110, 122
    Bible, 52–54
    Christianity, 54, 63–66, 84–88
    France, 10, 69–70
    Greece (ancient), 30–32
    Hammurabi Code, 22–23, 53
    Marseille, France, 8, 117–18, 166–68, 187
    media, 70, 104, 118, 146–47
    Middle Ages, 73–76, 84
    Rome (ancient), 41–44
Critique of Pure Reason (Kant), 110–11
Croix-de-Feu (right-wing group), 91
Cruyff, Johan, 129
Cubaynes (prison official), 272

Dallari, Patrick, 221
Damiens, François, 86–87, 157
"Dans la Simca 1000" (song), 59–60
Danton, Georges-Jacques, 126
Darkness at Noon (Koestler), 165
Darnton, Robert, 95–96
David, Christian, 168
death penalty. *See also* executions; guillotine
    abolition efforts, 96–97, 110–11, 122, 127,
        133, 136–39, 141–43, 152–55, 157,
        165–66, 177–78, 181–82, 214–19,
        225–27, 230–31, 249–50, 252–53, 255,
        258, 265, 267, 270, 277–83
    alternatives to, 139–40, 252
    ancient law, 22–23
    Bible, 52–54
    botched executions, 2–3, 108
    Christianity, 54, 63–66, 84
    country statistics, listed, 157, 287–88
    deterrence argument, 217–18, 219
    England, 84
    extenuating circumstances concept, 195,
        199, 209, 216
    France, 48, 50, 73–76, 91, 104, 136, 156–57,
        170, 177–82, 210–11, 213
    Goudareau, Jean, 219
    Greco, Marc, 191
    Greece (ancient), 30–32
    highwaymen, 95
    innocence argument, 88, 214
    media, 142–43, 152, 153, 235, 253, 277, 279,
        280
    Middle Ages, 73–76, 84
    minors, 211
    politics, 84–88, 156–57, 180, 191, 216–19,
        231, 250–51, 253, 256–59, 277,
        280–83, 285–86
    popular culture, 125–26, 151–53, 215,
        218–19, 259, 280–81
    Protestant reformation, 84–88
    public execution, banning of, 152, 153,
        265
    Rome (ancient), 41–44
    support for, 110–11, 124, 210–11, 215–19,
        222–23, 224, 231, 278
    violence, 43, 96–97, 122
    women, 156
decapitation, life after, 154–55
Déclaration des droits de l'homme et du citoyen
    (France), 98
Declaration of Independence (U.S.), 98
Defferre, Gaston, 130, 168–70, 177, 187

de Gaulle, Charles, 36, 48–50, 91, 146, 156–57,
    177, 257, 280
de Gaulle, Yvonne, 157
Deibler, Anatole, 264–65
Deibler, Antoine, 265
Deibler, Louis, 264–65
Dei delitti e delle pene (On Crimes and
    Punishments, Beccaria), 96, 97, 110
De la peine de mort en matière politique
    (Guizot), 137
Delarue, Jacques, 123n
de Lignières, Dassy, 154
Demades, 30
Denmark, 157
Desfourneaux, Jules–Henri, 265
Desmoulins, Camille, 126
Détective (magazine), 70
deterrence argument, death penalty, 217–18,
    219
Deville, Micheline, 237
Devolvé, Guillaume, 252, 253
di Francia, Josée, 185–86
Diodotus, 32, 137
disability pension
    Azzarello, Jean–Louis, 92
    Djandoubi, Hamida, 37, 39, 46, 80–81
Discipline and Punish (*Surveiller et punir*,
    Foucault), 195
discrimination, France, 10, 47, 147–48, 224,
    229–30
divorce law, 91
Djandoubi, Ahmed, 55
Djandoubi, Ali, 24, 55–56, 57, 106, 107, 201–2,
    208, 222, 275
Djandoubi, Cherifa, 24, 46
Djandoubi, Hamida. *See also* Djandoubi,
        Hamida trial
    arrest of, 162–63, 189
    birth of, 7
    Bousquet, Elisabeth and, 25, 27, 28, 29, 45,
        46–48, 50–51, 60, 61–62, 67–68,
        106–7, 162, 205
    Bousquet, Marie–Josée, 190
    childhood of, 55–56
    clemency request, 256–58, 262, 268–70
    confession of, 171–76, 184
    disability pension, 37, 39, 46, 59–60, 80–81
    employment, 58–59, 81, 82–83, 101
    execution of, 272–74
    France, immigration to, 7
    friendships of, 34–35, 57–58, 106, 186–87,
        222, 241

girlfriends
Amaria M. and, 78–79, 81–83, 89, 101–3,
104–7, 171–76, 193–94, 196–97,
200–201
Annie V. and, 77–78, 89, 101–3, 104–7,
171–76, 193–94, 196–97, 200–201,
205
Houria S., 158–62, 183, 192–93
health of, 55, 189, 221–22
injury of, 10–11, 33, 132–33, 164, 195–96,
238, 244
interrogation of, 164, 171
Marseille, France, 9–10
media, 70
money of, 210
onomastics, 56–57
personality of, 81, 83
possessions of, 208–10
prison life, 221–22
prostitution, 62, 67–68, 71–72, 102, 106,
184–85, 224
psychiatric evaluations, 196, 205–6, 209,
222–23
rehabilitation of, 39–40, 45
substance abuse, 55, 57
violence, 40, 51, 62, 68, 101–3, 105–6,
160–62, 196–97, 229, 233–34
women and, 24–25, 159
Djandoubi, Hamida trial. See also Djandoubi,
Hamida
Amaria M. testimony, 240
Annie V. testimony, 240
appeals court process, 251–52, 253
Bousquet family, 190–91
Chauvy, Yves, 234–35
crime reconstruction, 206–7
death penalty, 242, 243, 244–46, 247,
249–50
Djandoubi, Hamida testimony and
statement, 238–39, 245
Goudareau, Jean and defense, 187–88,
208–10, 222–24, 243–45
Houria S. testimony, 240
jury deliberations, 245–46
jury selection, 237, 250
media, 228, 235, 237, 239, 240, 241, 249
opening of, 236–37
police testimony, 240
prosecution tactics, 243
psychiatric testimony, 239–40
public opinion, 236
racism, 229–30

witnesses, 237–38
women, 233–34, 250
Djandoubi, Hédi, 7, 35, 46
Dorkel, Jean–Baptiste, 228–29
Dos, Michel, 61–62
Dostoyevsky, Fyodor, 140, 165, 223
Draco, 30
Dreyfus, Alfred, 140
drugs, 50, 55
dueling, 169
Dumas, Alexandre (*père*), 8, 109, 113, 159
Dunkel, Ernst, 118, 188
Duport, Adrien, 110

Edict of Milan, 64
Edmonds, Paul, 222
Eichmann, Adolf, 216–17
Eichmann in Jerusalem (Arendt), 216–17
Eiffel Tower, 151
Eliezar ben Azariah, 53–54
England, 84, 85, 108–9, 165–66, 178, 218
Enlightenment, 96, 98, 138, 177
Erasmus, 84
Erblinger, Marthe, 142
Estaing, France, 14
États Généraux, 97, 98
Euxene (Phocaean sea captain), 26–27
executioners, 262–67, 279–80
executions. See also death penalty; guillotine
of Djandoubi, Hamida, 272–74
executioners, 262–65, 279–80
methods of, 95–96, 217
prehistoric, 13
private, 152–53
rituals of, 3–4
extenuating circumstances concept, 195, 199,
209, 216

Faculté de Paris, 98
Fages, Aimé, 145
Fallières, Armand, 141–42
family notification, Bousquet, Elisabeth,
189–90
feminism, 91, 182, 190–91, 193, 202, 232–34.
See also women
Ferrandini, Thomas, 205
Le Figaro (newspaper), 129, 211, 228, 230
Le Figaro Littéraire (journal), 178
Finland, 157
firing squad, 156, 157, 188, 225
Fitch, John, 123
Foreign Legion. See French Foreign Legion

Foucault, Michel, 195, 279
Fournier, Dr., 155
Foyer Ariane (women's shelter, Marseille), 67, 68–69, 90, 101
France
　abortion legalized, 203
　Algeria, 35–37, 38, 46, 49, 165
　archaeology, 12–13
　crime, 10, 69–70
　death penalty, 48, 50, 73–76, 85–87, 91, 104, 110–11, 136–37, 140–43, 151–52, 155–57, 170, 177–82, 210–11, 213
　discrimination in, 10, 47, 147–48, 224, 229–30
　economy of, 15, 146–47
　immigration to, 8–9, 15, 36–37, 38, 146, 147–48
　legal system, 119–20, 130, 136, 141, 171, 195–96, 224, 232–34, 236, 238, 251–52, 256–58
　media, 129
　politics in, 48–50, 90–92, 104, 110–11, 137, 141–43, 146–48, 157, 177–78
　social unrest in, 97
　women, 48, 50, 67, 68–69, 202–4, 232–34
France-Soir (newspaper), 280
Franco, Francisco, 210–11, 279
Franklin, Benjamin, 139
Free French Forces, 48–49. See also French Resistance The French Connection (film), 8, 167
French Empire, 8, 35–37
French Foreign Legion, 92–93, 179, 191
Frenchmen: One More Effort If You Wish to Be Republicans (Sade), 69, 97, 122
French Resistance, 15–16, 28, 38, 49, 91, 157, 169, 191. See also Free French Forces
French Revolution, 91–92
　death penalty abolished in, 127
　events of, 97–98
　Reign of Terror, 92, 122, 123–25, 127, 128, 153, 157, 264
　violence, 123–25
Front de Libération Nationale (FLN), 36
Front National (political party), 147–48, 281, 285–86
Fulvia, 43
Furman, William Henry, 180
Furman v. Georgia, 180, 216

Gallimard, Michel, 166
Garceau, Norbert, 278
Georgia, United States, 284
gibbet, 108–9
Gicquel, Roger, 215
Gilmore, Gary, 225
Girousse, Jean-Claude, 120, 183
Giscard d'Estaing, Valéry, 90–91, 182, 196, 203, 210, 216, 226, 230, 231, 250–51, 253, 255, 256, 257, 258, 260–61, 268, 280, 281
gladiatorial contests, 42–43
gnostic groups, 73–74, 75
Goethe, Johann Wolfgang von, 126
Gorgias (Plato), 31, 217
Goudareau, Jean
　career of, 37–39
　clemency appeal, 257–58, 260–61, 268–69
　death penalty opinion, 219, 231
　Djandoubi, Hamida defense, 187–88, 208–10, 222–24, 231–32, 236, 237, 240, 241, 242, 243–45, 246, 247, 249–50, 254
　Djandoubi, Hamida execution, 272, 273, 274, 275
　Djandoubi, Hamida pension, 37, 39, 46, 58, 60, 186–87
　extenuating circumstances concept, 195–96
　media, 249
　politics, 49, 254
Goya, Francisco, 188
Gratian of Bologna, 73
Greco, Marc, 191, 254
Greece (ancient), death penalty, 30–32
Gregg, Tony, 216
Gregg v. Georgia, 216, 225
Guérini, Antoine, 118, 168, 170
Guérini, Barthélemy, 170
Guérini, Mémé, 118, 170
Guiard, Marie-Solange, 69, 90, 101
Guillot (mechanic), 123
Guillotin, Catherine, 95
Guillotin, Joseph-Ignace, 95, 96, 153
　career of, 98–99
　guillotine invention, 108, 112, 113, 114, 123, 127
　politics, 128
guillotine. See also death penalty; executions
　antiquity, 26, 108
　botched executions with, 2–3, 262
　conception of, 99–100
　construction of, 1–2, 112–13, 123, 271–72

efficiency of, 122–23, 127
forerunners of, 108–9
inspections of, 262, 267
politics of, 110–12
popular culture, 125–26, 151–53, 259
tests of, 113–15
Guiraud, Martine, 89
Guizot, François, 136–37, 141, 165
gunrunning, 33–34

Hackman, Gene, 8
Hair (musical), 218
Halifax Gibbet, 108–9
Halimi, Gisèle, 202
Hammurabi (king of Babylon), 21–23, 53
harkis, 36, 78, 146, 197, 257
Havana Conference (1946), 167
Henri IV (king of France), 75–76
Henry, Patrick, 212–13, 215, 224, 225–27, 228,
    231, 235, 277
Henry VIII (king of England), 85, 263
heretics, 73
heroin epidemic, 8, 166–68
highwaymen, 95
Himmler, Heinrich, 16
A History of the Guillotine (Kershaw), 123n
History of the Peloponnesian War
    (Thucydides), 31–32
Hitler, Adolf, 147
Hobbes, Thomas, 85
Holland, 141, 157, 259
homosexuality, 52
Hôpital de la Conception (Marseille), 11, 20,
    33, 39
Hôpital de la Timone (Marseille), 72
Hôpital Édouard (Toulouse), 89
hostage taking, 48, 178–82, 210, 212–13
Hôtel de Ville (Paris), 114
Houria S.
    defense of, 224
    Djandoubi, Hamida and, 158–63, 183,
        192–93, 197, 198, 275
    pregnancy of, 202–4
    self-esteem, 208
    testimony of, 240, 248, 249
The House of the Dead (Dostoyevsky), 223
Hugo, Victor, 2, 80, 114, 138–39, 141, 282
Hugon, Maryse, 17, 18, 191n
Hugo Obermaier Society (Regensburg,
    Germany), 13n
Humanae vitae (On Human Life, Paul VI),
    252–53

The Hunchback of Notre Dame (Hugo), 138
Hundred Years' War, 147
Hussein, Omar, 153

The Idiot (Dostoyevsky), 140
Il Caffè (journal), 96
immigration, to France, 8–9, 15, 36–37, 38,
    146, 147–48
innocence argument, death penalty, 88
Iran, 153
Islam, 36, 222
Italy, 97, 109, 156, 157, 167
Izoret, Émile, 93

"Je suis pour" (song), 218
Joan of Arc, 147–48
Joubert, Alberte, 59
Journal des États Généraux (newspaper), 99
Judaism, 53–54, 140
juge d'enfants, 247
juge d'instruction, 120, 148, 183, 184, 272. See
    also Llaurens, Françoise
Julian (emperor of Rome), 64
jury selection, Hamida Djandoubi trial, 237
Justinian (emperor of Rome), 41

Kant, Immanuel, 110–11, 195, 225
Kanzari, Mohamed, 107
Kennedy, John F., 168
Kershaw, Alister, 123n
Kervella, Marie-Claude, 83, 105–6, 161, 201,
    240–41, 253
kidnapping, 212–13
King, Martin Luther, Jr., 182
Koestler, Arthur, 165–66

"Le Lac" (Lamartine), 137–38
Laetoli site (Tanzania), 12
Lafayette, Marquis de, 114
Lafout, Odette, 17, 50
L'Agonie de la peine de mort (Naud), 178
Laguiller, Arlette, 281
La Marseillaise (anthem), 91–92, 114
La Marseillaise (newspaper), 129, 130–31,
    176, 235, 241, 249, 277
Lamartine, Alphonse de, 137–38, 139
Lampérière, Louise, 156
Lancre, Pierre de, 74
Langogne, France, 17–18, 50
Languille, Henri, 155
Le Provençal (newspaper), 130, 131, 176, 235,
    277

Lascaux caves, France, 12–13
"*L'Assassin assassiné*" (song), 218
The Last Days of a Condemned Man (Hugo), 138
Lateran councils, 73
La Tête et les jambes (TV show), 244
Latour, Justin, 69
Laval, Pierre, 156, 230–31
Laws (Plato), 31
League Against Capital Punishment, 165
Léauté, Jacques, 217–18, 219, 226
le Belge, François, 118
Lecanuet, Jean, 217
Le Figaro (newspaper), 129, 211, 228, 230
Le Figaro Littéraire (journal), 178
Lefranc, Pierre Berge, 256, 272
legal system (France), 119–20, 130, 136, 141, 171, 195–96, 224, 232–34, 236, 238, 251–52, 256–58
"*Le Lac*" (Lamartine), 137–38
Le Manchec, Lucie, 60, 186–87
le Mat, Jacky, 118
Le Méridional (newspaper), 130, 146–47, 235, 249, 277
Le Monde (newspaper), 129, 228, 230, 277
Le Nouveau Détective (magazine), 70
Le Nouvel Observateur (news magazine), 222–23, 227, 279
Le Parisien (newspaper), 129
Le Pen, Jean-Marie, 146–47, 148, 281, 285–86
Le Petit Journal (newspaper), 142
Le Point (news magazine), 227
Les Aberrations sexuelles d'un monstre (film), 196
Les Actes des Apôtres (newspaper), 99
Les Chevaliers du Fiel (group), 59–60
Les Misérables (Hugo), 138
Le Soir (newspaper), 130, 237
Les Quatres Fils Aymon (puppet show), 108
Lévesque, René, 228
Libdom, Karl, 279
Libération (newspaper), 129, 153, 228, 231
Liebling, A. J., 117
"life" imprisonment, 252
Ligurian people, 26–27, 108
Lisle, Rouget de, 91–92, 114
Little Red Riding Hood (nursery story), 95–96
Llaurens, Françoise, 183, 184, 194, 195, 200, 206, 207, 208, 209–10, 220, 223, 224. See also *juge d'instruction*
Locke, John, 85
Lombard, Paul, 214, 215, 252

Lorraine, France, 74
L'Osservatore romano (newspaper), 253
Louis, Antoine, 112–13, 114, 127, 128
Louis XIV (king of France), 85–86, 170
Louis XV (king of France), 86–87
Louis XVI (king of France), 97, 98, 113, 124–25, 264
Louis XVIII (king of France), 137
Louis-Philippe (king of France), 140–41
Louvre (Paris), 23
Luciano, Lucky, 167, 168
Luther, Martin, 84
Lutte Ouvrière (political party), 281

Mabelly (official witness), 272
Maghreb, emigration from, 8–9. See also immigration
Maine, Henry, 22, 217
Malraux, André, 187
Manias, Nicole, 148, 149
Manias, Pierre, 148–50, 185
mannaia (historical decapitation machine), 109
Marat, Jean-Paul, 153
Marie-Antoinette (queen of France), 97, 124, 125, 264
Marra, Catina, 133
Marra, Danièle, 133
Marra, Francesco, 133
La Marseillaise (anthem), 91–92, 114
La Marseillaise (newspaper), 129, 130–131, 176, 235, 241, 249, 277
Marseille, ou la mauvaise réputation (Boura), 166
Marseille, Battle of, 16
Marseille, France
    Bousquet family, 14–15
    crime, 8, 117–18, 166–68
    criminal lawyers, 187
    described, 7–8, 19–20, 25, 80, 196–97
    economy of, 15
    ethnicities of, 27, 47
    history of, 26–27
    immigration to, 8–9, 15, 36–37, 38
    media, 129–31, 170, 235
    police department brutality, 183–84
    politics in, 168–70
    women's services in, 67, 68–69
    World War II, 15–17
Maurel (prison official), 272
McCoy, Alfred W., 166–67
McKay, Claude, 47

media
  crime, 70, 104, 118, 146–47
  death penalty, 142–43, 152, 153, 235, 253, 277, 279, 280
  Djandoubi, Hamida execution, 277
  Djandoubi, Hamida trial, 228, 235, 237, 239, 240, 241, 249
  executioners, 266–67
  French journalism, 129
  Goudareau, Jean, 249
  Louis XVI (king of France), 124–25
  Marseille, France, 129–31, 170
Medjikian, Ohannès, 101
Mémoires de messire Jacques de Chastenet (Chastenet), 109
Ménesclou, Louis, 154
mental illness defense, 195, 199, 209
Mercier, Louis-Sébastien, 125
Le Méridional (newspaper), 130, 146–47, 235, 249, 277
Merlin, Dr., 159, 205, 239
Mesmer, Franz, 98
Mesopotamia, 21–23
Metaphysical Elements of Justice (Kant), 110–11
Le Métier de bourreau (Delarue), 123n
Meurthe, Boulay de la, 127
Meyssonnier, Fernand, 267n
Michelin, Marguerite-Marie, 193
Middle Ages, death penalty, 73–76, 84
Milan, Edict of, 64
Milieu (criminal organization), 148, 168
minors, death penalty, 211
mistral, 10, 19, 35
mitigating circumstances concept. *See* extenuating circumstances concept
Mitterrand, François, 36, 90–91, 169, 181–82, 196, 280, 281
monarchists, 123, 124
Le Monde (newspaper), 129, 228, 230, 277
Montagu, Basil, 139n
Montand, Yves, 211
Montesquieu, Charles de Secondat, baron de, 86, 96
Montmorency, Henri de, 109
Morant, Gaston, 120, 134
More, Thomas, 84–85
Moreau (Judge), 112
Morellet, Abbé, 97
Morocco, 7
Morton, earl of, 109
Mosaic Law, 53

Moulin, Josy, 149
mountaineering, 234
Mouvement Fédéralist Européen, 196
Mussolini, Benito, 167
Les Mystères de Marseille (Zola), 15
Mytilene (Athenian colony), 32

Napoleon Bonaparte (emperor of France), 127, 136, 137, 141, 195
Napoleonic Code *(Code civil des français)*, 136
Napoleon III (emperor of France), 141
National Assembly (France), 98, 99, 110, 111, 124, 127, 137, 141, 143, 168, 169, 170, 253, 260, 280, 282
Le National (newspaper), 38
Naud, Albert, 156, 178, 230–31
Nazi Germany, Vichy France, 15–17, 118. *See also* Vichy government
Ne pleure pas, hurle! (Perasso), 232
Nero (emperor of Rome), 42
New Testament. *See* Bible
Nice, France, 10, 12
Nice-Matin (newspaper), 129
Nobel Prize in Literature (1957), 166
Norway, 141, 157
Nostradamus, 131
Notre Dame de Bon Voyage (rehabilitation center, La Ciotat, France), 39, 45
Notre-Dame de la Garde (Marseille), 80
Le Nouveau Détective (magazine), 70
Le Nouvel Observateur (news magazine), 222–23, 227, 279
Nuremberg Trials, 177

Oberg, Karl, 15–16
Obermaier, Hugo, 13
Obrecht, André, 262, 265, 266, 271
Obrecht, Georges, 262
Obrecht, Marcelle Louise, 262
Old Testament. *See* Bible
Olduvai Gorge (Tanzania), 12
Olympique de Marseille (soccer team), 33
On Cain and Abel (Saint Ambrose), 64
On Crimes and Punishments *(Dei delitti e delle pene,* Beccaria), 96, 97, 110
On Human Life *(Humanae vitae,* Paul VI), 252–53
onomastics, 56–57
Opinions of Different Authors upon the Punishment of Death (Montagu), 139n
Organisation de l'Armée Secrète, 157

Origen, 63–64
Orves, Honoré Étienne d', 28
L'Osservatore romano (newspaper), 253

Pache, Nadine, 206
pacifism, 63–64
Pamiers, France, 2
Panzani, Alex, 241
Paris Exposition Universelle of 1889 (Paris, France), 151
Le Parisien (newspaper), 129
Paris-Match (magazine), 152, 267
Paris-Soir (magazine), 152
parole, 252
parrains (crime bosses), 118
Pasolini, Pier Paolo, 239
Patel, Noël, 19, 28, 29, 60–61, 61n, 190, 201
Paul, Saint, 63
Paul VI (pope), 252–53
Peigné-Delacourt, Achille, 26
La Peine de mort: Esquisse historique et juridique (Savey-Casard), 13n
Pelletier, Nicolas-Jacques, 112, 114–15, 122, 271
Peloponnesian War, 30–31
penal colonies, 140, 142, 267
penitentiary system, 139–40, 178–79
Perasso, Éliane, 190–91, 232, 242
Peres, Shimon, 228
"perpetual" imprisonment, 252
Perrault, Gilles, 214, 279
Pétain, Philippe, 156
Pétition des citoyens domiciliés à Paris (Guillotin), 98–99
Le Petit Journal (newspaper), 142
Le Petit Marseillais (newspaper), 16
Peyrefitte, Alain, 258, 259
Philippeville massacres (Algeria), 36
Phocaea (city-state), 26–27
Piedelièvre, Dr., 155
pieds-noirs (French nationals born in Algeria), 36, 145, 146, 197
pigs, 74–75, 75n
Plato, 31, 41, 217
Le Point (news magazine), 227
police testimony, Djandoubi, Hamida trial, 240
Politics of Heroin in Southeast Asia (McCoy), 166–67
Pollak, Émile, 213, 229–30, 249, 254–55, 256, 257, 258, 260–61, 269, 272, 275–76

Pollak, Nicole, 255, 269, 278
Pompidou, Georges, 50, 90, 91, 177, 178, 181–82, 203, 216
popular culture
    death penalty, 125–26, 151–53, 215, 218–19, 259, 280–81
    guillotine, 125–26, 151–53, 259
pornography, 196, 209
Portais, Jean, 278
Portugal, 141, 157
Poulidor, Raymond, 280
prehistoric executions, 13
Prejean, Helen, 153
prejudice, France, 10, 47, 147–48, 224, 229–30
prison systems, 139–40
Procès de Bobigny, 202
Propriano, Corsica, 116, 121
prostitution, 193
    Bousquet, Elisabeth, 62, 67–68
    criminal investigations and, 135
    Djandoubi, Hamida, 62, 67–68, 71–72, 102, 106, 184–85, 244
    Manias, Pierre, 185–86
Protestant reformation, 84–88
Protis (Greek sea captain), 27
Le Provençal (newspaper), 130, 131, 176, 235, 277
Prunier, Théotime, 154
psychiatric evaluations, Djandoubi, Hamida, 196, 205–6, 209, 222–23
psychiatric testimony, Djandoubi, Hamida trial, 239–40
public execution, banning of, 152, 153, 265
Le Pull-over rouge (Perrault), 214, 279

Quakers, 97
Les Quatres Fils Aymon (puppet show), 108
The Question, 86

Rabin, Yitzhak, 228
racism, France, 10, 47, 147–48, 224, 229–30
Rambla, Marie-Dolorès, 103–4, 184, 214
Ranucci, Christian, 104, 134–35, 184, 214–15, 226, 228, 234–35, 236, 249, 251, 252, 271, 279
rape, 202, 232–34
Ravaillac, François, 75–76, 86
Ray, Martha, 139n
Reflections on Hanging (Koestler), 165–66

Réflexions sur la guillotine (Camus), 166
Reign of Terror, 92, 122, 123–25, 127, 128,
    153, 157, 264. *See also* French
    Revolution
religion. *See* Christianity
The Republic (Plato), 31
The Republic of the Massalians (Aristotle), 26
Resistance. *See* French Resistance
Revolution of 1830, 137
Revolution of 1848, 140–41
Ribière, René, 169
Rigaud, Father, 17
Rihet, Alphonse, 272
Rimbaud, Arthur, 33–34
Rivele, Stephen, 168
Robespierre, Maximilien, 110, 123–24,
    126–27, 128
Roch, Nicolas, 264
Rochefoucauld, François de la, 274
Roman Catholic Church. *See* Christianity
Rombaud, Jean, 263
Rome (ancient)
    Christianity, 63–65
    French law, 120, 136, 256–57
    laws in, 41–44, 52
Rousseau, Jean-Jacques, 124
Rousseau (prison official), 272
Rousseau, Michel, 278
Rouvet, Riou, 240
Rush, Benjamin, 139
Russia, 140

Sade, Marquis de, 69, 97, 122, 165
Saidi, Hocine, 272
Saint-Claude, France, 74
Saint-Fargeau, Le Peletier de, 98
Salendre, Yves, 119, 198
Salò, or the 120 Days of Sodom (film), 239
Sanhedrin, 54
Sanson, Charles, Jr., 264
Sanson, Charles Henri, 95, 111–12, 113,
    114–15, 125, 154, 264
Sanson, Charles Jean-Baptiste, 264
Sanson, Henri-Clément, 264
Sanson de Longval, Charles, 263, 264
Sardou, Michel, 68, 71, 72, 218
Sarkozy, Nicolas, 286
Sarti, Lucien, 168
Savey-Casard, Paul, 13n
Saylens (Ligurian tribe), 26–27
Schabas, William A., 13n
Schaumburg, clock tower in, 109

Schmidt, Tobias, 113, 127
Scotland, 109
"Scottish Maiden," 109
A Season in Hell (Rimbaud), 33–34
Sebag, Jean-Claude, 196, 197, 207
Seghers, Anna, 15
Seneca, 41
Sharia law, 153
Shelley, Percy Bysshe, 109
Siberia, 140
Sicily, 167
Siméon (lawyer), 236
Simon of Cyrene, 248
Sin-muballit (king of Babylon), 21
soccer, 33
The Social Contract (Rousseau), 124
socialism, 91
Socialist Party, 170
Société Nationale de Construction pour les
    Travailleurs (housing agency), 46
Socrates, 30–31
Soemmering, S. T., 154
Le Soir (newspaper), 130, 237
Soleilland, Albert, 142
Solonian Constitution (ancient Greece), 30
Somalia, 153
Sonacotras housing, 46, 48, 81
Spain, 210–11, 279
Spanish Civil War, 165
Sparta, Greece (ancient), 30–31
Spirito, François, 118
The Spirit of the Laws (Montesquieu), 86
state-assisted suicide, 189
Steinem, Gloria, 182
Stendhal, 109
Stockholm syndrome, 197–98
Stone Age culture, archaeology, 12–13
The Stranger (Camus), 165, 184, 269
substance abuse, 50, 55
Sud-Ouest (newspaper), 129
Sue, Pierre, 154
suicide, 87, 90, 189
suicide (state-assisted), 189
Suidas, 30
Summa contra gentiles (Aquinas), 65–66
Summa theologiae (Aquinas), 65
Supreme Court (U.S.), 180, 216, 225
Surveiller et punir (Discipline and Punish,
    Foucault), 195
Suttel, René, 159, 205, 222–23
Sweden, 157, 279
Switzerland, 157

Tacitus, 126
Tanzania, archaeology in, 12
Tarfon, 54
Ten Commandments, 53
Tennis Court Oath, 97
Teper, Doug, 284
Terra Amata (prehistoric village, France), 12
The Terrible and Deserved Death of Francis Ravilliack, 75–76
terrorism, 210–11
Tertullian, 63
Terzian, Cathy, 145
La Tête et les jambes (TV show), 244
Thain, Jean, 144–46, 148–50, 164
The Third Reich (record album), 147
Thiroux, Gabriel, 131
Thomas Cook and Company (travel agency), 151
Thucydides, 31–32
Time magazine, 156, 168
Tolstoy, Leo, 151
torture, 119. *See also* violence
    Algerian War, 147
    confession and, 86
    crime scene, 130–32
    Djandoubi, Hamida, 105, 162, 164, 224
    French Revolution, 98
Tosti, Dr., 272
Toulouse, France, 74, 109
Tragédie à Clairvaux (Vigo), 181
Traité sur la tolérance (Voltaire), 87–88
Trenet, Charles, 38
Tres de Mayo (Goya), 188
trial. *See* Djandoubi, Hamida trial
Trudeau, Pierre, 130
Tunisia, 7, 34, 46, 55–56
Turlesque, Georges, 164
Twain, Mark, 8
Twelve Tables (Roman criminal code), 41–42
2001: A Space Odyssey (film), 12

United Nations, 177, 211
United States, 16, 170, 216, 217, 225, 284
U.S. Bureau of Narcotics, 167–68
Universal Declaration of Human Rights (United Nations), 177
Ur-Nammu (king of Sumaria), 21
Urukagina (king of Babylon), 21
Utopia (More), 84–85

Valazé, 123
Veil, Simone, 91, 203–4

Verlaine, Paul, 33–34
Viaux-Peccate, Stéphane, 259
Vichy government, France, 15–17, 49, 91, 118, 156, 165, 230–31
Vidou, Pierre, 120, 134, 189, 190, 191
Viennet, Georgie, 255
violence. *See also* torture
    criminal reform, 85–86
    death penalty, 43, 96–97, 122
    Djandoubi, Hamida, 40, 51, 62, 68, 101–3, 105–6
    French Revolution, 123–25
    La Marseillaise (anthem), 92
    psychiatric testimony, 239–40
Vitrolles, France, 146–47, 148
Voltaire, 87–88, 96, 97, 279
Voyage to the End of the Night (Céline), 230
Vuillet, François, 131, 184
Vuillet, Henri, 237, 238–39, 240–42, 245, 247, 272

Wars of Religion, 75
Weidmann, Eugène, 152, 153, 265
West Germany, 156, 157
wheel, 95
William Rufus (William II, king of England), 84
William the Conqueror (king of England), 84
witchcraft, 52, 74, 75, 95–96
witnesses, Djandoubi, Hamida trial, 237–38
women. *See also* feminism
    Djandoubi, Hamida and, 24–25, 159
    execution of, 156
    France, 48, 50, 67, 68–69, 91, 202–4, 232–34
    trial, 250
World Cup (1974), 129, 130
World War II, 193, 262
    de Gaulle, Charles, 48–49
    France, 37–38, 165, 169
    Luciano, Lucky, 167
    Marseille, 15–17, 118
    outbreak of, 155–56
    war crimes, 177

Yahiaoui, Mohamed, 278

Zampa, Tany, 118
Zola, Émile, 15
Züchner, Christian, 13n